Garfield hams it up

BY JIM DAVIS

Ballantine Books • New York

2016 Ballantine Books Trade Paperback Edition

Published in the United States by Ballantine Books, an imprint of Random House,
a division of Penguin Random House LLC, New York.

BALLANTINE and the HOUSE colophon are registered trademarks of Penguin Random House LLC.

Originally published in slightly different form in the United States by Ballantine Books,
an imprint of Random House, a division of Penguin Random House LLC, in 1997.

ISBN 978-0-345-52606-9
eBook ISBN 978-0-8041-7767-2

Printed in the United States of America on acid-free paper

randomhousebooks.com

9 8 7 6 5 4 3 2 1

First Colorized Edition

DEAR FLABBY

Snappy answers to sappy questions: all your puny problems solved in 10 words or less!

Q: Dear Flabby, What can I do about my little brother? He's such a pest!
A: Have you tried a flyswatter?

Q: Dear Flabby, My boss is a mean, unappreciative slave driver who constantly belittles me. What can I do?
A: Shut up and get back to work!

Q: Dear Flabby, My dad insists I clean my room! How can I get out of this?
A: Get a new dad.

Q: Dear Flabby, Why are you so lazy?
A: Dear Loser, Why are you so stupid? Next question.

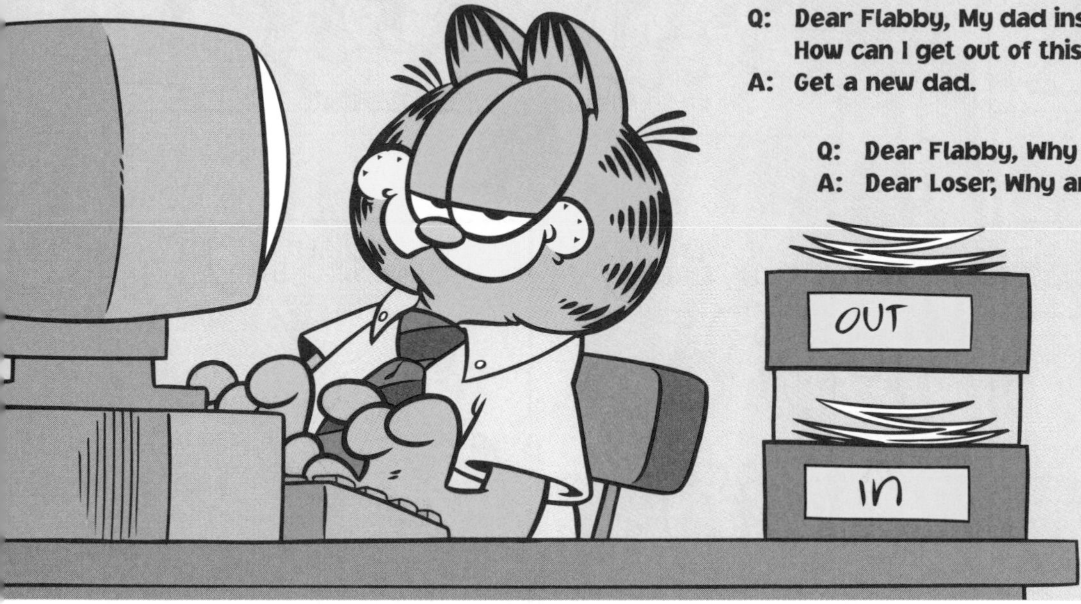

OUT
IN

Q: Help! I need to lose weight! How can I stop eating all the fattening foods I love?
A: Send them to me and I'll eat them for you.

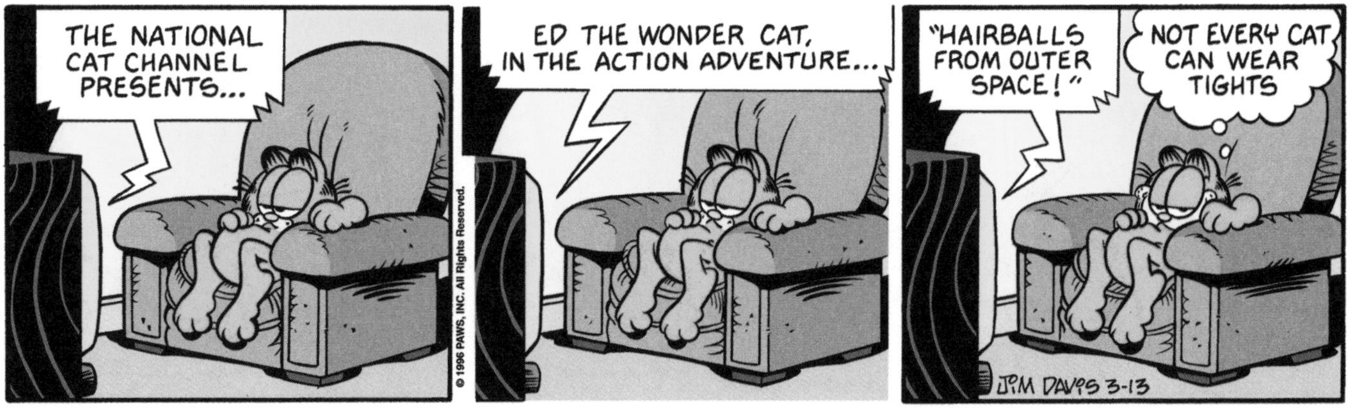

THE NATIONAL CAT CHANNEL PRESENTS...
ED THE WONDER CAT, IN THE ACTION ADVENTURE...
"HAIRBALLS FROM OUTER SPACE!"
NOT EVERY CAT CAN WEAR TIGHTS
JIM DAVIS 3-13

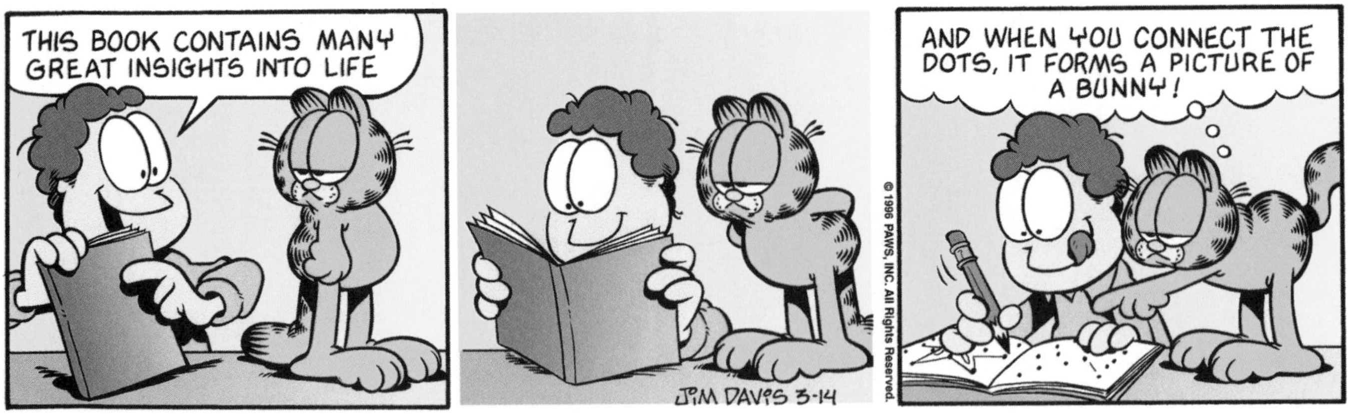
THIS BOOK CONTAINS MANY GREAT INSIGHTS INTO LIFE
JIM DAVIS 3-14
AND WHEN YOU CONNECT THE DOTS, IT FORMS A PICTURE OF A BUNNY!

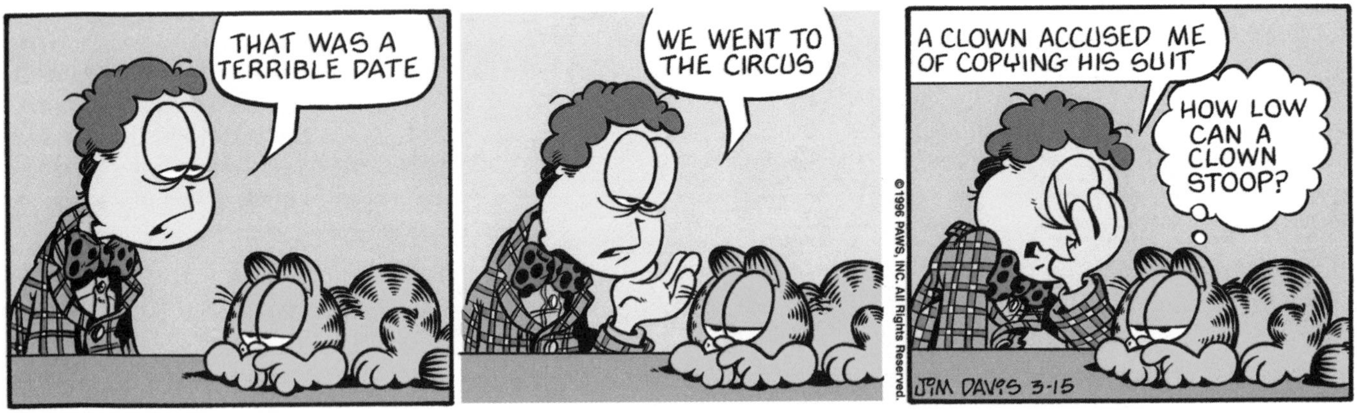
THAT WAS A TERRIBLE DATE
WE WENT TO THE CIRCUS
A CLOWN ACCUSED ME OF COPYING HIS SUIT
HOW LOW CAN A CLOWN STOOP?
JIM DAVIS 3-15

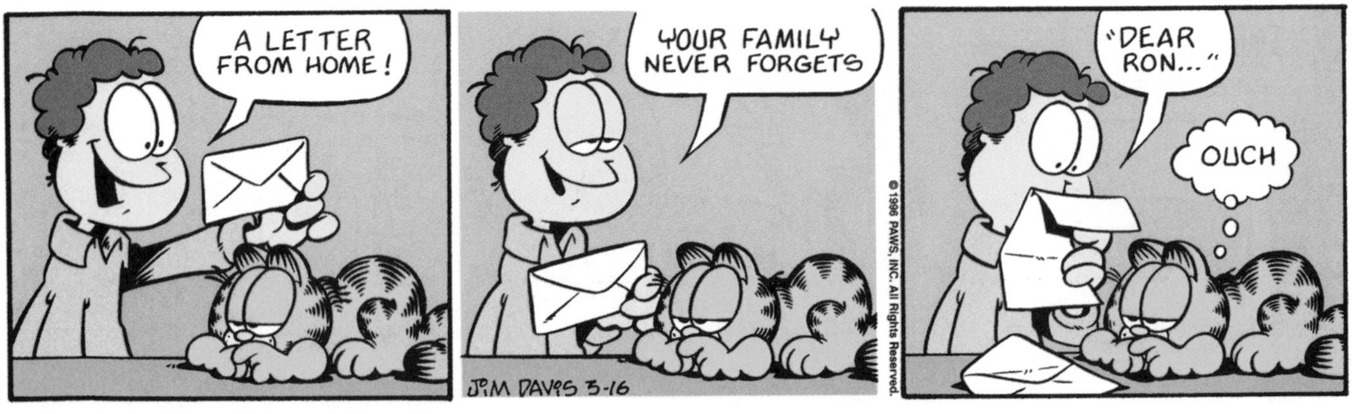
A LETTER FROM HOME!
YOUR FAMILY NEVER FORGETS
JIM DAVIS 3-16
"DEAR RON..."
OUCH

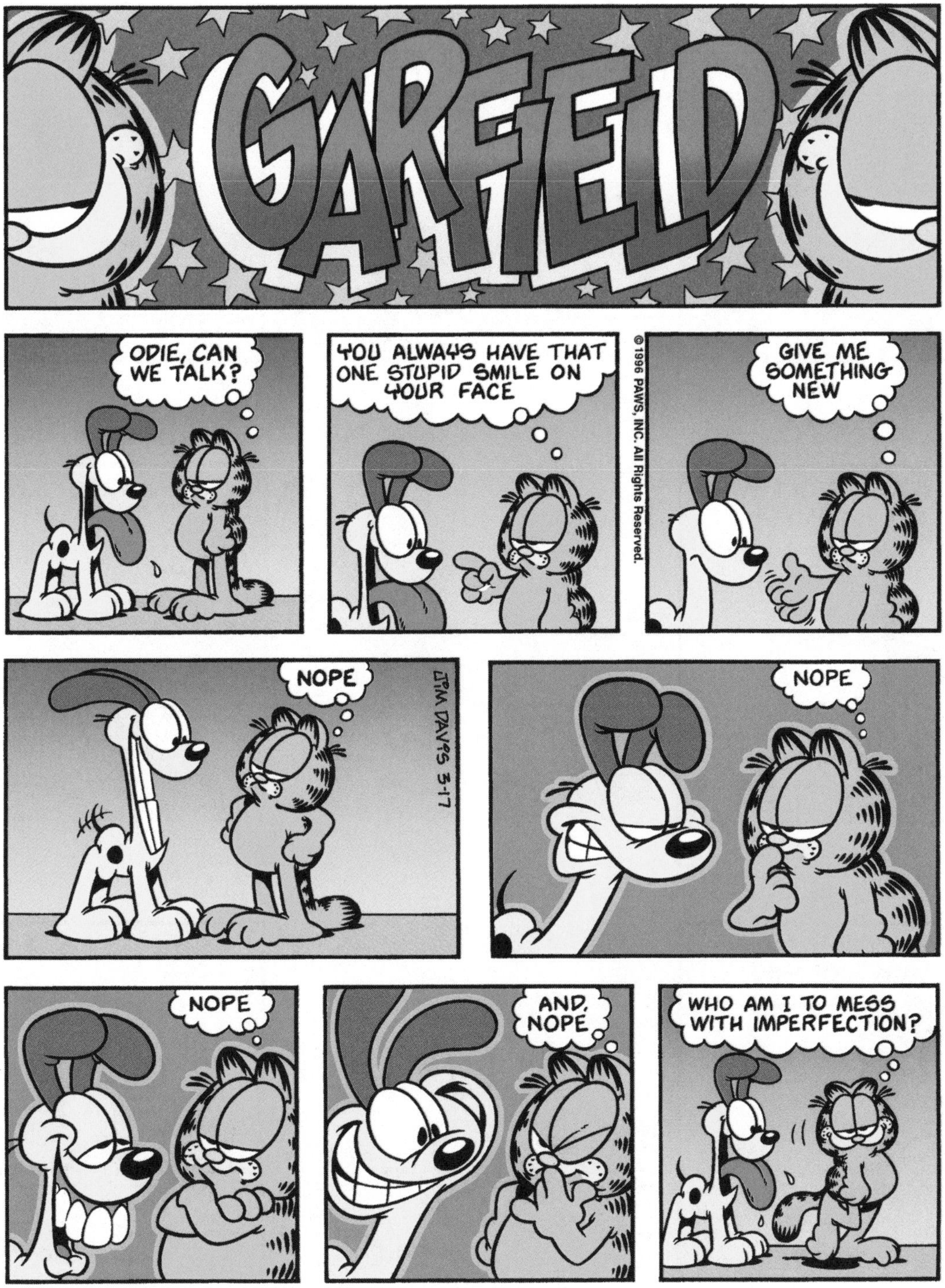
GARFIELD
ODIE, CAN WE TALK?
YOU ALWAYS HAVE THAT ONE STUPID SMILE ON YOUR FACE
© 1996 PAWS, INC. All Rights Reserved.
GIVE ME SOMETHING NEW
NOPE
JIM DAVIS 3-17
NOPE
NOPE
AND, NOPE
WHO AM I TO MESS WITH IMPERFECTION?

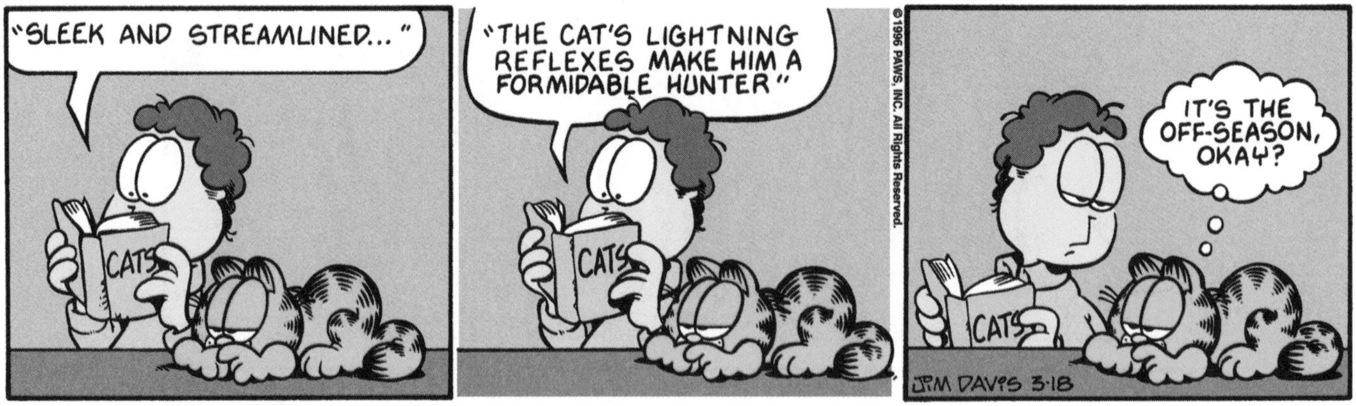
"SLEEK AND STREAMLINED..."
"THE CAT'S LIGHTNING REFLEXES MAKE HIM A FORMIDABLE HUNTER"
© 1996 PAWS, INC. All Rights Reserved.
IT'S THE OFF-SEASON, OKAY?
JIM DAVIS 3-18

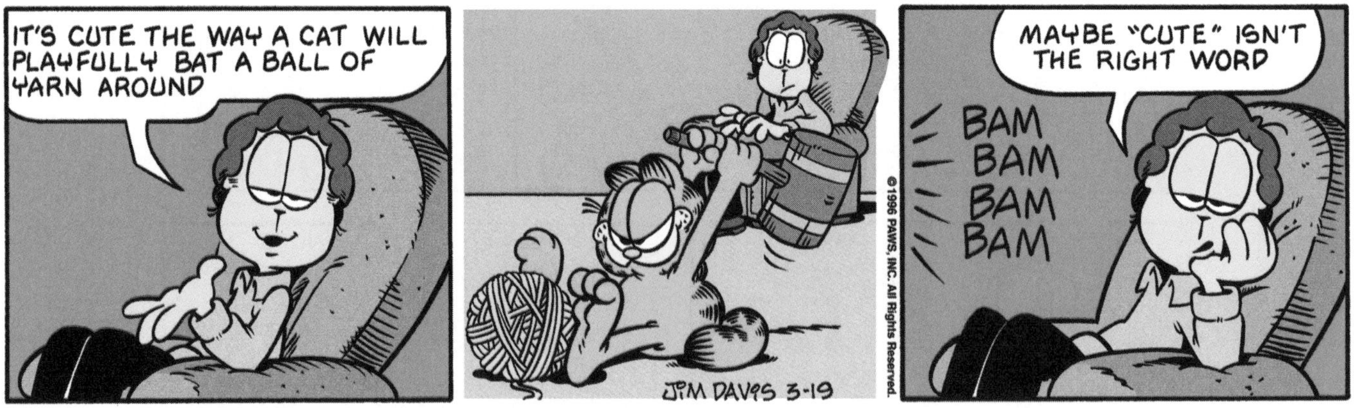
IT'S CUTE THE WAY A CAT WILL PLAYFULLY BAT A BALL OF YARN AROUND
JIM DAVIS 3-19
© 1996 PAWS, INC. All Rights Reserved.
MAYBE "CUTE" ISN'T THE RIGHT WORD
BAM BAM BAM BAM

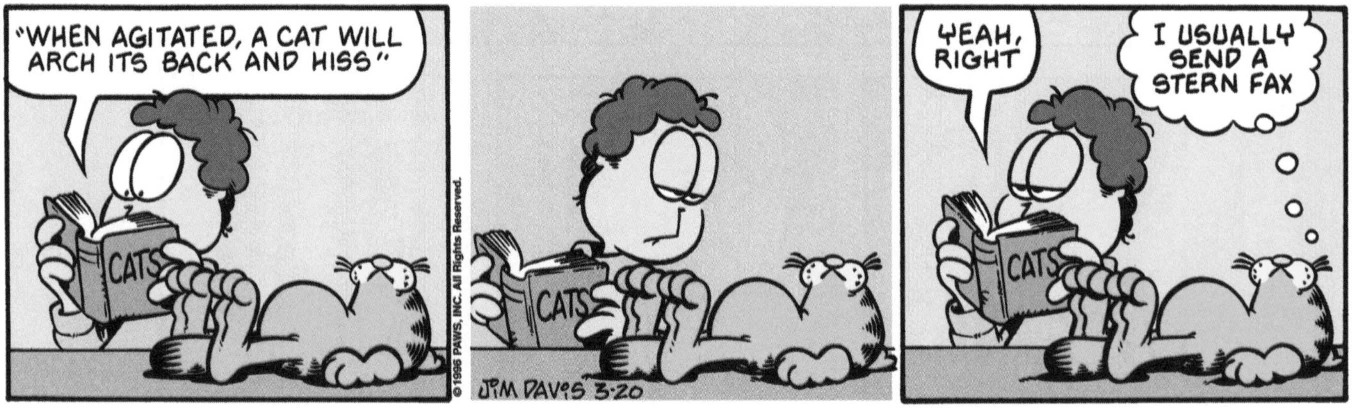
"WHEN AGITATED, A CAT WILL ARCH ITS BACK AND HISS"
© 1996 PAWS, INC. All Rights Reserved.
JIM DAVIS 3-20
YEAH, RIGHT
I USUALLY SEND A STERN FAX

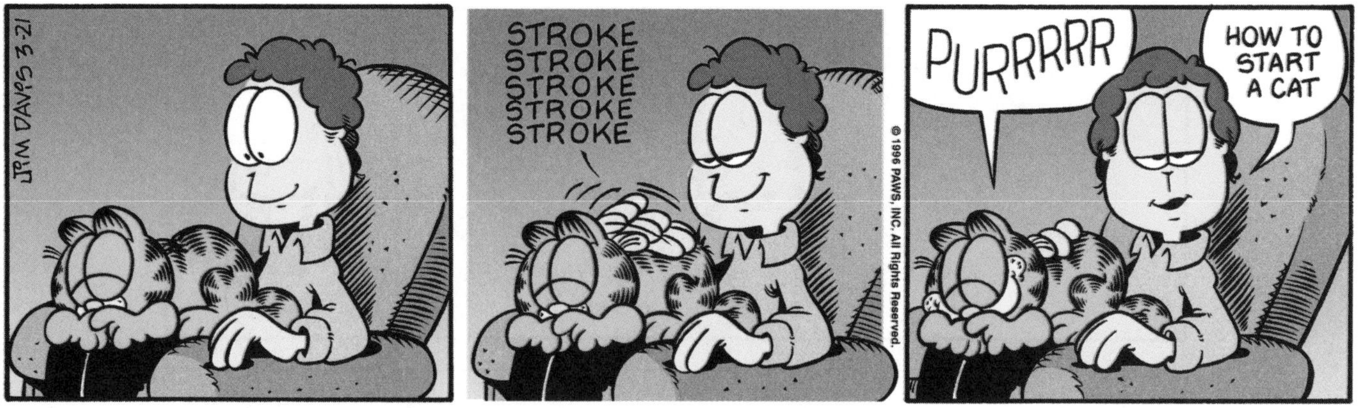
JIM DAVIS 3-21
STROKE
STROKE
STROKE
STROKE
STROKE
© 1996 PAWS, INC. All Rights Reserved.
PURRRRR
HOW TO START A CAT

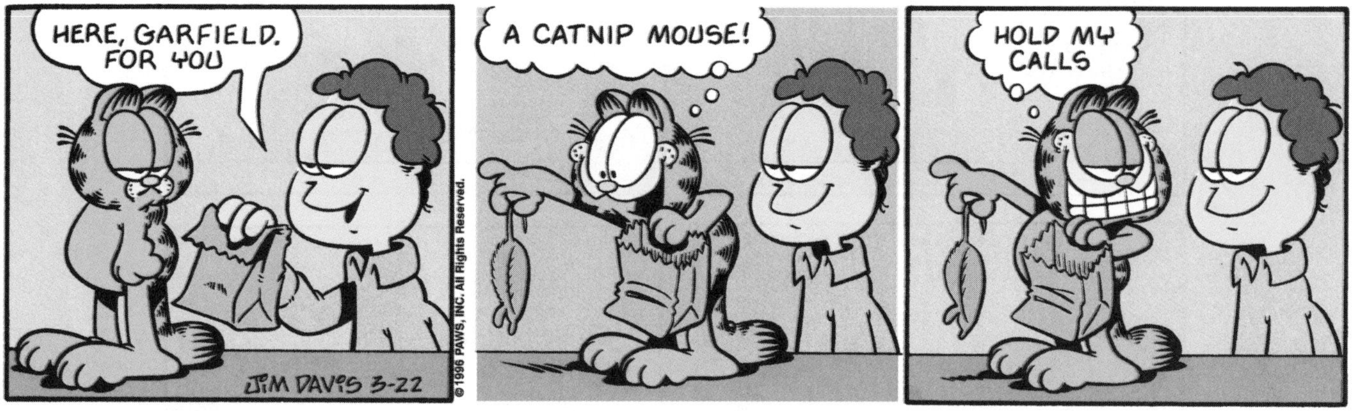
HERE, GARFIELD. FOR YOU
JIM DAVIS 3-22
© 1996 PAWS, INC. All Rights Reserved.
A CATNIP MOUSE!
HOLD MY CALLS

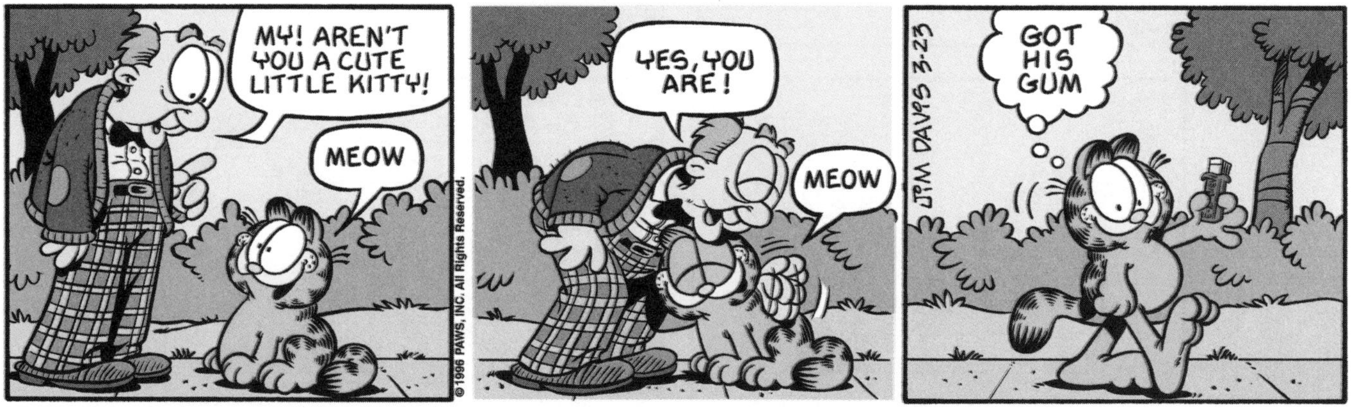
MY! AREN'T YOU A CUTE LITTLE KITTY!
MEOW
© 1996 PAWS, INC. All Rights Reserved.
YES, YOU ARE!
MEOW
JIM DAVIS 3-23
GOT HIS GUM

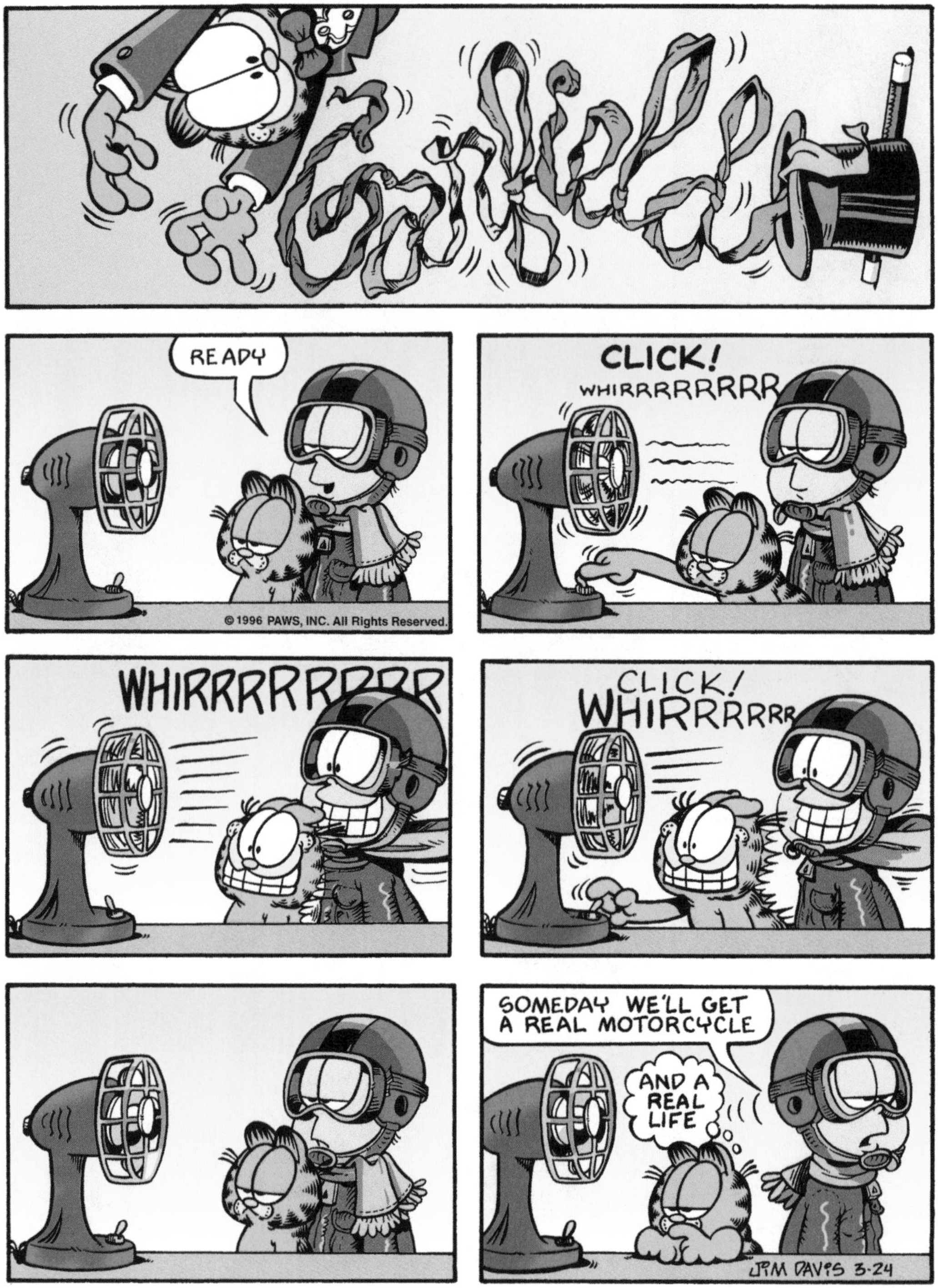

Garfield
READY
© 1996 PAWS, INC. All Rights Reserved.
CLICK!
WHIRRRRRRRR
WHIRRRRRRRR
CLICK!
WHIRRRRRR
SOMEDAY WE'LL GET A REAL MOTORCYCLE
AND A REAL LIFE
JIM DAVIS 3-24

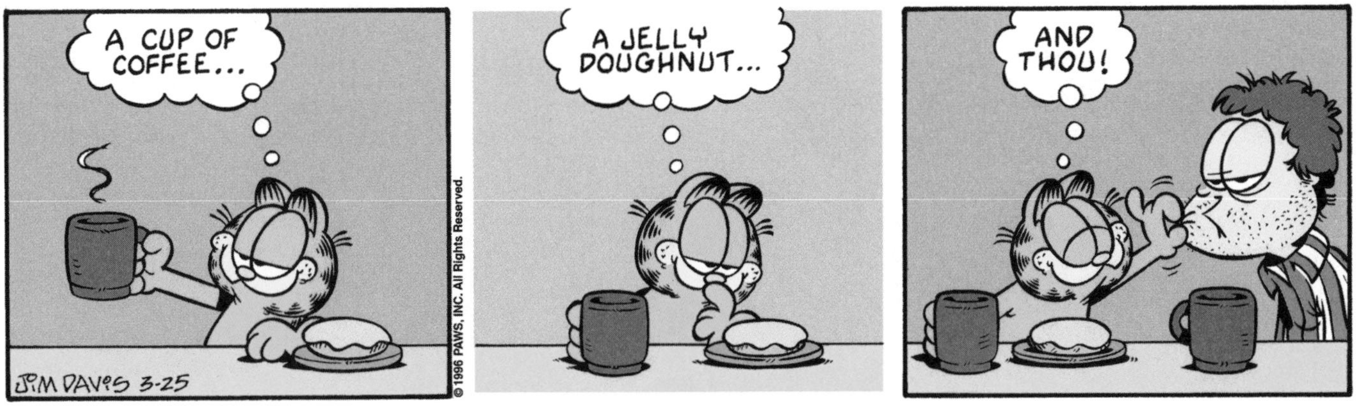
A CUP OF COFFEE...
JIM DAVIS 3-25
© 1996 PAWS, INC. All Rights Reserved.
A JELLY DOUGHNUT...
AND THOU!

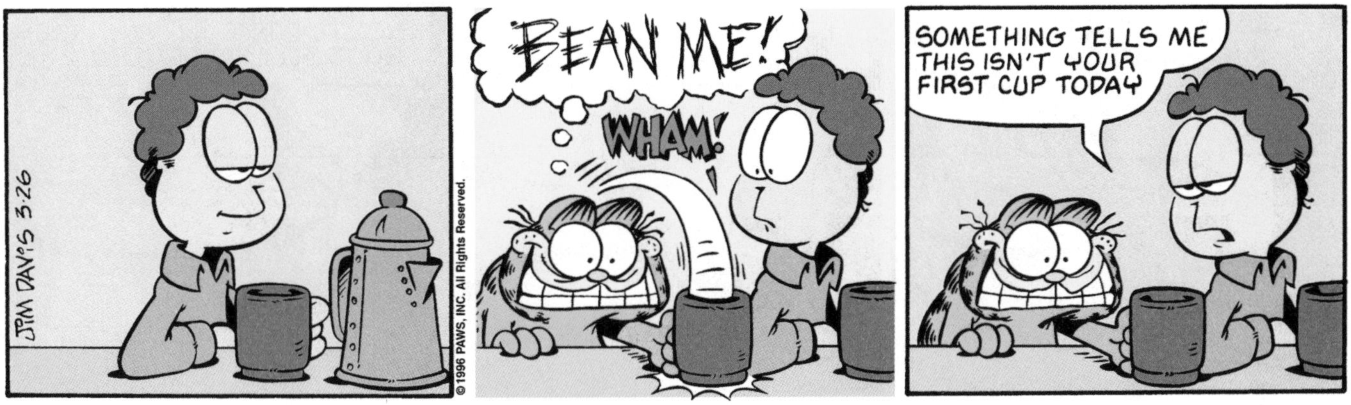
JIM DAVIS 3-26
© 1996 PAWS, INC. All Rights Reserved.
BEAN ME!
WHAM!
SOMETHING TELLS ME THIS ISN'T YOUR FIRST CUP TODAY

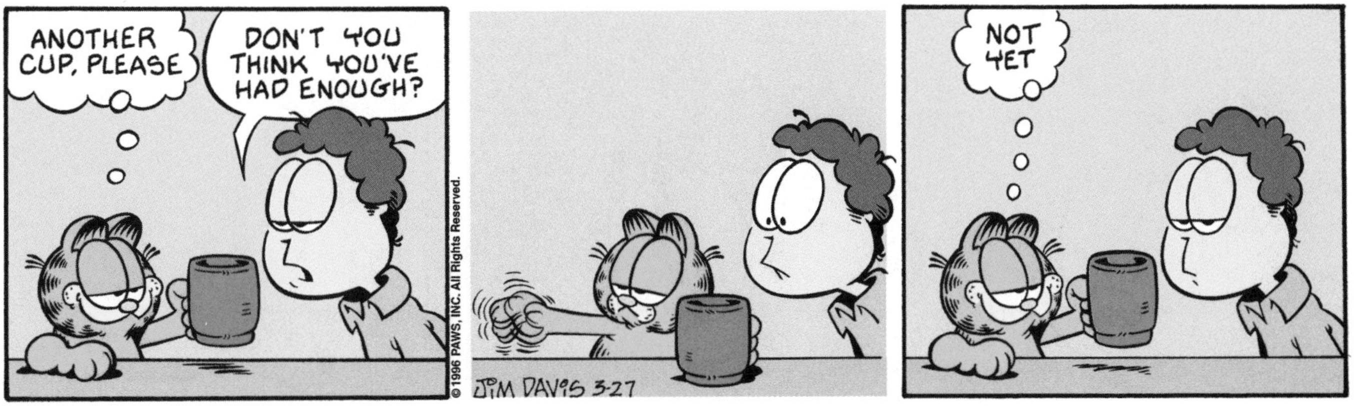
ANOTHER CUP, PLEASE
DON'T YOU THINK YOU'VE HAD ENOUGH?
© 1996 PAWS, INC. All Rights Reserved.
JIM DAVIS 3-27
NOT YET

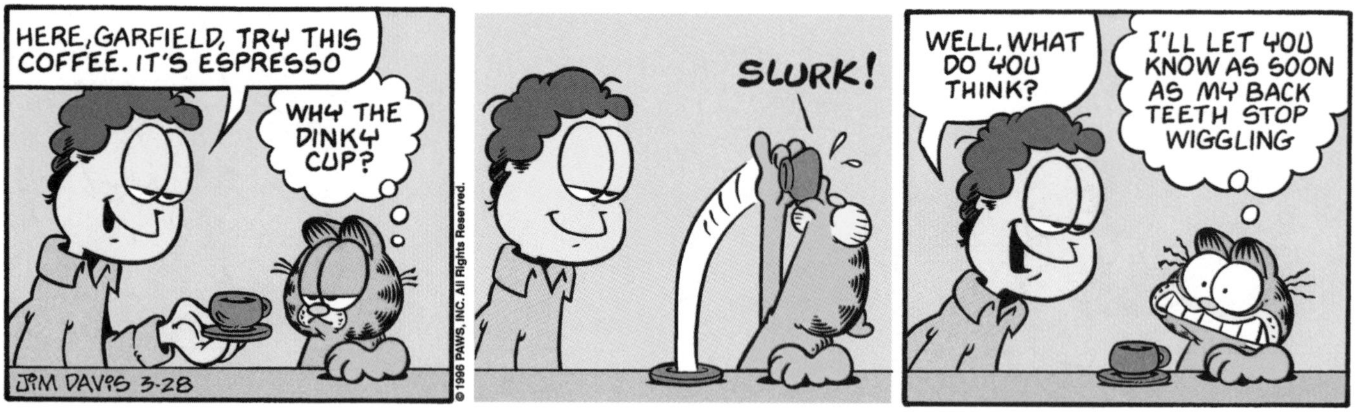
HERE, GARFIELD, TRY THIS COFFEE. IT'S ESPRESSO
WHY THE DINKY CUP?
JIM DAVIS 3-28
© 1996 PAWS, INC. All Rights Reserved.
SLURK!
WELL, WHAT DO YOU THINK?
I'LL LET YOU KNOW AS SOON AS MY BACK TEETH STOP WIGGLING

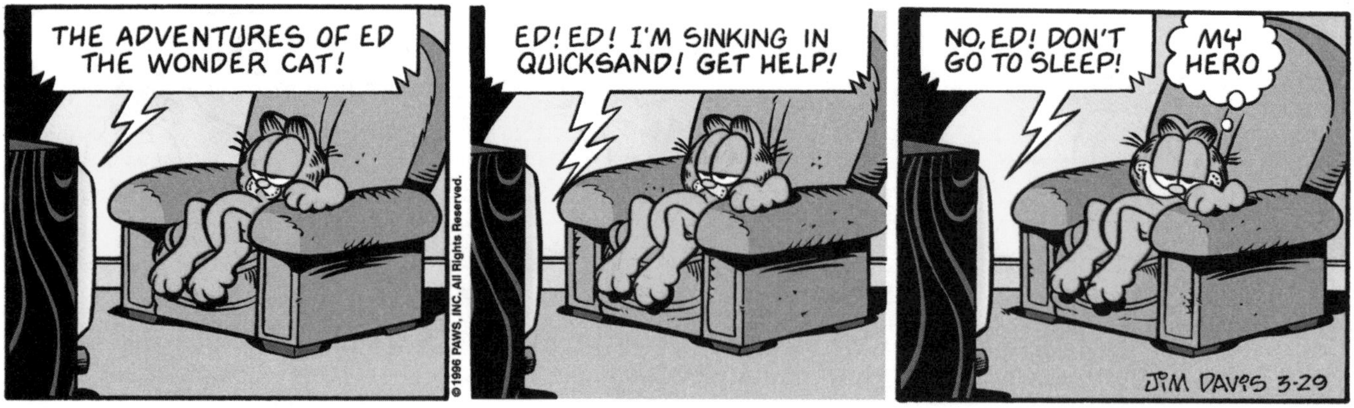
THE ADVENTURES OF ED THE WONDER CAT!
© 1996 PAWS, INC. All Rights Reserved.
ED! ED! I'M SINKING IN QUICKSAND! GET HELP!
NO, ED! DON'T GO TO SLEEP!
MY HERO
JIM DAVIS 3-29

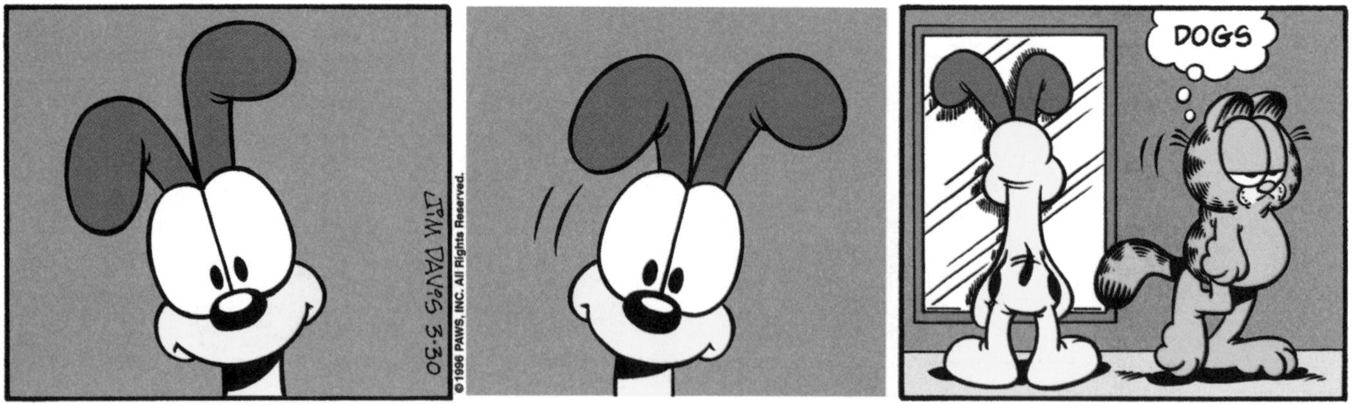
JIM DAVIS 3-30
© 1996 PAWS, INC. All Rights Reserved.
DOGS

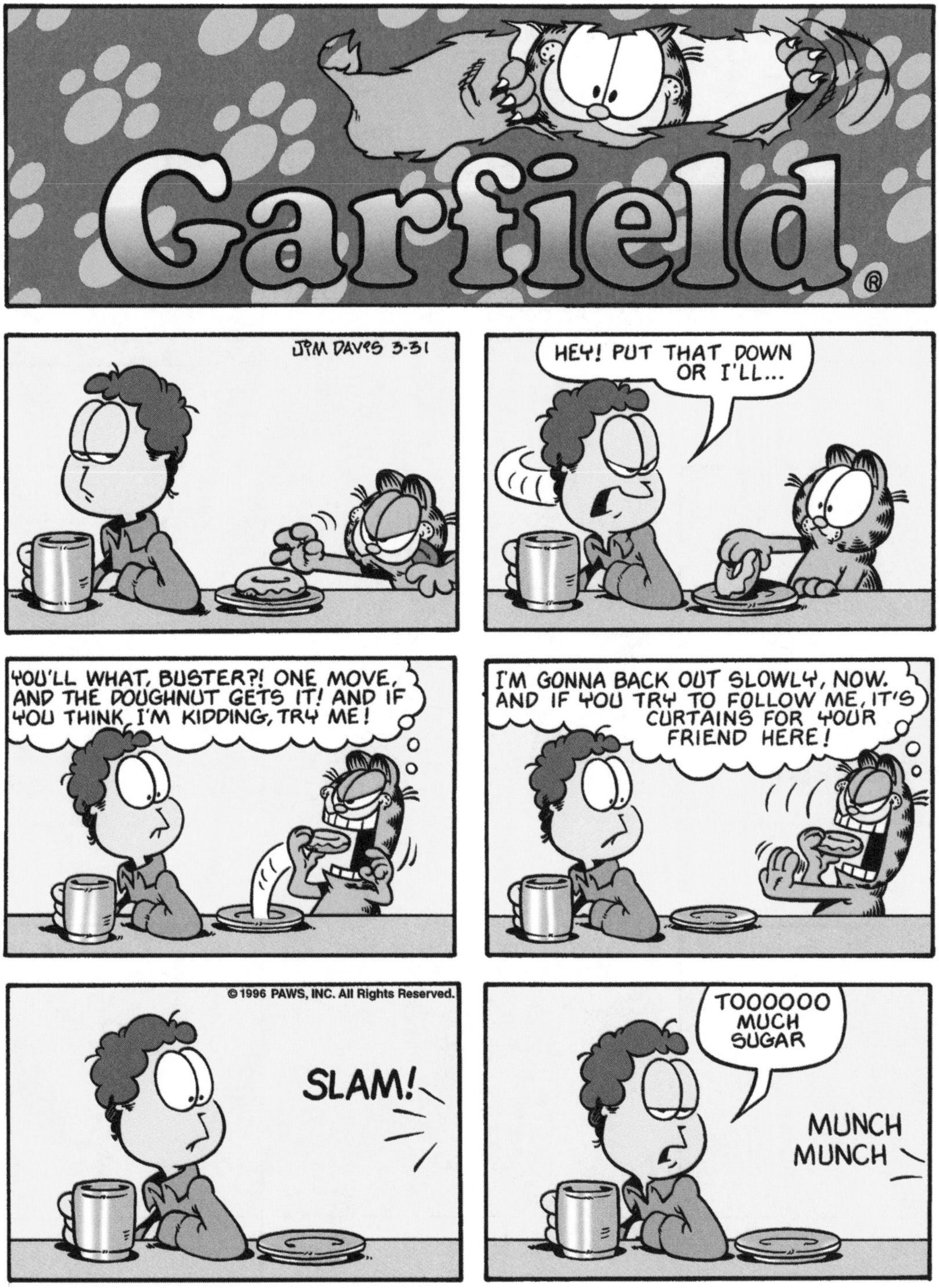
Garfield®
JIM DAVIS 3-31
HEY! PUT THAT DOWN OR I'LL...
YOU'LL WHAT, BUSTER?! ONE MOVE, AND THE DOUGHNUT GETS IT! AND IF YOU THINK I'M KIDDING, TRY ME!
I'M GONNA BACK OUT SLOWLY, NOW. AND IF YOU TRY TO FOLLOW ME, IT'S CURTAINS FOR YOUR FRIEND HERE!
SLAM!
TOOOOOO MUCH SUGAR
MUNCH MUNCH

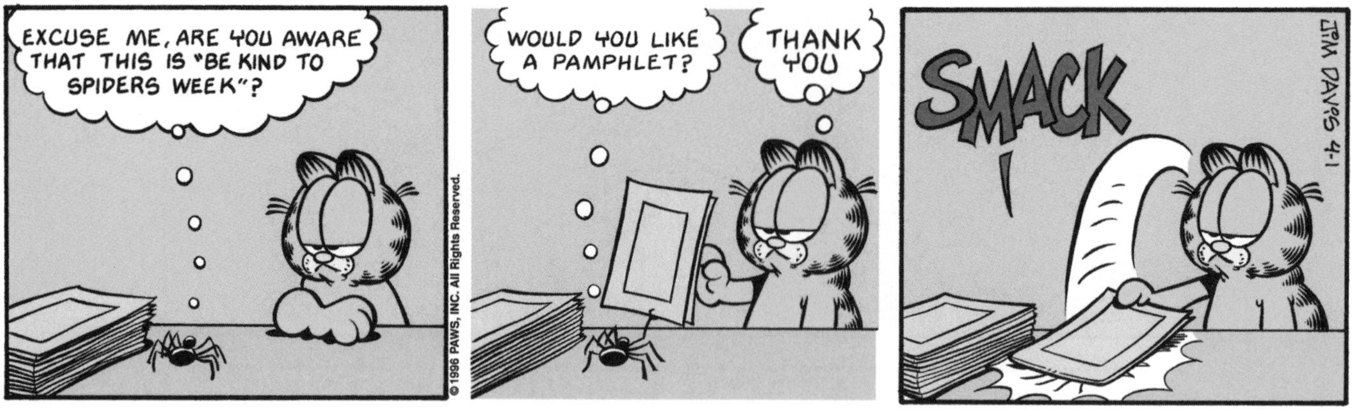
EXCUSE ME, ARE YOU AWARE THAT THIS IS "BE KIND TO SPIDERS WEEK"?
© 1996 PAWS, INC. All Rights Reserved.
WOULD YOU LIKE A PAMPHLET?
THANK YOU
SMACK
JIM DAVIS 4-1

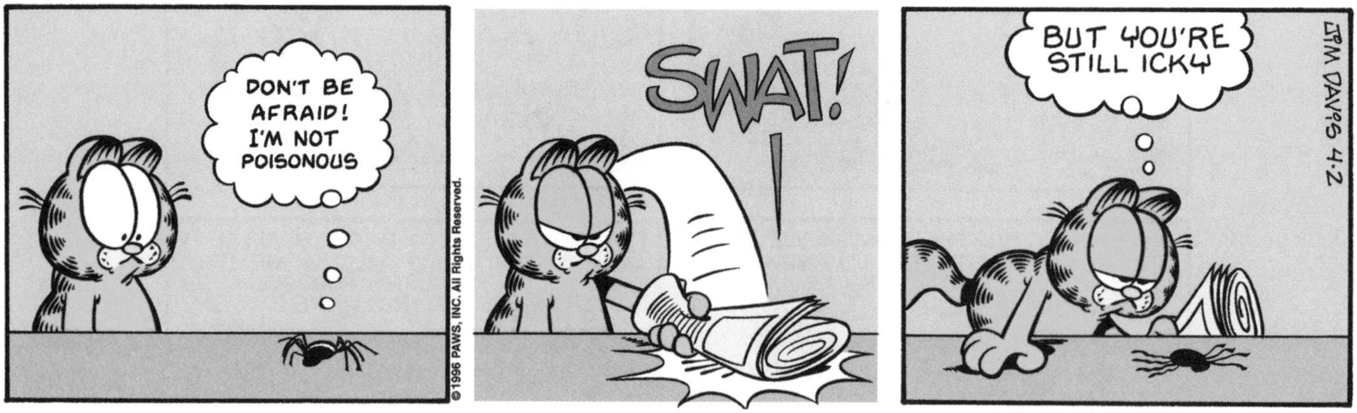
DON'T BE AFRAID! I'M NOT POISONOUS
© 1996 PAWS, INC. All Rights Reserved.
SWAT!
BUT YOU'RE STILL ICKY
JIM DAVIS 4-2

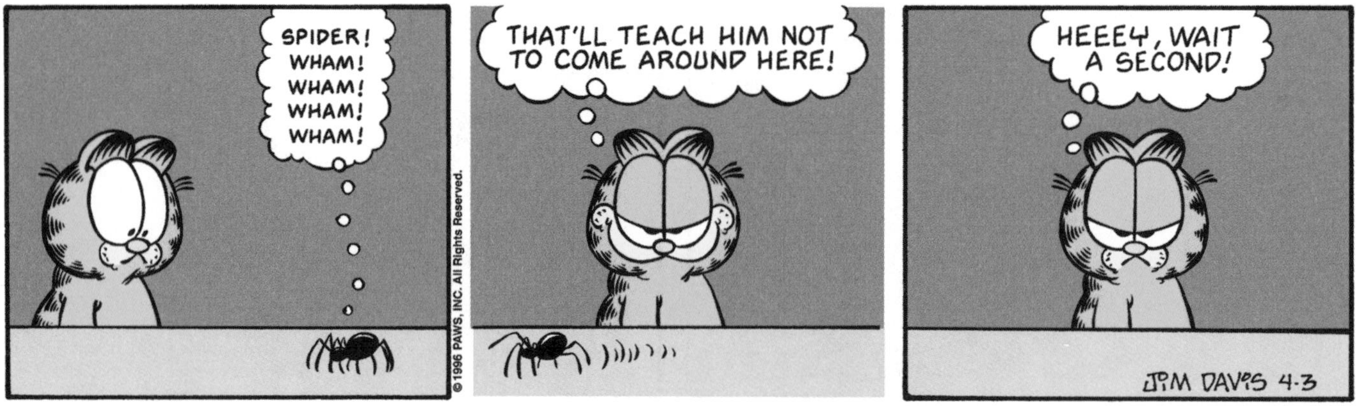
SPIDER! WHAM! WHAM! WHAM! WHAM!
© 1996 PAWS, INC. All Rights Reserved.
THAT'LL TEACH HIM NOT TO COME AROUND HERE!
HEEEY, WAIT A SECOND!
JIM DAVIS 4-3

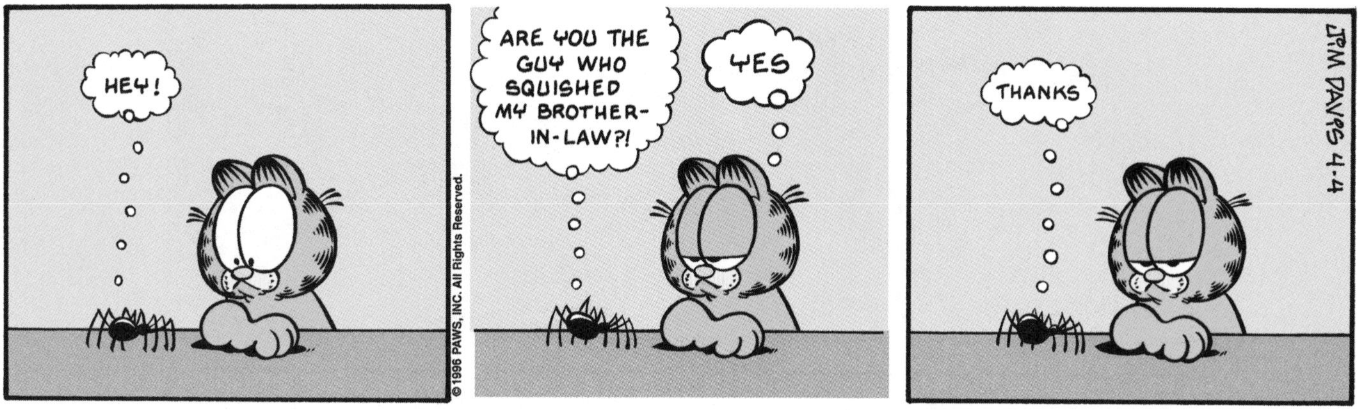
HEY!
ARE YOU THE GUY WHO SQUISHED MY BROTHER-IN-LAW?!
YES
THANKS
JIM DAVIS 4-4
© 1996 PAWS, INC. All Rights Reserved.

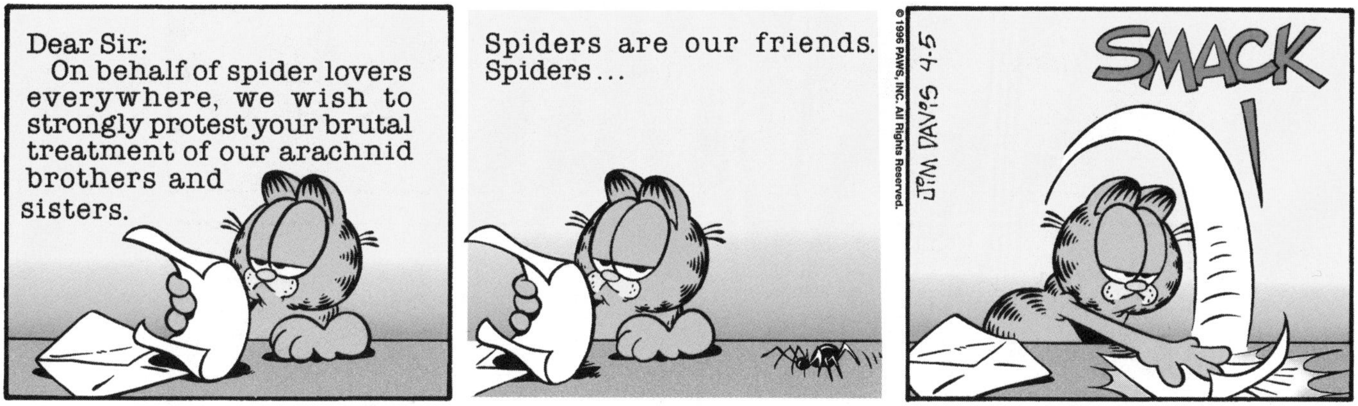
Dear Sir:
On behalf of spider lovers everywhere, we wish to strongly protest your brutal treatment of our arachnid brothers and sisters.
Spiders are our friends. Spiders...
SMACK
JIM DAVIS 4-5
© 1996 PAWS, INC. All Rights Reserved.

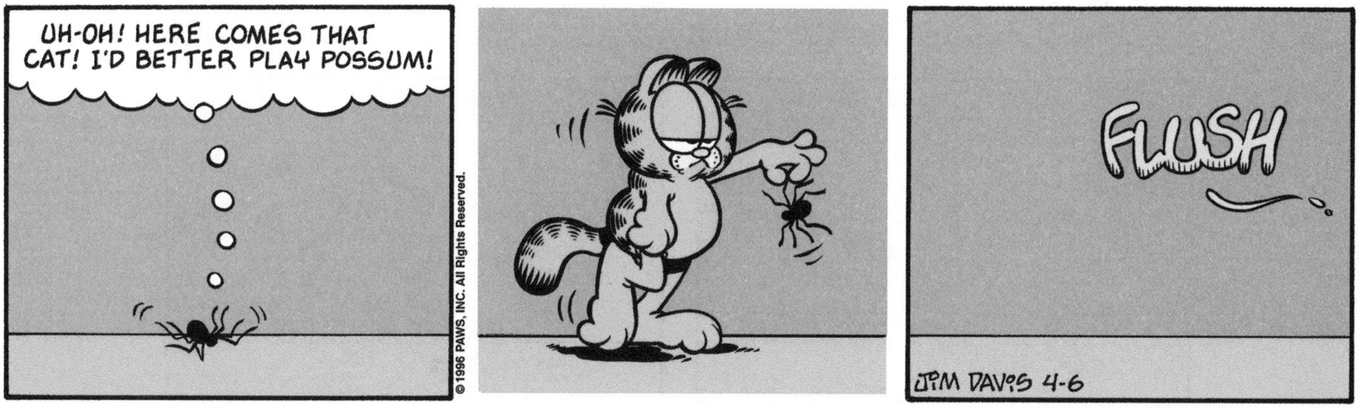
UH-OH! HERE COMES THAT CAT! I'D BETTER PLAY POSSUM!
FLUSH
JIM DAVIS 4-6
© 1996 PAWS, INC. All Rights Reserved.

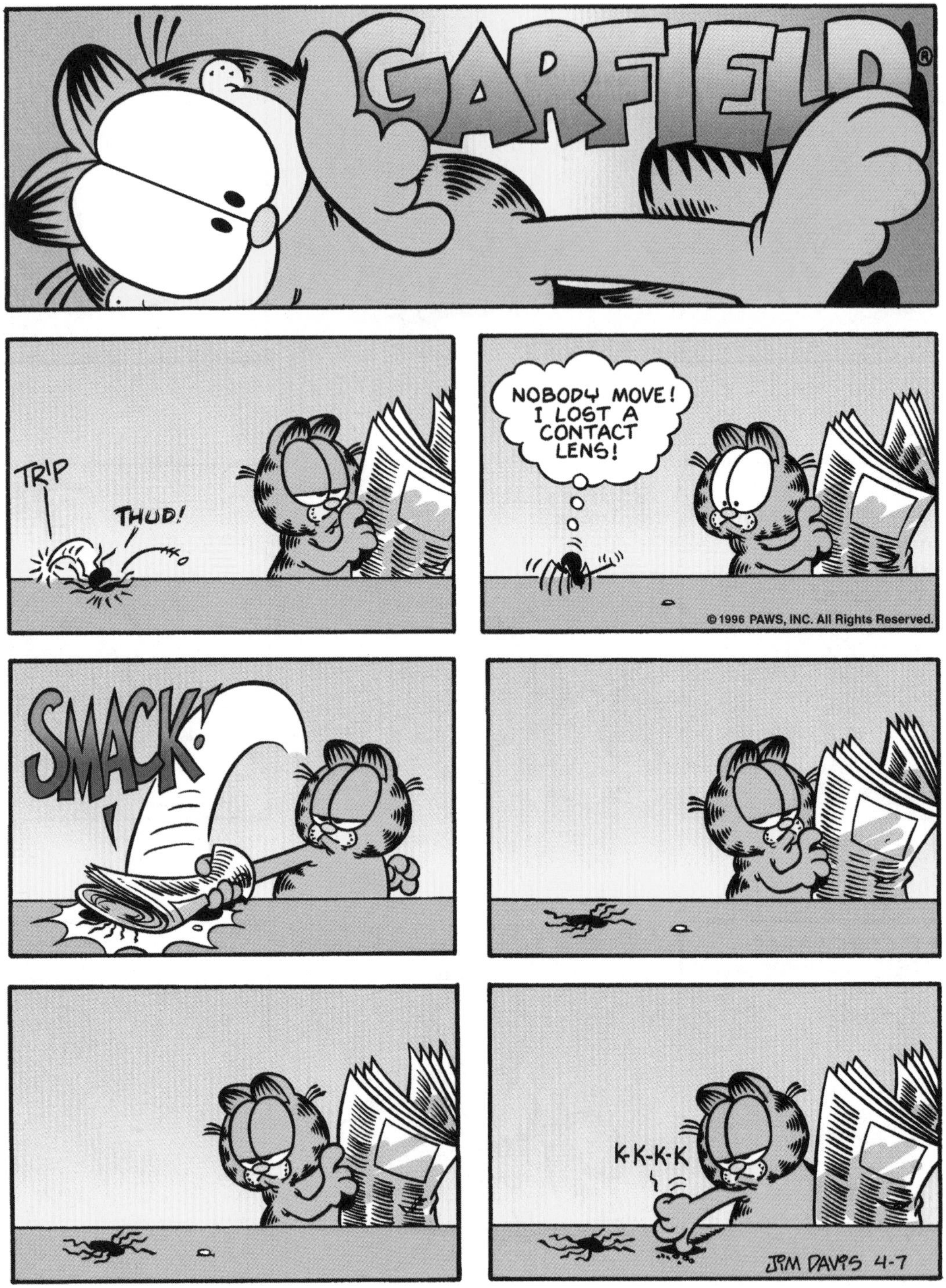
GARFIELD®
TRIP
THUD!
NOBODY MOVE! I LOST A CONTACT LENS!
© 1996 PAWS, INC. All Rights Reserved.
SMACK!
K-K-K-K
JIM DAVIS 4-7

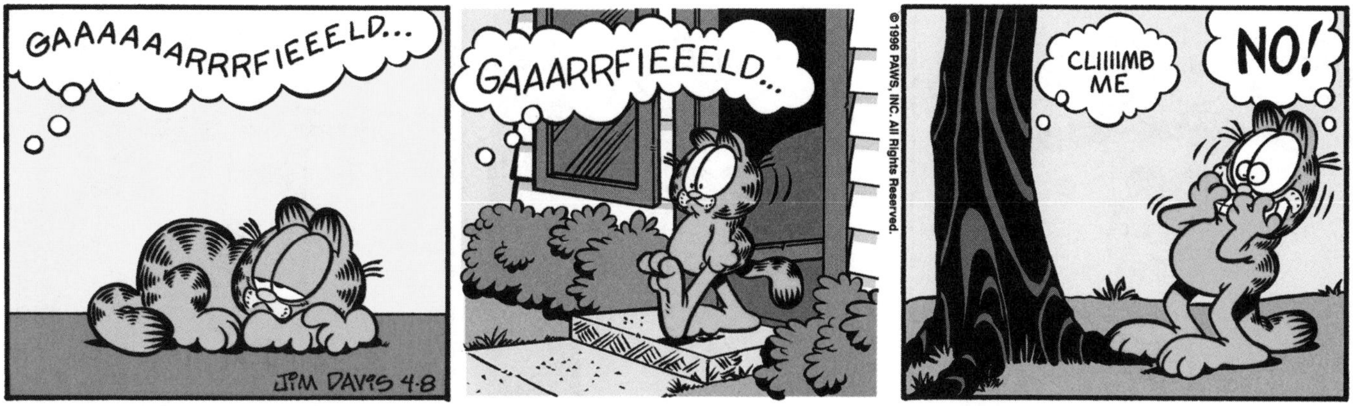
GAAAAAARRRRFIEEELD...
JIM DAVIS 4-8
GAAARRFIEEELD...
© 1996 PAWS, INC. All Rights Reserved.
CLIIIIMB ME
NO!

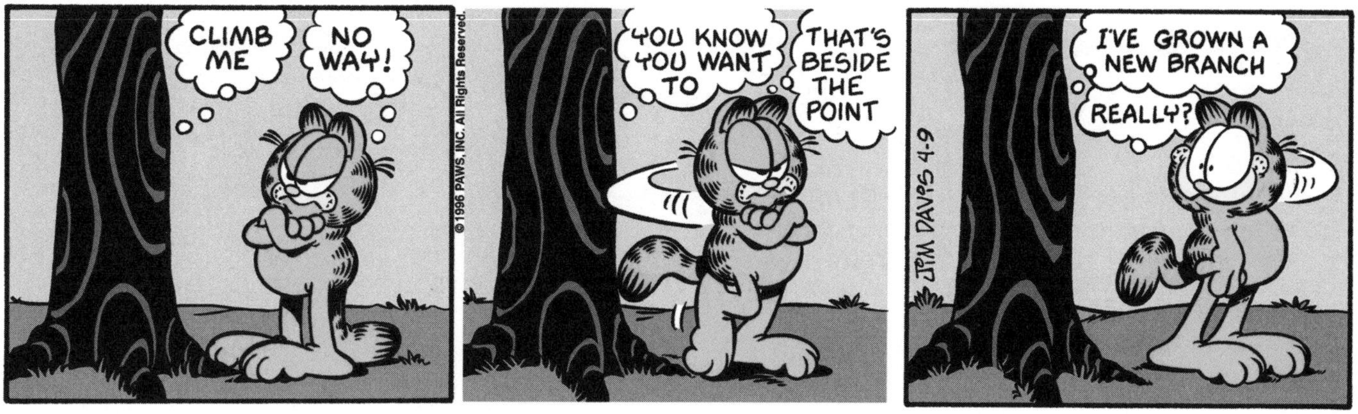
CLIMB ME
NO WAY!
© 1996 PAWS, INC. All Rights Reserved.
YOU KNOW YOU WANT TO
THAT'S BESIDE THE POINT
JIM DAVIS 4-9
I'VE GROWN A NEW BRANCH
REALLY?

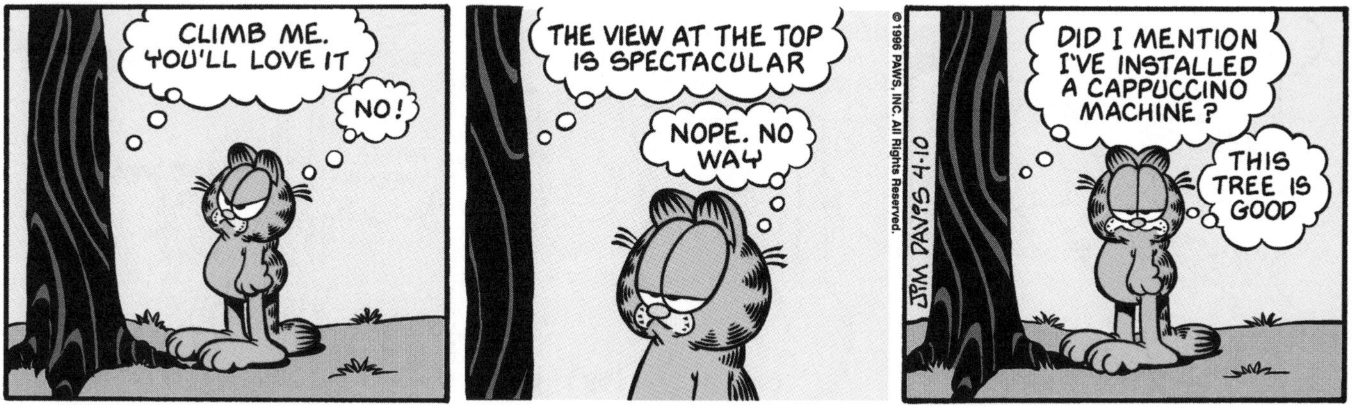
CLIMB ME. YOU'LL LOVE IT
NO!
THE VIEW AT THE TOP IS SPECTACULAR
NOPE. NO WAY
© 1996 PAWS, INC. All Rights Reserved.
JIM DAVIS 4-10
DID I MENTION I'VE INSTALLED A CAPPUCCINO MACHINE?
THIS TREE IS GOOD

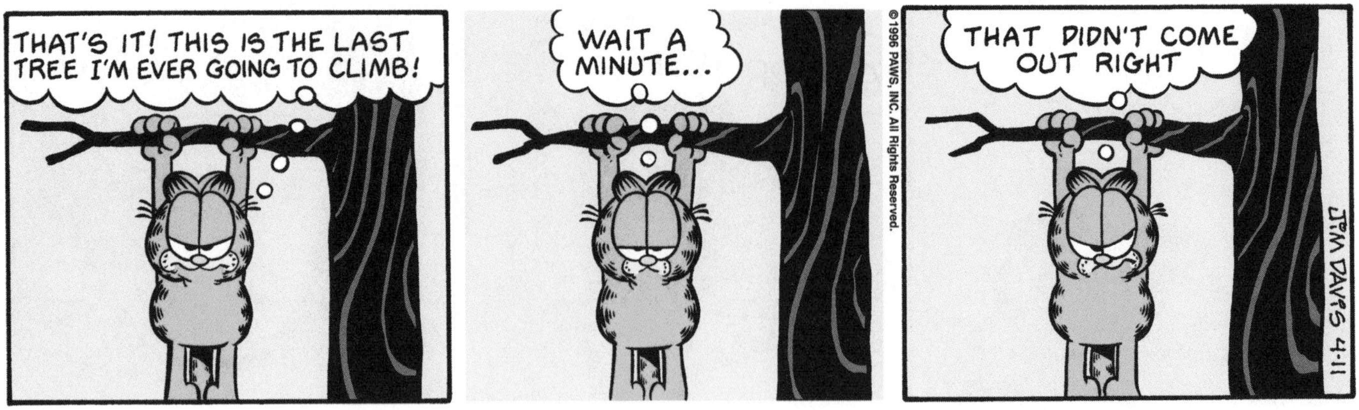
THAT'S IT! THIS IS THE LAST TREE I'M EVER GOING TO CLIMB!
WAIT A MINUTE...
© 1996 PAWS, INC. All Rights Reserved.
THAT DIDN'T COME OUT RIGHT
JPM DAVIS 4-11

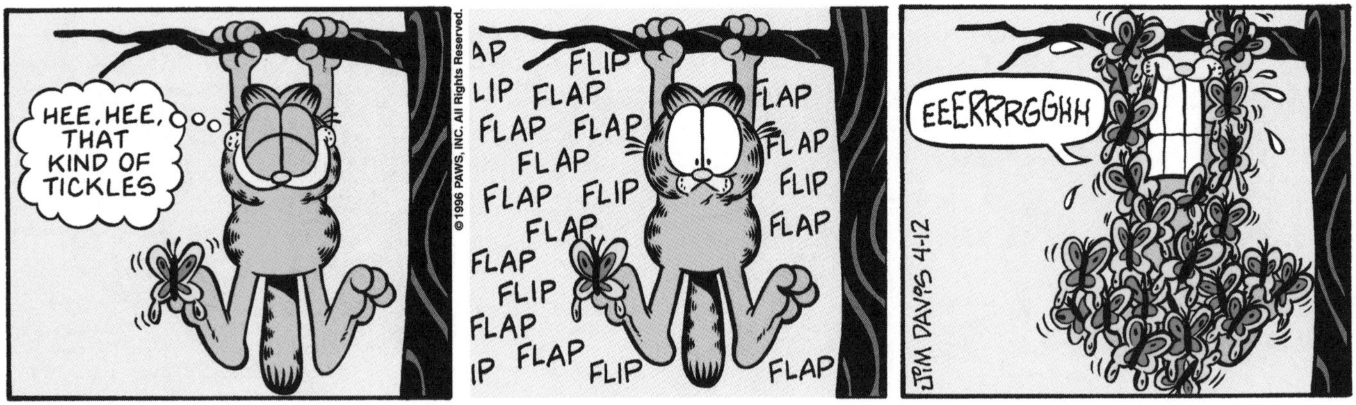
HEE, HEE, THAT KIND OF TICKLES
© 1996 PAWS, INC. All Rights Reserved.
FLIP FLAP FLAP FLAP FLAP FLIP FLAP FLAP FLIP FLAP FLAP FLIP FLAP FLIP FLAP FLAP
EEERRRGGHH
JPM DAVIS 4-12

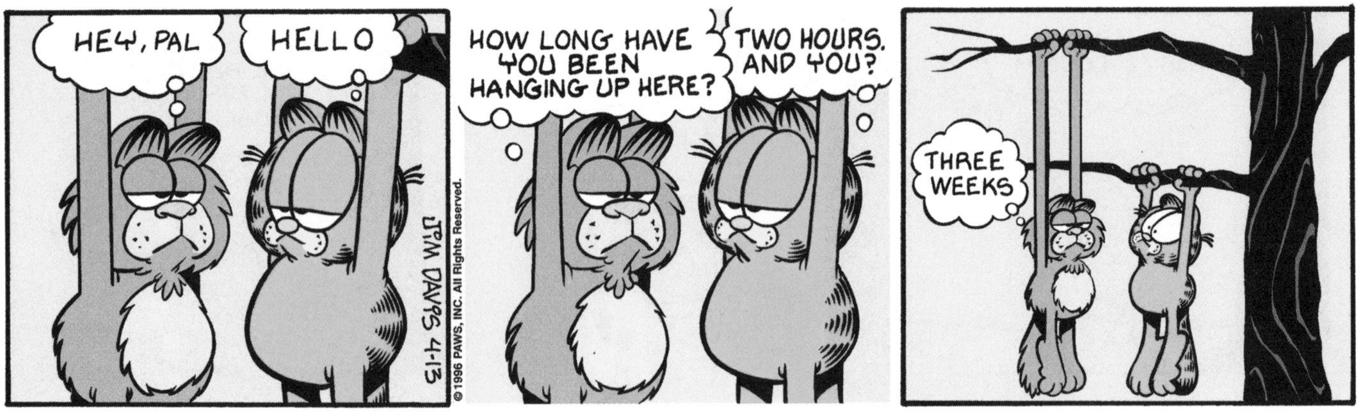
HEY, PAL
HELLO
JPM DAVIS 4-13
© 1996 PAWS, INC. All Rights Reserved.
HOW LONG HAVE YOU BEEN HANGING UP HERE?
TWO HOURS. AND YOU?
THREE WEEKS

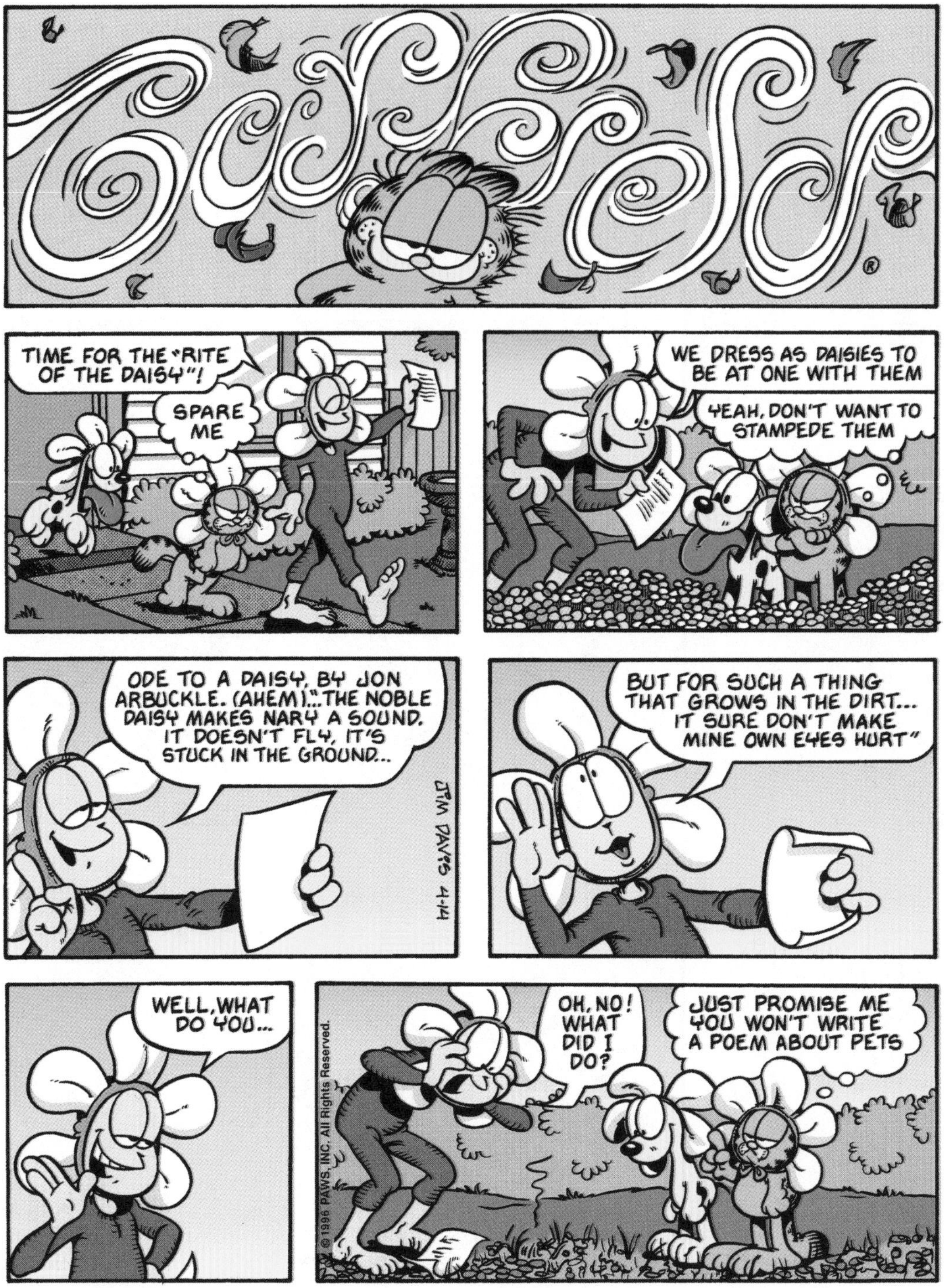
GARFIELD®
TIME FOR THE "RITE OF THE DAISY"!
SPARE ME
WE DRESS AS DAISIES TO BE AT ONE WITH THEM
YEAH, DON'T WANT TO STAMPEDE THEM
ODE TO A DAISY, BY JON ARBUCKLE. (AHEM)..."THE NOBLE DAISY MAKES NARY A SOUND. IT DOESN'T FLY, IT'S STUCK IN THE GROUND...
JIM DAVIS 4-14
BUT FOR SUCH A THING THAT GROWS IN THE DIRT... IT SURE DON'T MAKE MINE OWN EYES HURT"
WELL, WHAT DO YOU...
OH, NO! WHAT DID I DO?
JUST PROMISE ME YOU WON'T WRITE A POEM ABOUT PETS

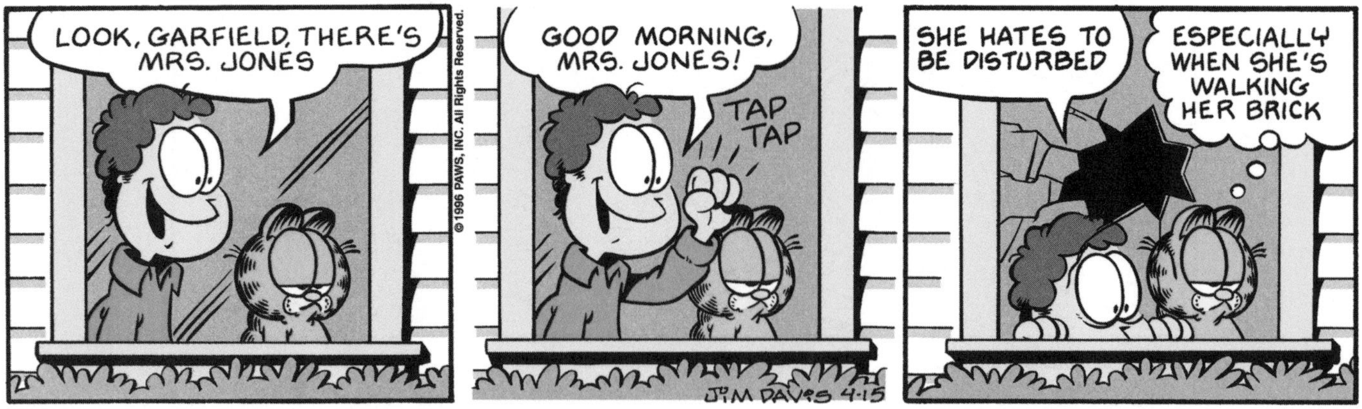
LOOK, GARFIELD, THERE'S MRS. JONES
© 1996 PAWS, INC. All Rights Reserved.
GOOD MORNING, MRS. JONES!
TAP TAP
JIM DAVIS 4-15
SHE HATES TO BE DISTURBED
ESPECIALLY WHEN SHE'S WALKING HER BRICK

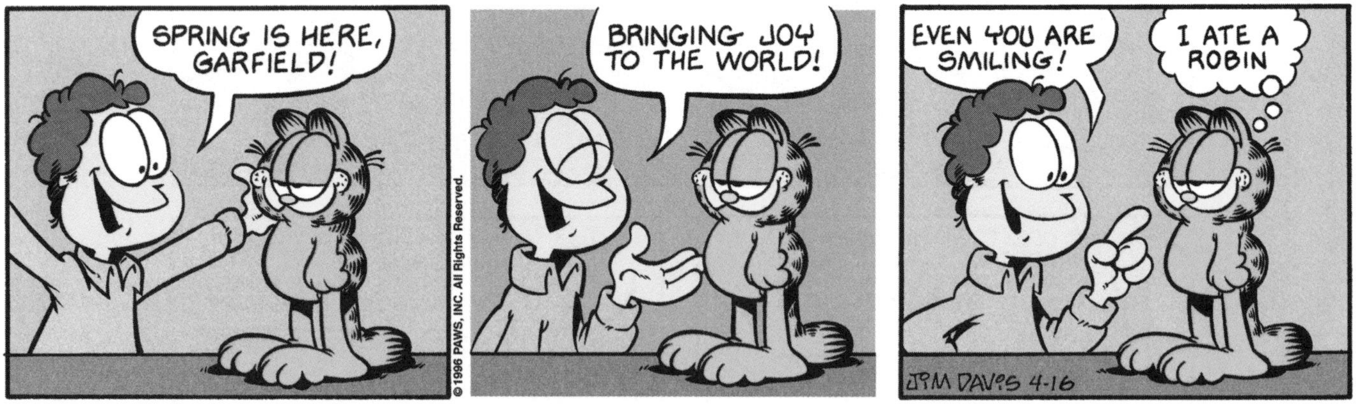
SPRING IS HERE, GARFIELD!
© 1996 PAWS, INC. All Rights Reserved.
BRINGING JOY TO THE WORLD!
EVEN YOU ARE SMILING!
I ATE A ROBIN
JIM DAVIS 4-16

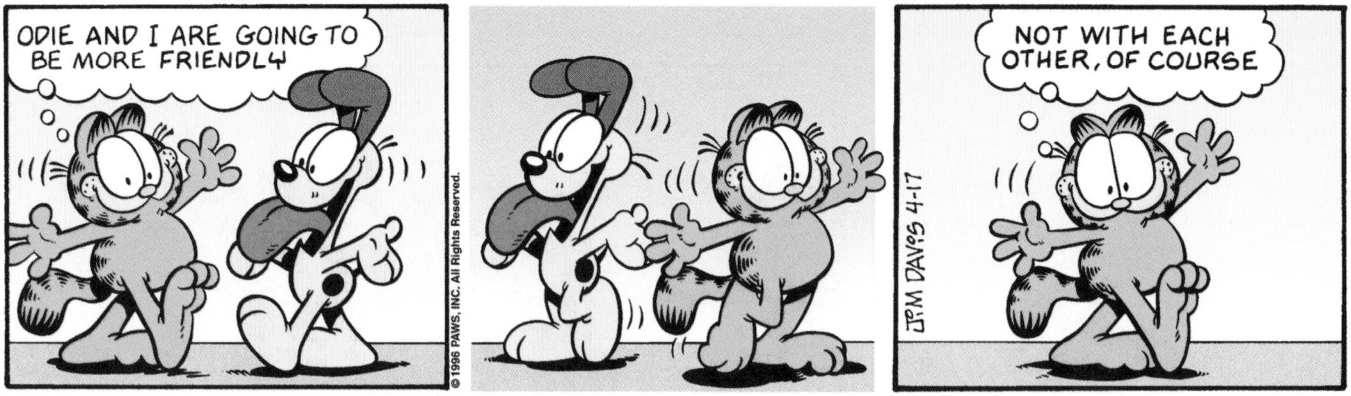
ODIE AND I ARE GOING TO BE MORE FRIENDLY
© 1996 PAWS, INC. All Rights Reserved.
JIM DAVIS 4-17
NOT WITH EACH OTHER, OF COURSE

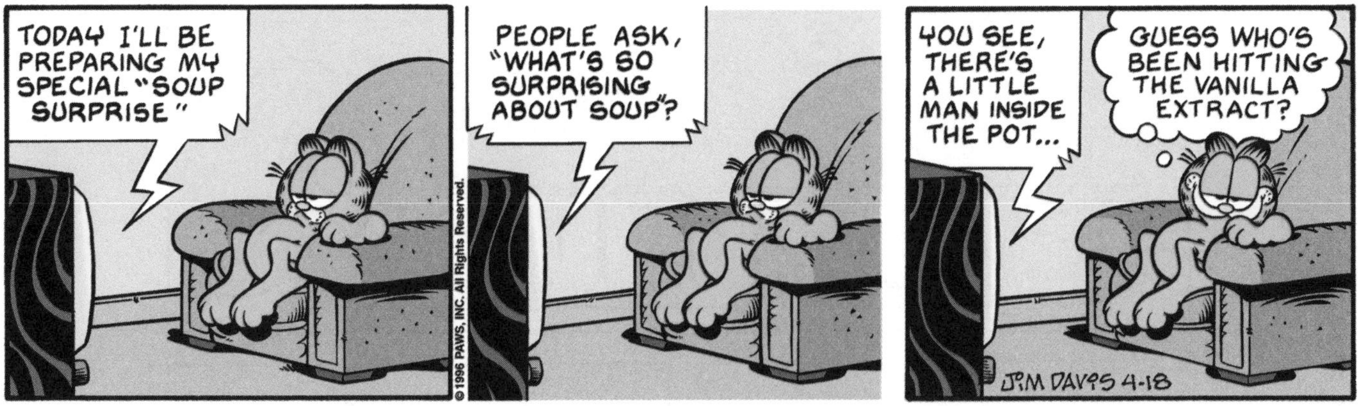
TODAY I'LL BE PREPARING MY SPECIAL "SOUP SURPRISE"
PEOPLE ASK, "WHAT'S SO SURPRISING ABOUT SOUP"?
YOU SEE, THERE'S A LITTLE MAN INSIDE THE POT...
GUESS WHO'S BEEN HITTING THE VANILLA EXTRACT?
© 1996 PAWS, INC. All Rights Reserved.
JIM DAVIS 4-18

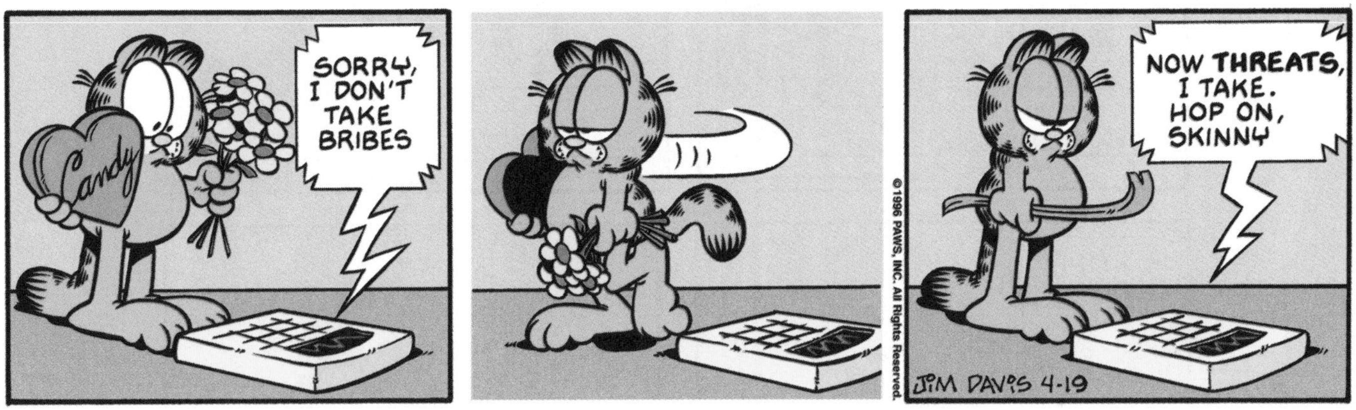
Candy
SORRY, I DON'T TAKE BRIBES
NOW **THREATS**, I TAKE. HOP ON, SKINNY
© 1996 PAWS, INC. All Rights Reserved.
JIM DAVIS 4-19

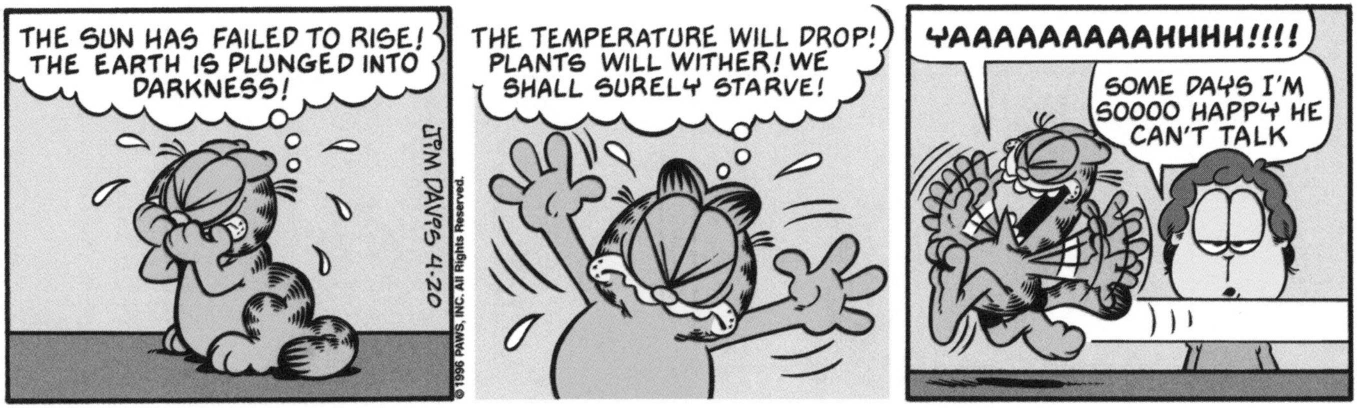
THE SUN HAS FAILED TO RISE! THE EARTH IS PLUNGED INTO DARKNESS!
JIM DAVIS 4-20
© 1996 PAWS, INC. All Rights Reserved.
THE TEMPERATURE WILL DROP! PLANTS WILL WITHER! WE SHALL SURELY STARVE!
YAAAAAAAAAHHHH!!!!
SOME DAYS I'M SOOOO HAPPY HE CAN'T TALK

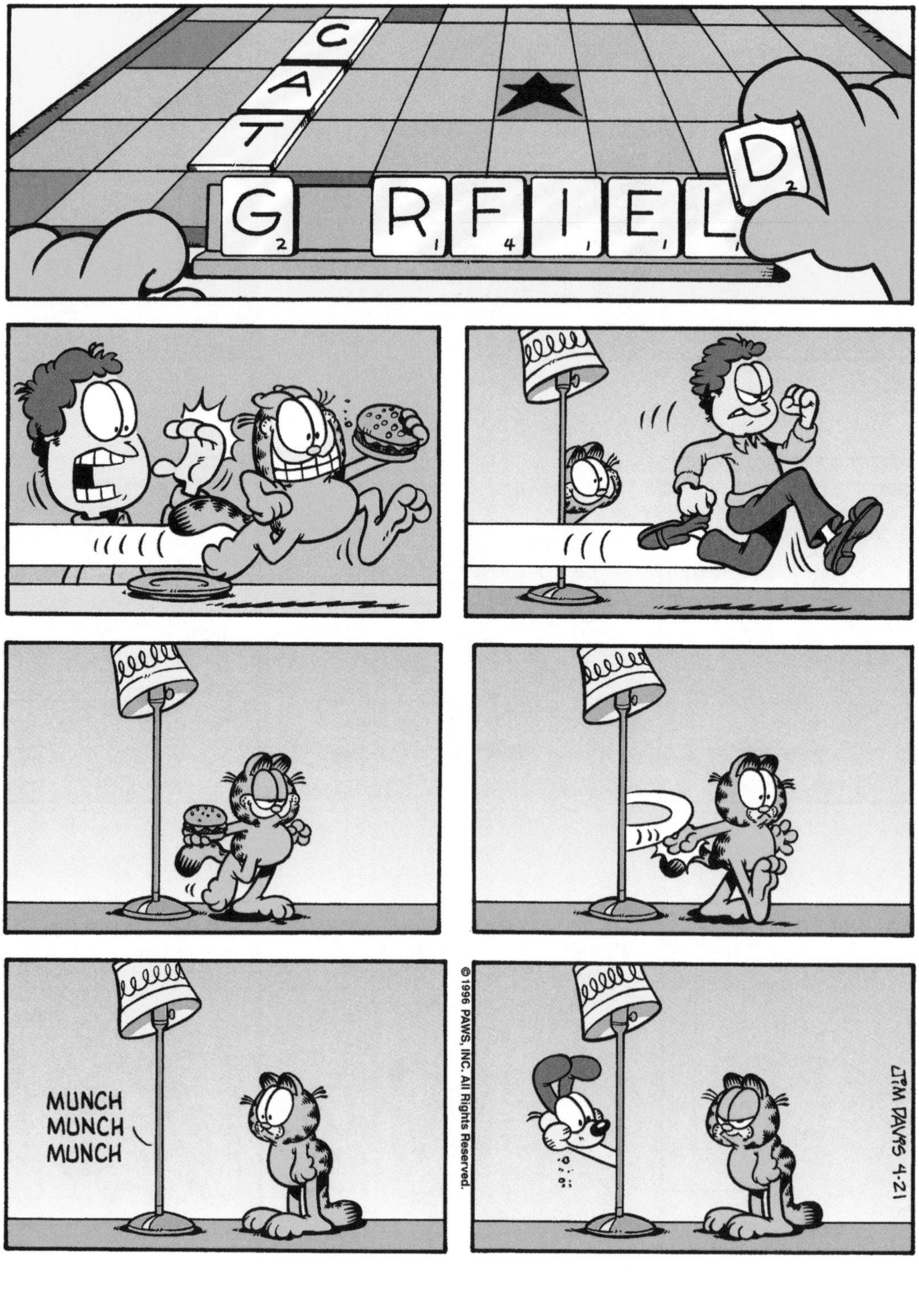

C
A
T
G RFIELD
MUNCH
MUNCH
MUNCH
JIM DAVIS 4-21

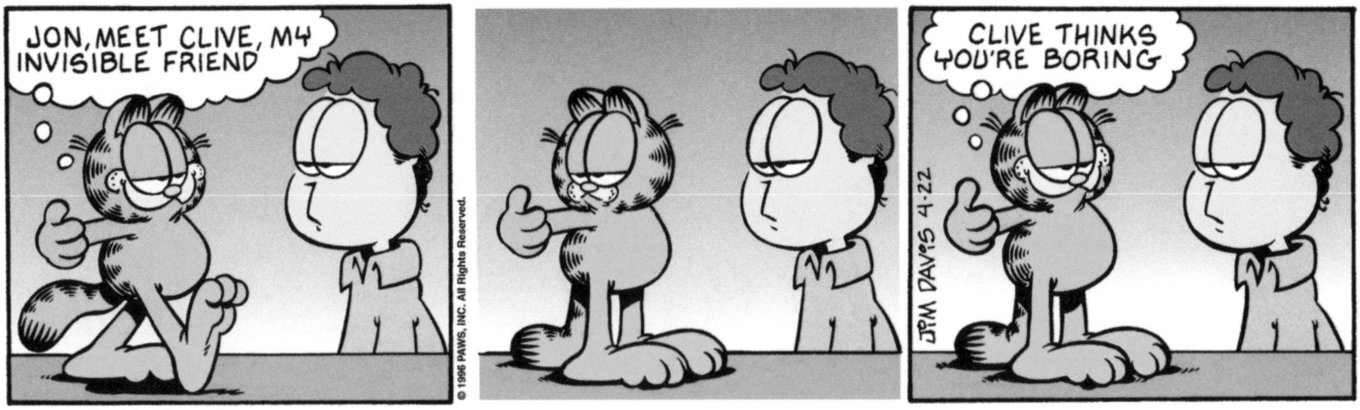
JON, MEET CLIVE, MY INVISIBLE FRIEND
CLIVE THINKS YOU'RE BORING
© 1996 PAWS, INC. All Rights Reserved.
JIM DAVIS 4-22

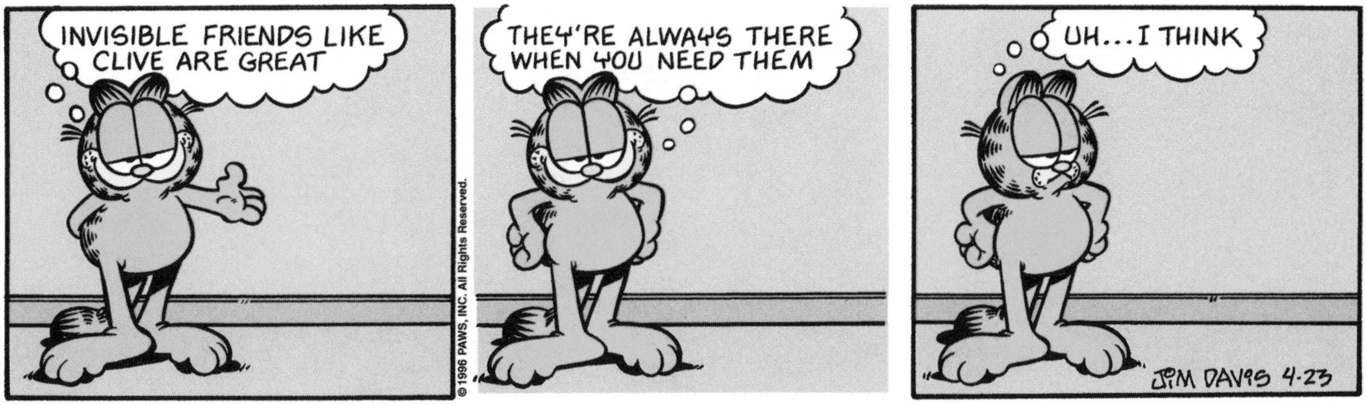
INVISIBLE FRIENDS LIKE CLIVE ARE GREAT
THEY'RE ALWAYS THERE WHEN YOU NEED THEM
UH... I THINK
© 1996 PAWS, INC. All Rights Reserved.
JIM DAVIS 4-23

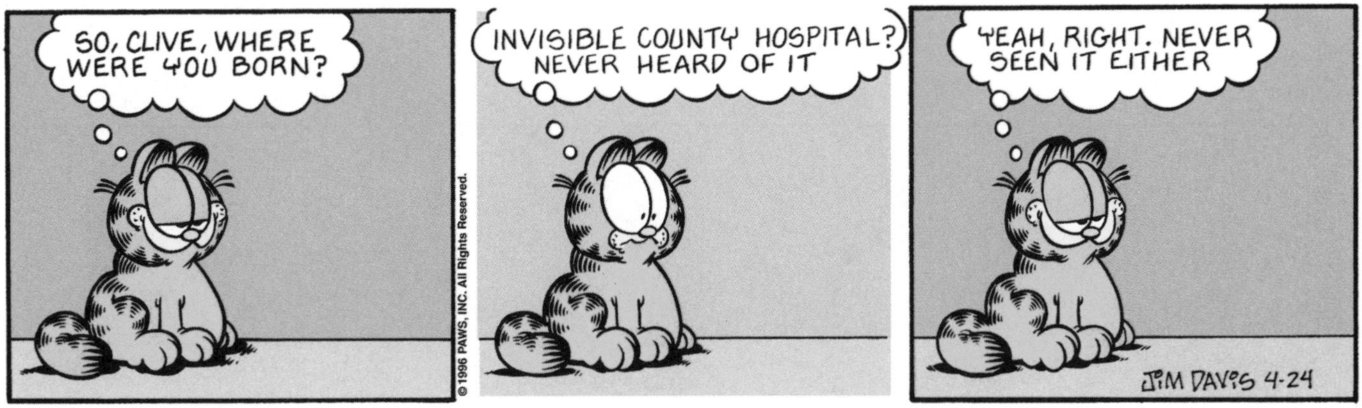
SO, CLIVE, WHERE WERE YOU BORN?
INVISIBLE COUNTY HOSPITAL? NEVER HEARD OF IT
YEAH, RIGHT. NEVER SEEN IT EITHER
© 1996 PAWS, INC. All Rights Reserved.
JIM DAVIS 4-24

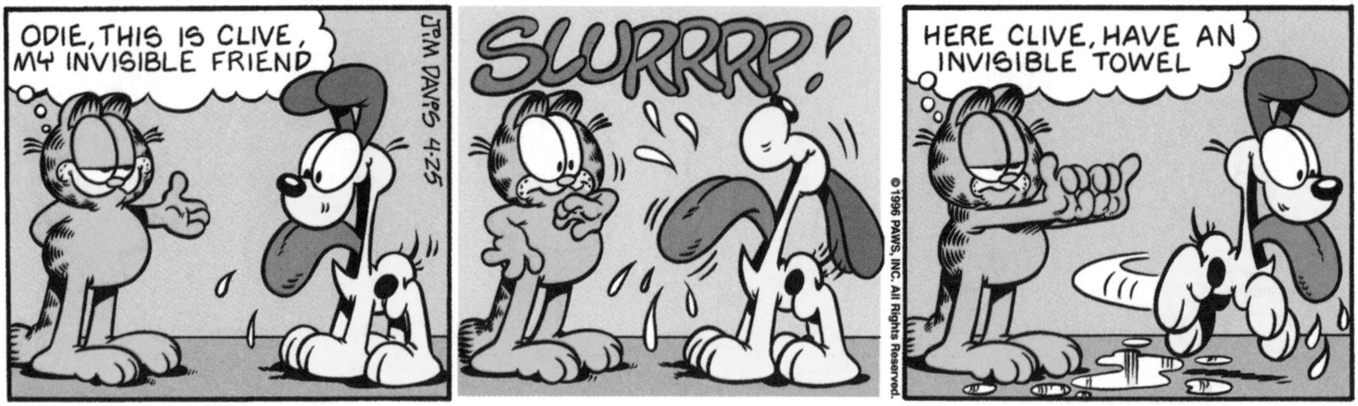
ODIE, THIS IS CLIVE, MY INVISIBLE FRIEND
JIM DAVIS 4-25
SLURRRP!
© 1996 PAWS, INC. All Rights Reserved.
HERE CLIVE, HAVE AN INVISIBLE TOWEL

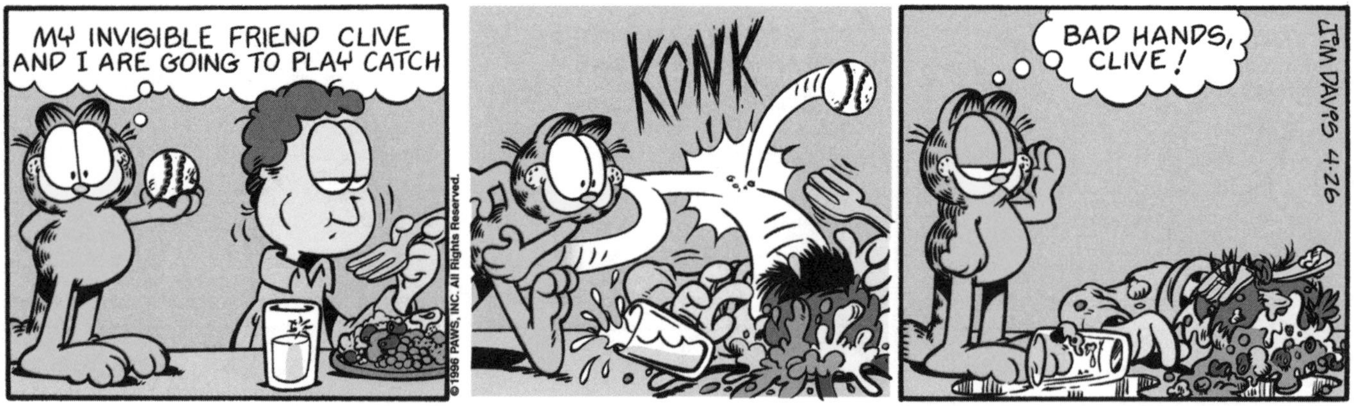
MY INVISIBLE FRIEND CLIVE AND I ARE GOING TO PLAY CATCH
© 1996 PAWS, INC. All Rights Reserved.
KONK
BAD HANDS, CLIVE!
JIM DAVIS 4-26

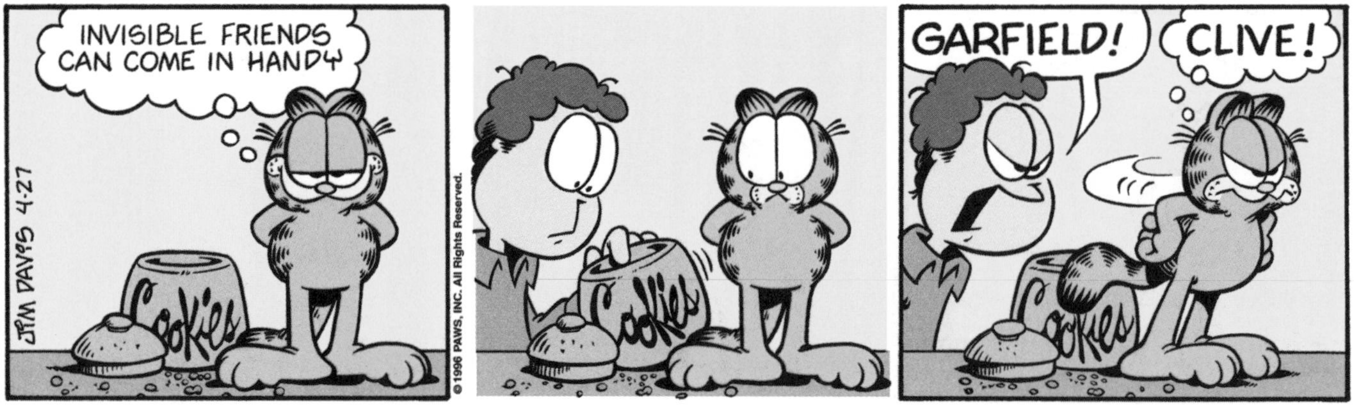
INVISIBLE FRIENDS CAN COME IN HANDY
JIM DAVIS 4-27
Cookies
© 1996 PAWS, INC. All Rights Reserved.
GARFIELD!
CLIVE!

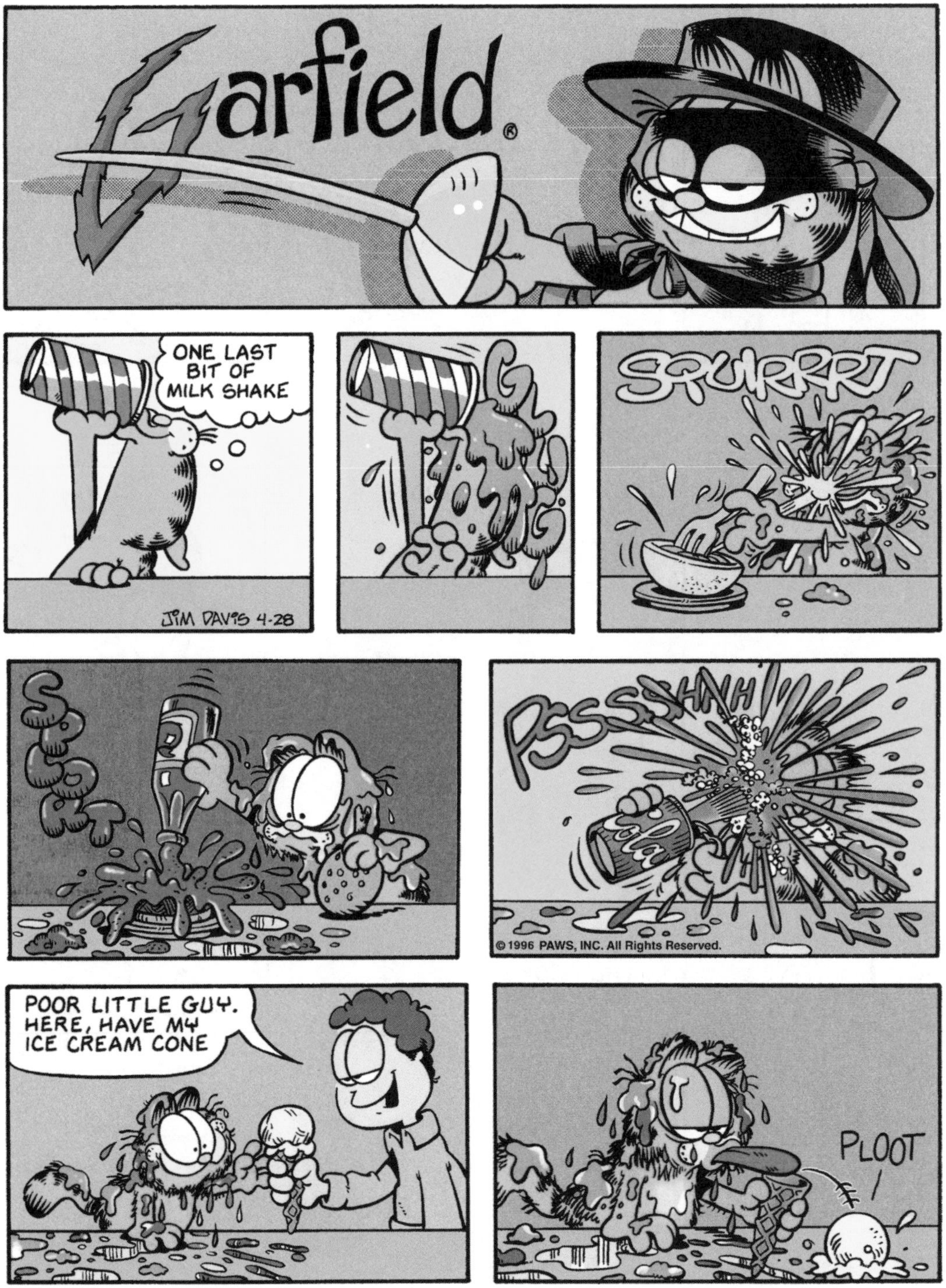
Garfield®
ONE LAST BIT OF MILK SHAKE
JIM DAVIS 4-28
SQUIRRRT
© 1996 PAWS, INC. All Rights Reserved.
POOR LITTLE GUY. HERE, HAVE MY ICE CREAM CONE
PLOOT

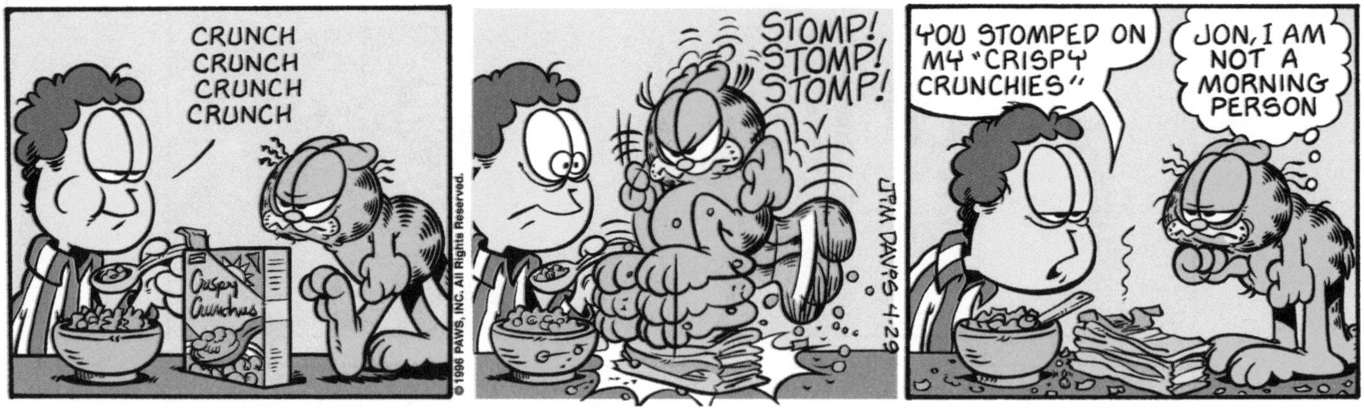
CRUNCH CRUNCH CRUNCH CRUNCH
Crispy Crunchies
© 1996 PAWS, INC. All Rights Reserved.
STOMP! STOMP! STOMP!
JIM DAVIS 4-29
YOU STOMPED ON MY "CRISPY CRUNCHIES"
JON, I AM NOT A MORNING PERSON

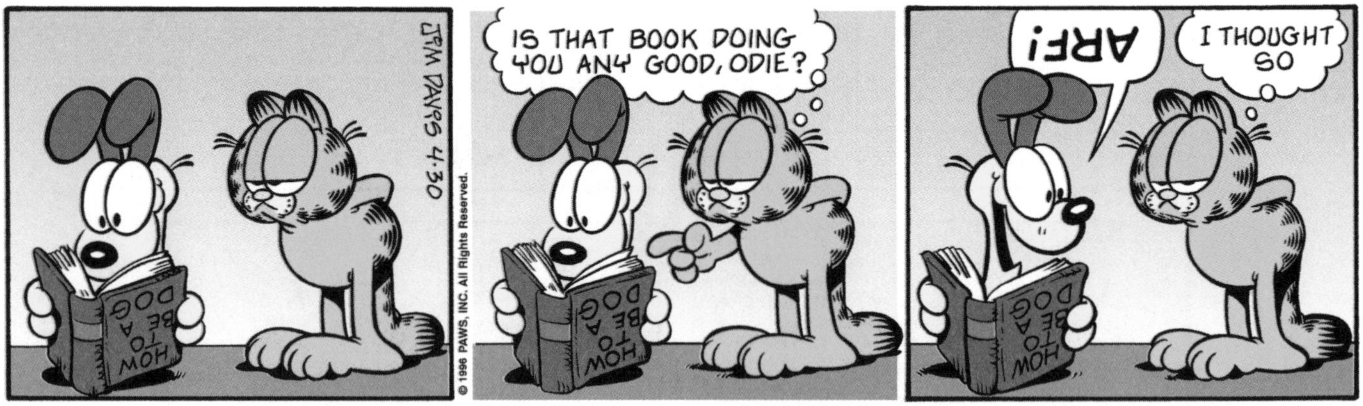
JIM DAVIS 4-30
HOW TO BE A DOG
© 1996 PAWS, INC. All Rights Reserved.
IS THAT BOOK DOING YOU ANY GOOD, ODIE?
ARF!
I THOUGHT SO

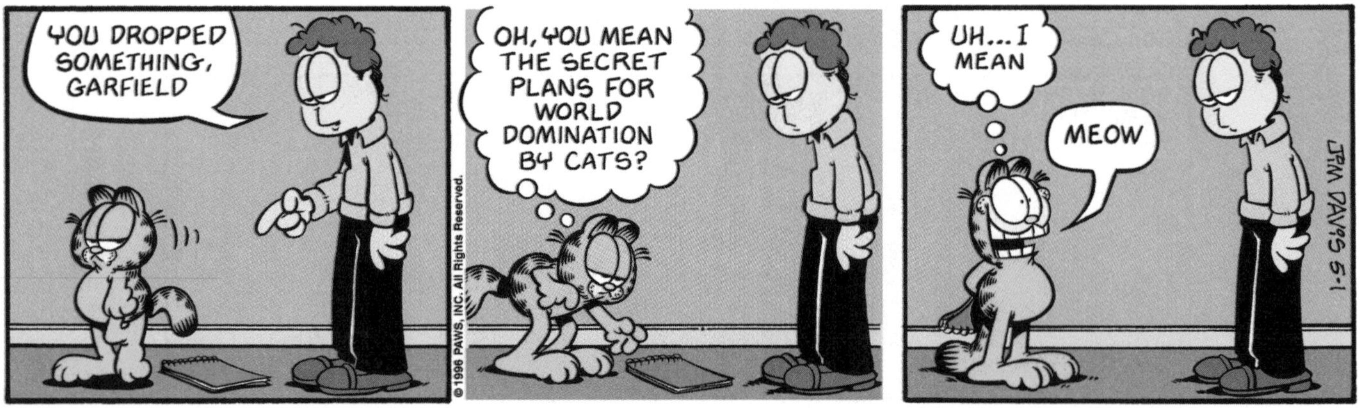
YOU DROPPED SOMETHING, GARFIELD
© 1996 PAWS, INC. All Rights Reserved.
OH, YOU MEAN THE SECRET PLANS FOR WORLD DOMINATION BY CATS?
UH... I MEAN
MEOW
JIM DAVIS 5-1

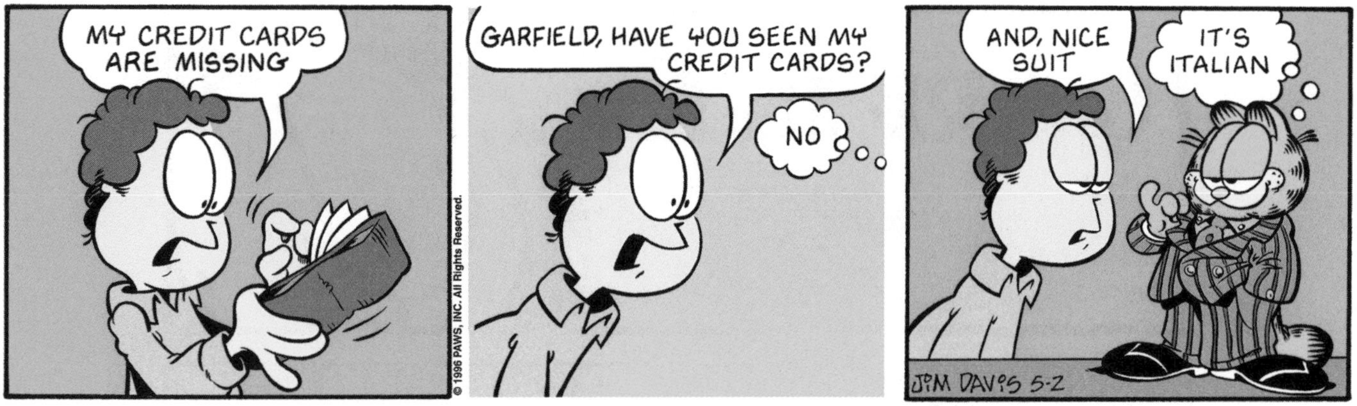
MY CREDIT CARDS ARE MISSING
© 1996 PAWS, INC. All Rights Reserved.
GARFIELD, HAVE YOU SEEN MY CREDIT CARDS?
NO
AND, NICE SUIT
IT'S ITALIAN
JIM DAVIS 5-2

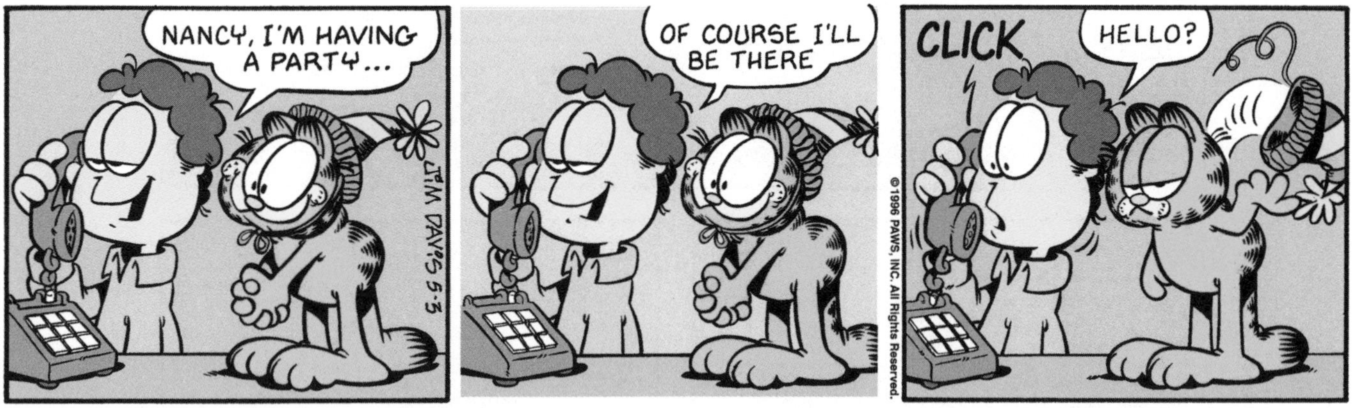
NANCY, I'M HAVING A PARTY...
JIM DAVIS 5-3
OF COURSE I'LL BE THERE
© 1996 PAWS, INC. All Rights Reserved.
CLICK
HELLO?

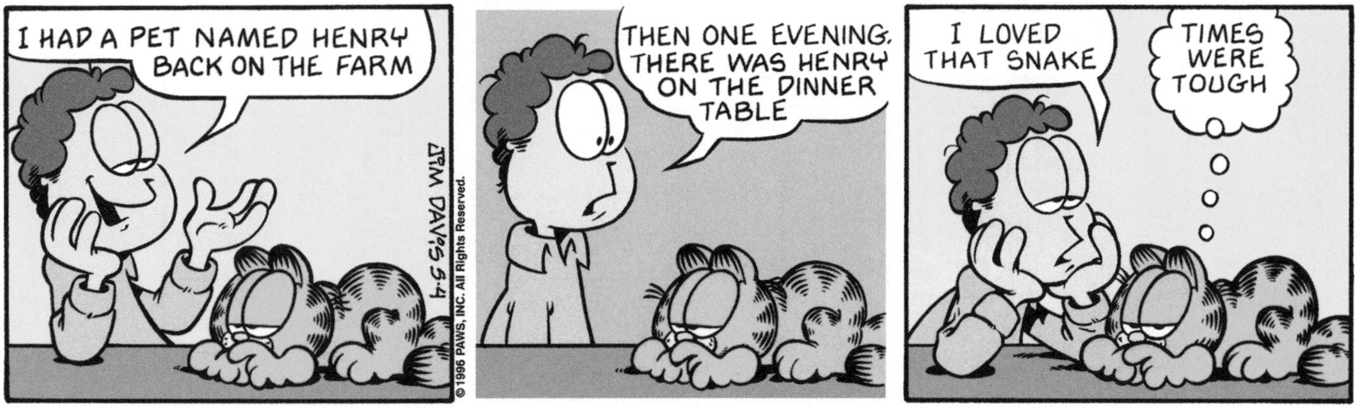
I HAD A PET NAMED HENRY BACK ON THE FARM
JIM DAVIS 5-4
© 1996 PAWS, INC. All Rights Reserved.
THEN ONE EVENING, THERE WAS HENRY ON THE DINNER TABLE
I LOVED THAT SNAKE
TIMES WERE TOUGH

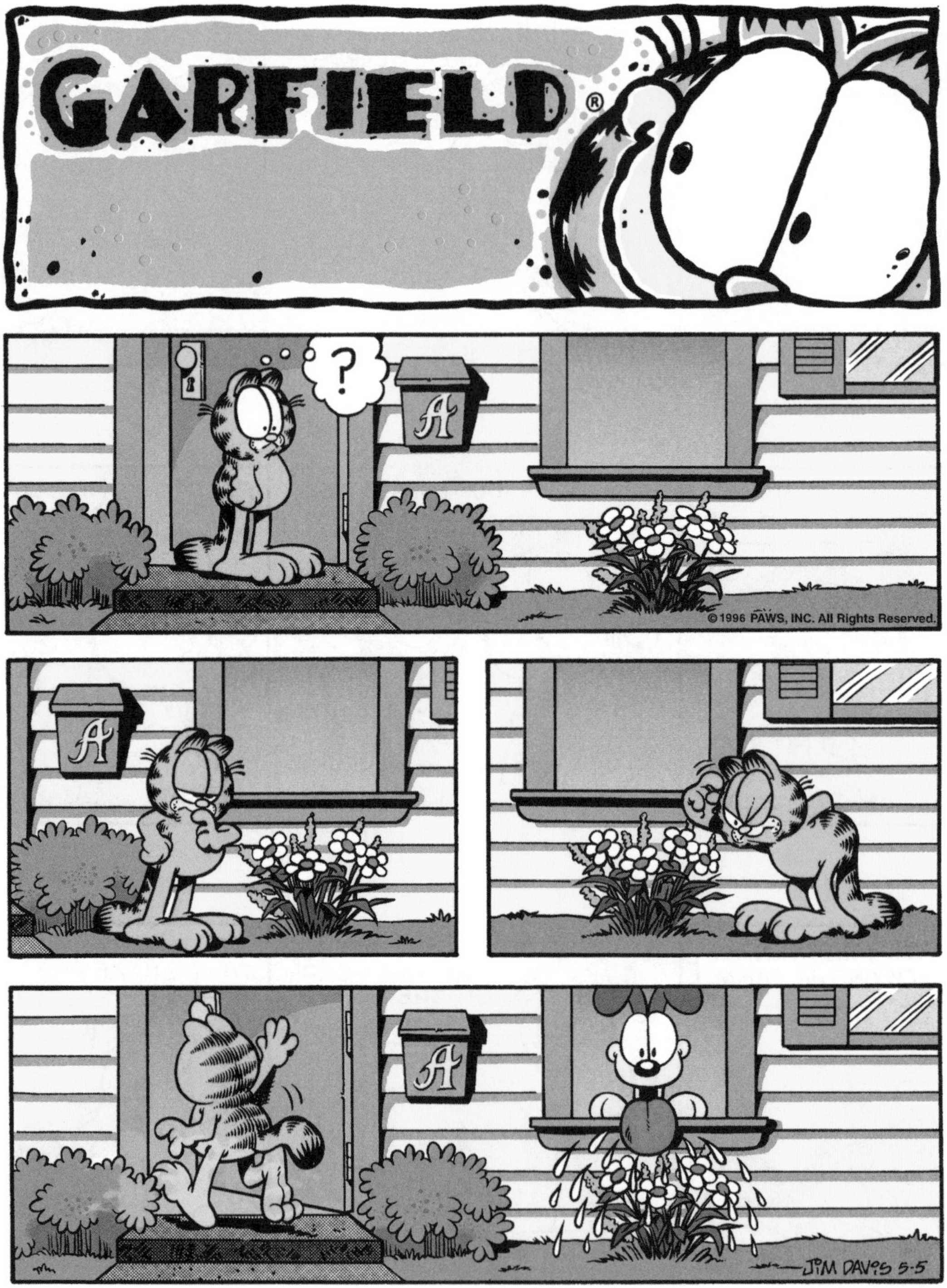
GARFIELD®
?
© 1996 PAWS, INC. All Rights Reserved.
JIM DAVIS 5-5

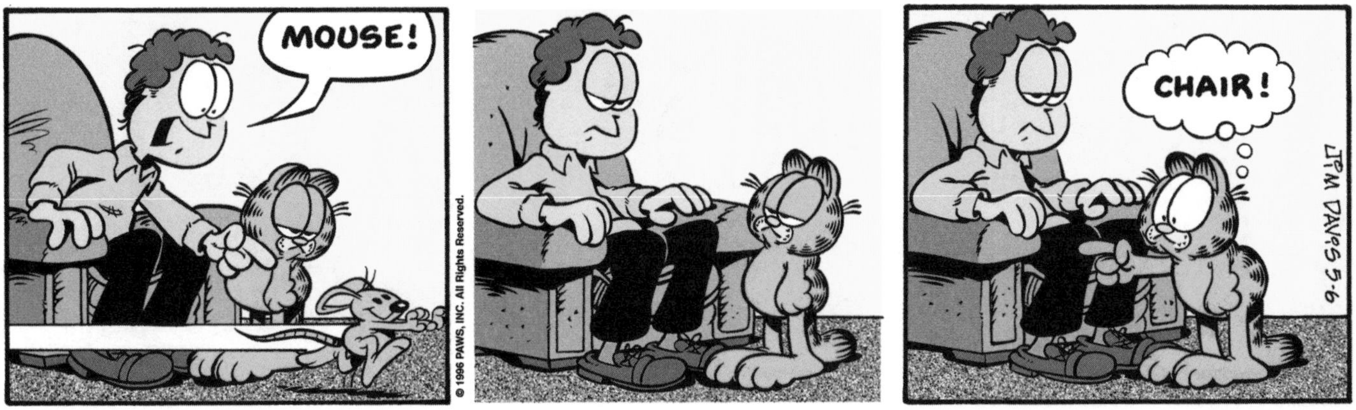
MOUSE!
© 1996 PAWS, INC. All Rights Reserved.
CHAIR!
JIM DAVIS 5-6

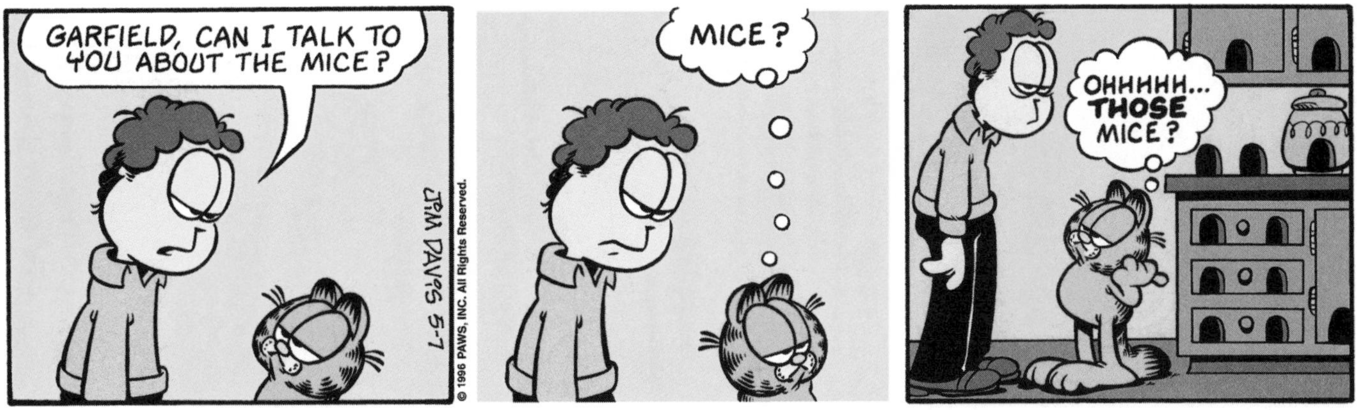
GARFIELD, CAN I TALK TO YOU ABOUT THE MICE?
JIM DAVIS 5-7
© 1996 PAWS, INC. All Rights Reserved.
MICE?
OHHHHH... **THOSE** MICE?

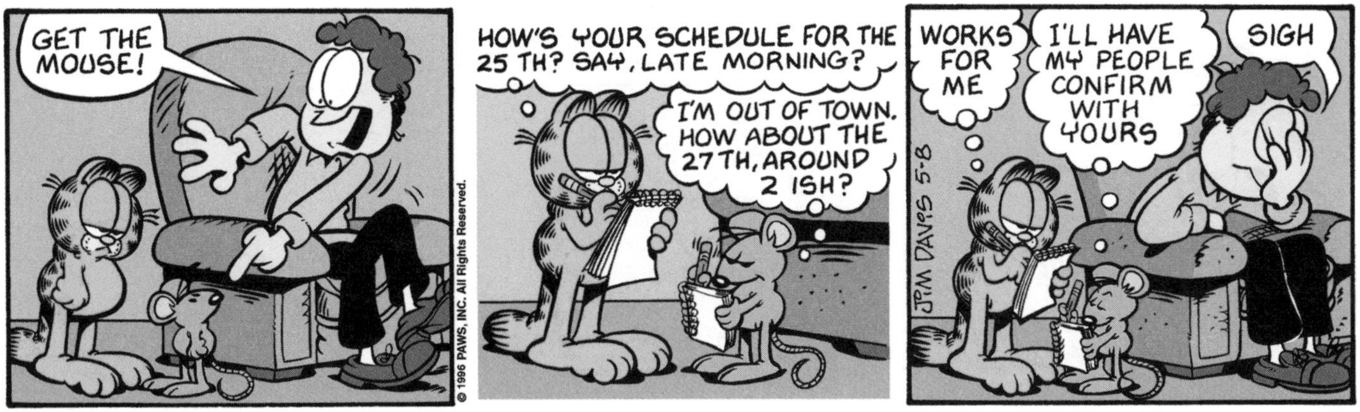
GET THE MOUSE!
© 1996 PAWS, INC. All Rights Reserved.
HOW'S YOUR SCHEDULE FOR THE 25 TH? SAY, LATE MORNING?
I'M OUT OF TOWN. HOW ABOUT THE 27 TH, AROUND 2 ISH?
WORKS FOR ME
I'LL HAVE MY PEOPLE CONFIRM WITH YOURS
SIGH
JIM DAVIS 5-8

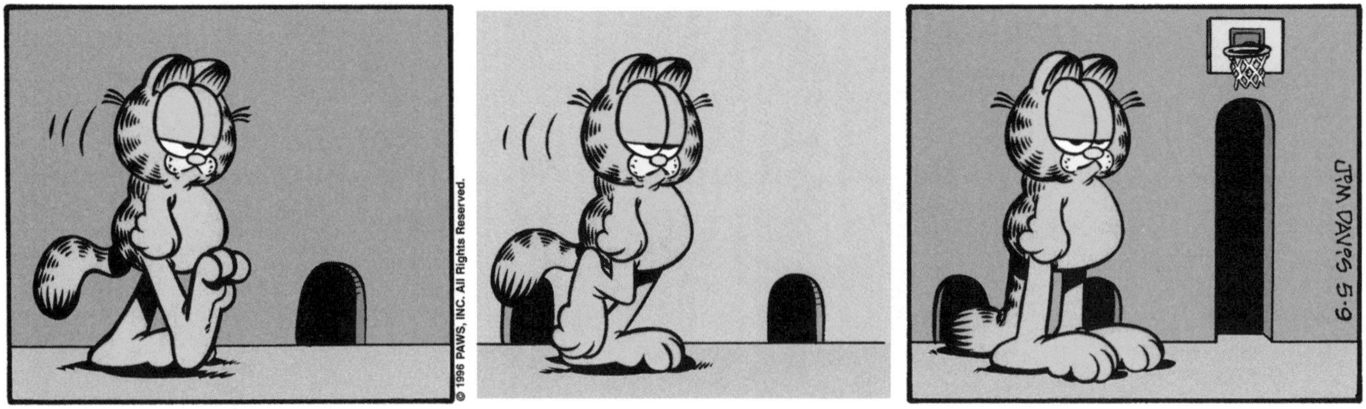
© 1996 PAWS, INC. All Rights Reserved.
JIM DAVIS 5-9

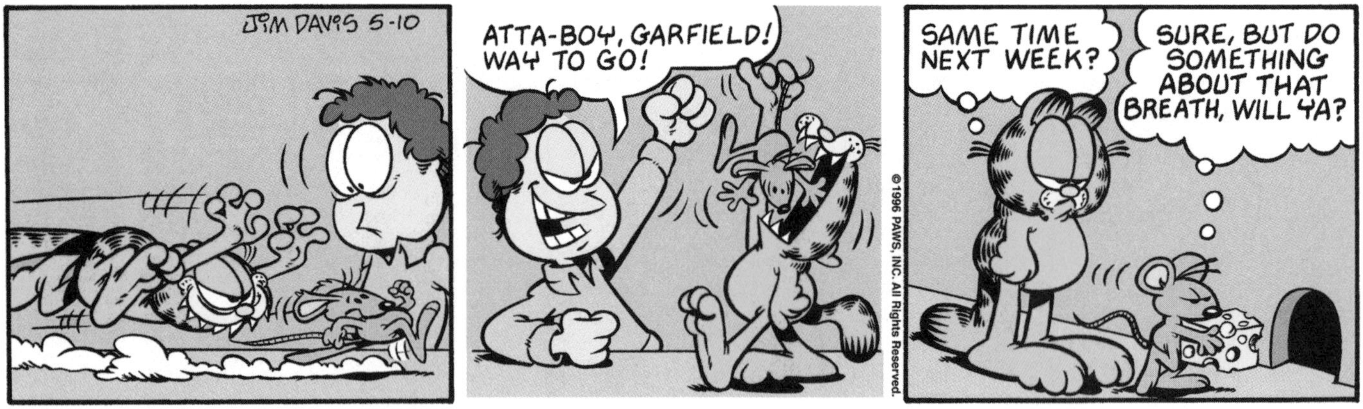
JIM DAVIS 5-10
ATTA-BOY, GARFIELD! WAY TO GO!
© 1996 PAWS, INC. All Rights Reserved.
SAME TIME NEXT WEEK?
SURE, BUT DO SOMETHING ABOUT THAT BREATH, WILL YA?

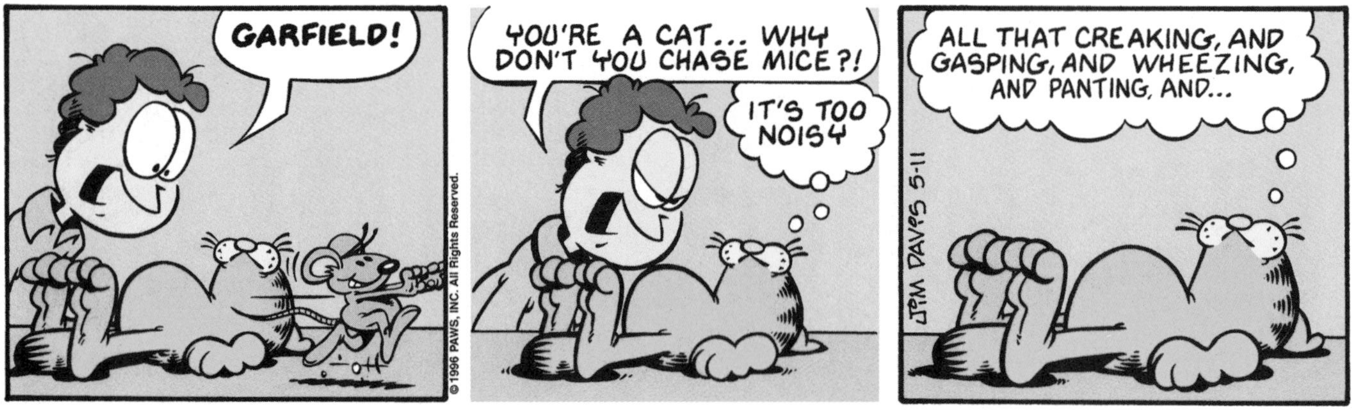
GARFIELD!
© 1996 PAWS, INC. All Rights Reserved.
YOU'RE A CAT... WHY DON'T YOU CHASE MICE?!
IT'S TOO NOISY
JIM DAVIS 5-11
ALL THAT CREAKING, AND GASPING, AND WHEEZING, AND PANTING, AND...

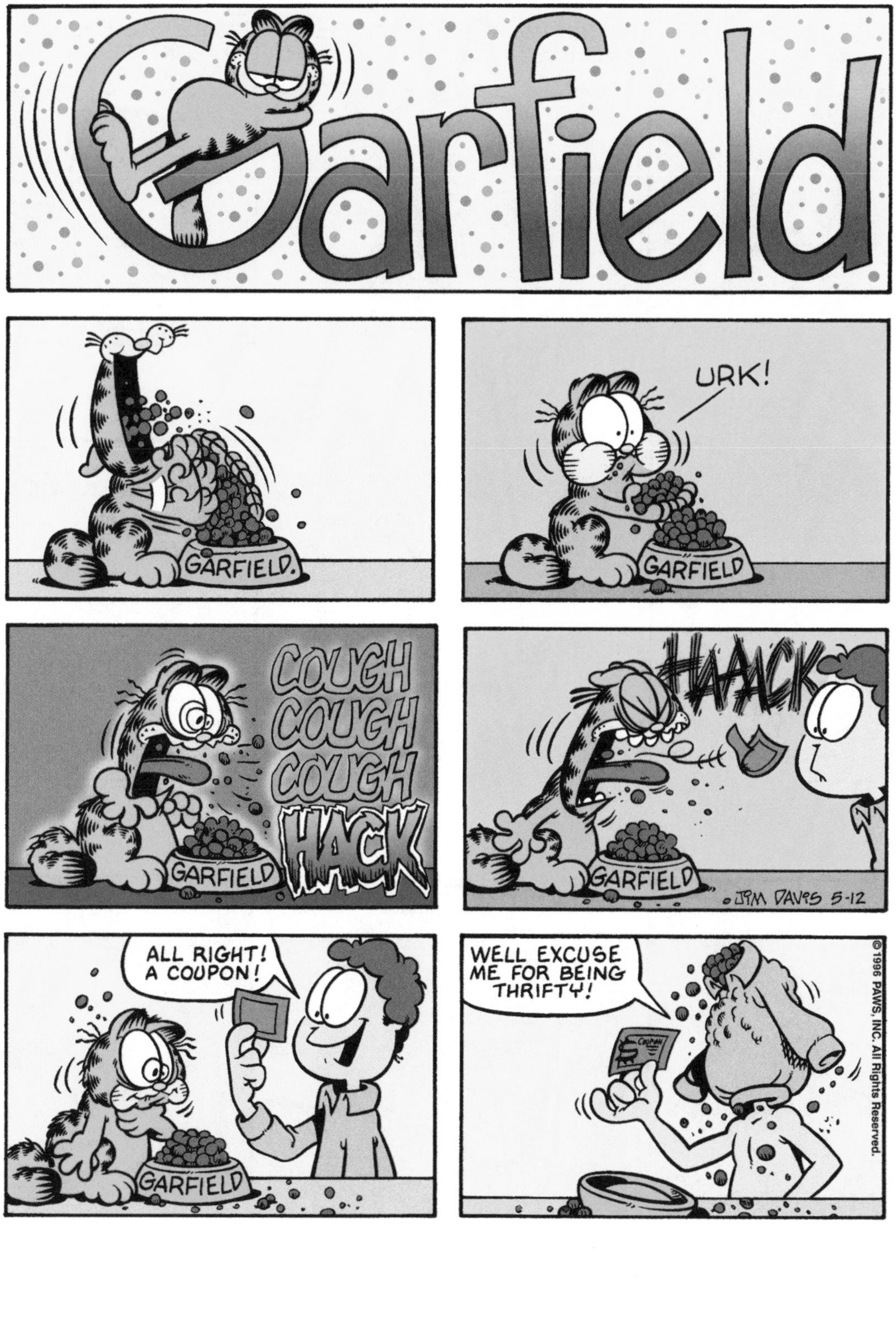
Garfield
GARFIELD
URK!
GARFIELD
COUGH
COUGH
COUGH
HACK
GARFIELD
HAACK
GARFIELD
JIM DAVIS 5-12
ALL RIGHT! A COUPON!
GARFIELD
WELL EXCUSE ME FOR BEING THRIFTY!
COUPON
© 1996 PAWS, INC. All Rights Reserved.

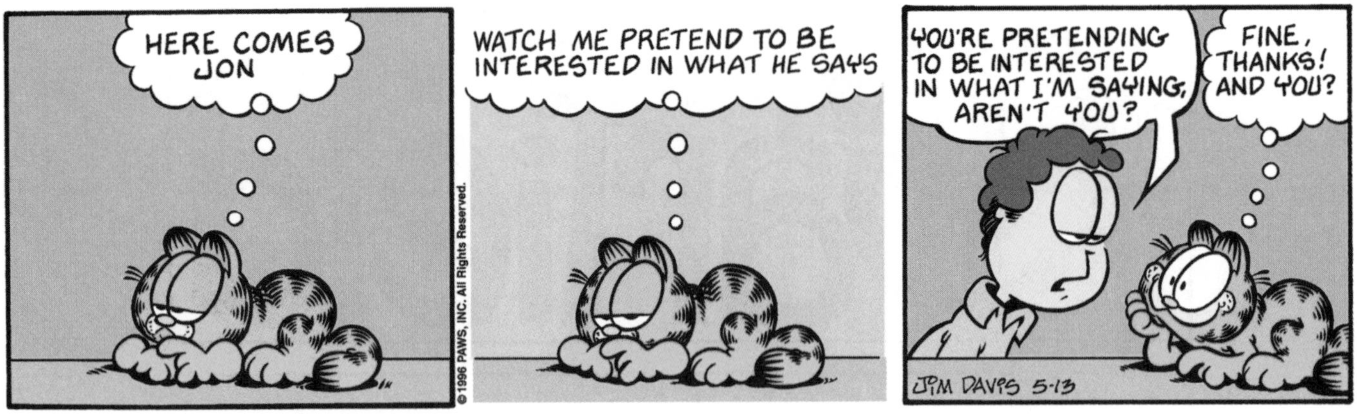
HERE COMES JON
WATCH ME PRETEND TO BE INTERESTED IN WHAT HE SAYS
© 1996 PAWS, INC. All Rights Reserved.
YOU'RE PRETENDING TO BE INTERESTED IN WHAT I'M SAYING, AREN'T YOU?
FINE, THANKS! AND YOU?
JIM DAVIS 5-13

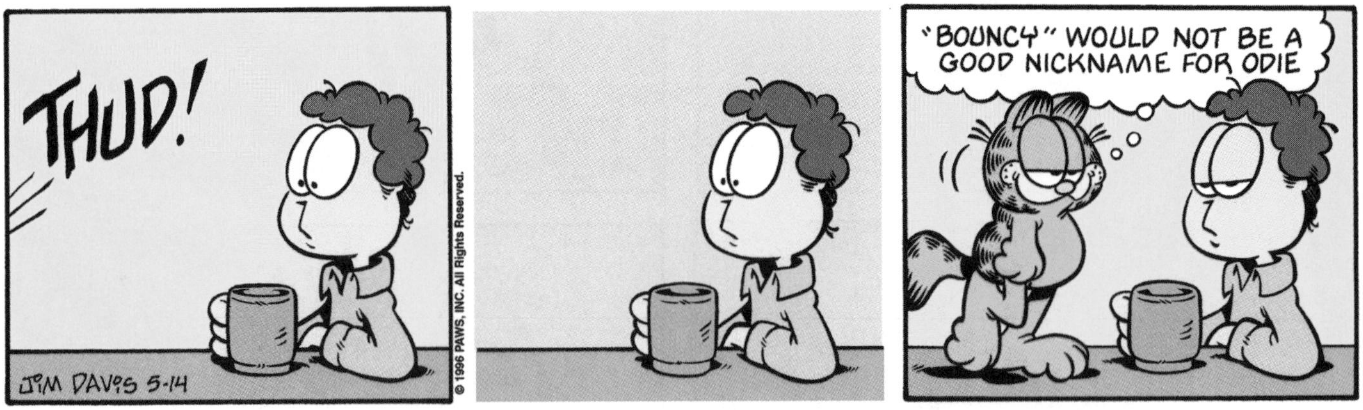
THUD!
JIM DAVIS 5-14
© 1996 PAWS, INC. All Rights Reserved.
"BOUNCY" WOULD NOT BE A GOOD NICKNAME FOR ODIE

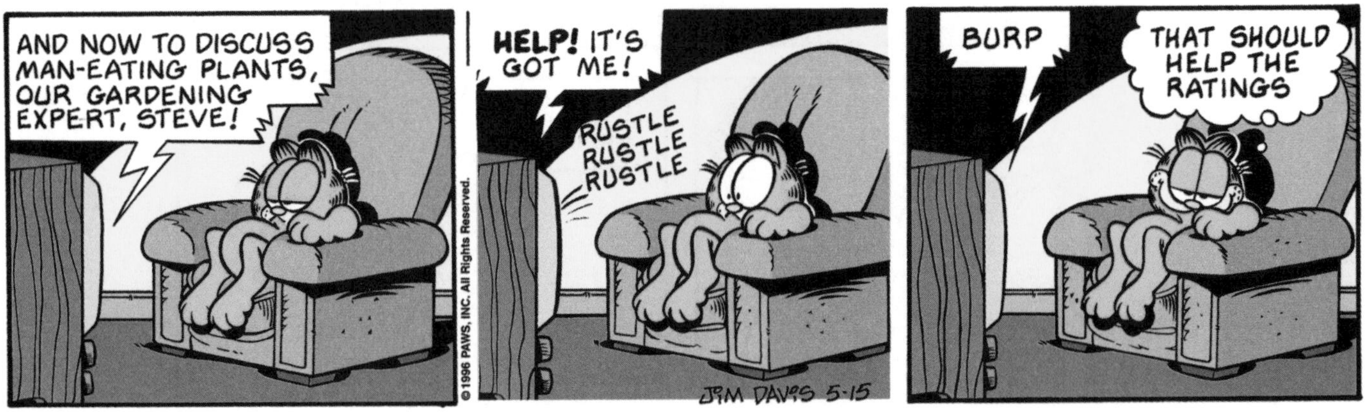
AND NOW TO DISCUSS MAN-EATING PLANTS, OUR GARDENING EXPERT, STEVE!
© 1996 PAWS, INC. All Rights Reserved.
HELP! IT'S GOT ME!
RUSTLE RUSTLE RUSTLE
JIM DAVIS 5-15
BURP
THAT SHOULD HELP THE RATINGS

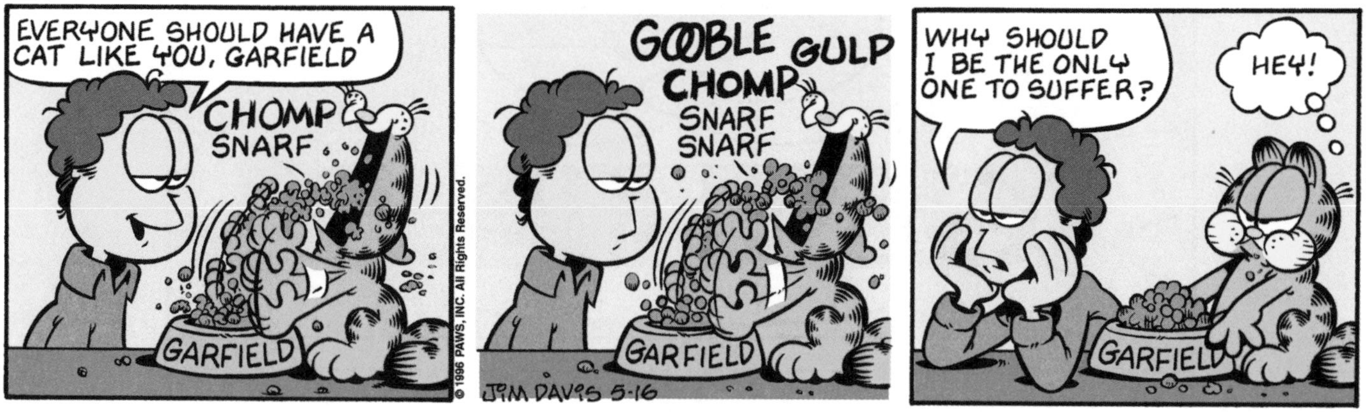
EVERYONE SHOULD HAVE A CAT LIKE YOU, GARFIELD
CHOMP
SNARF
GARFIELD
© 1996 PAWS, INC. All Rights Reserved.
GOOBLE
GULP
CHOMP
SNARF
SNARF
GARFIELD
JIM DAVIS 5-16
WHY SHOULD I BE THE ONLY ONE TO SUFFER?
HEY!
GARFIELD

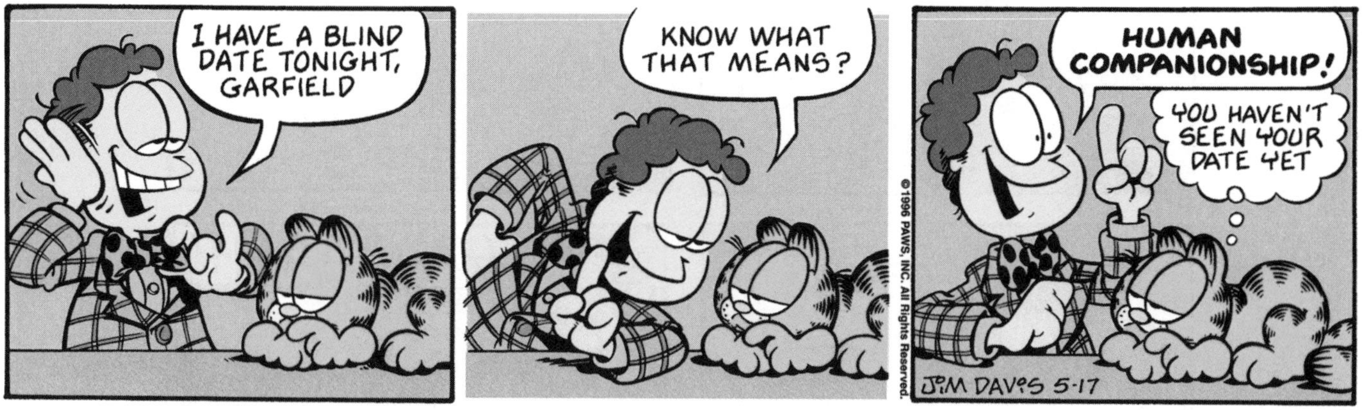
I HAVE A BLIND DATE TONIGHT, GARFIELD
KNOW WHAT THAT MEANS?
© 1996 PAWS, INC. All Rights Reserved.
HUMAN COMPANIONSHIP!
YOU HAVEN'T SEEN YOUR DATE YET
JIM DAVIS 5-17

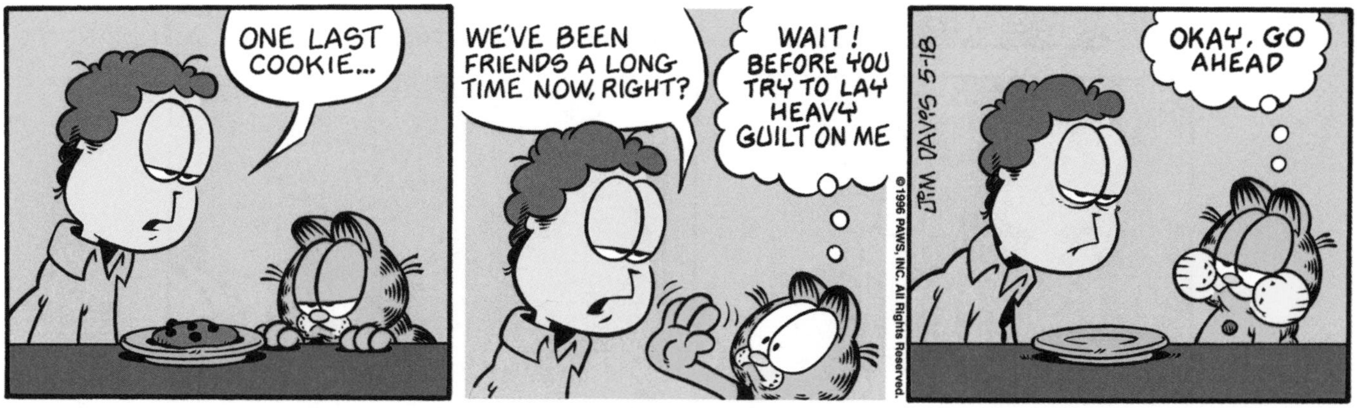
ONE LAST COOKIE...
WE'VE BEEN FRIENDS A LONG TIME NOW, RIGHT?
WAIT! BEFORE YOU TRY TO LAY HEAVY GUILT ON ME
JIM DAVIS 5-18
© 1996 PAWS, INC. All Rights Reserved.
OKAY, GO AHEAD

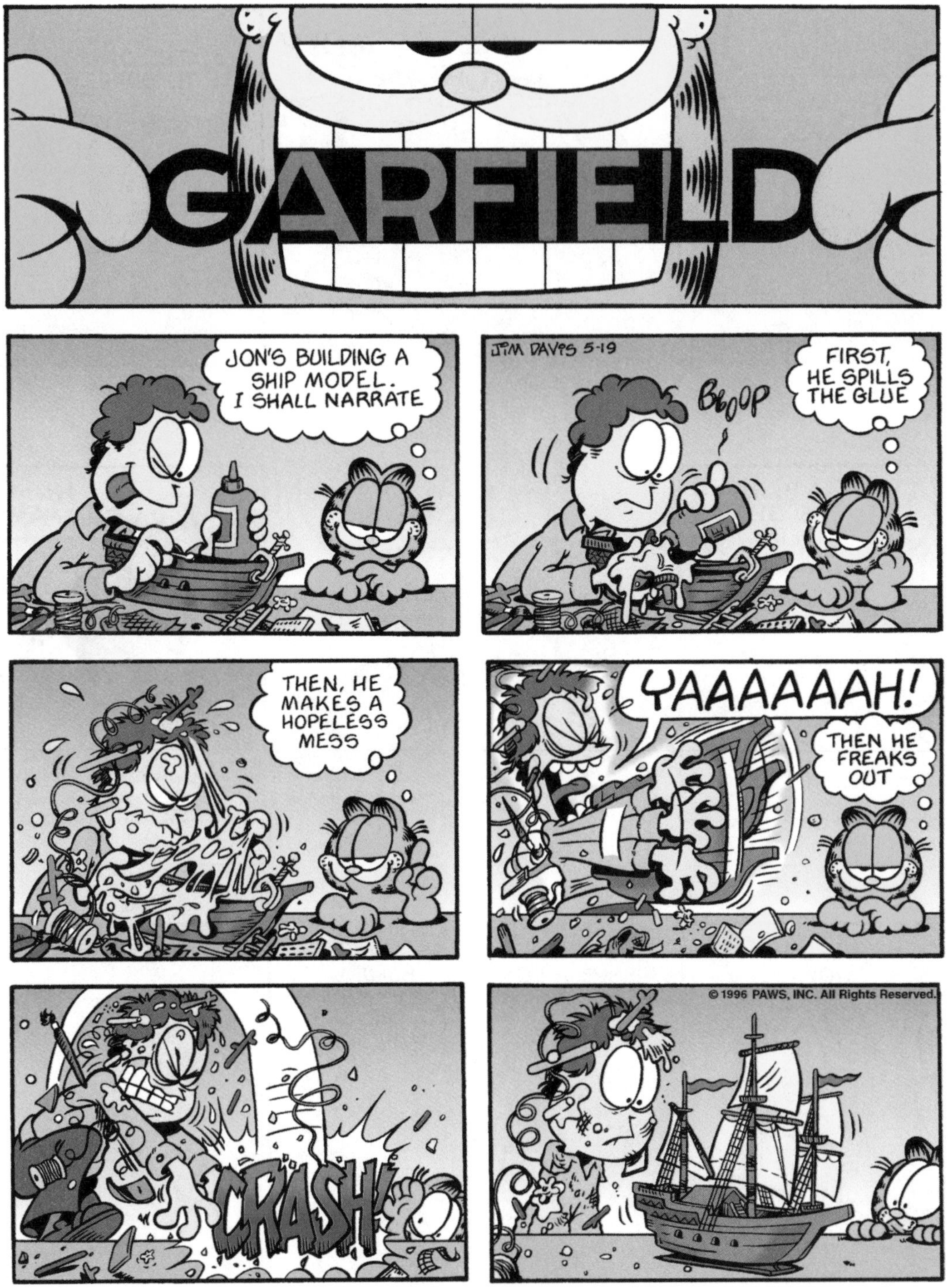
GARFIELD
JON'S BUILDING A SHIP MODEL. I SHALL NARRATE
JIM DAVIS 5-19
BLOOP
FIRST, HE SPILLS THE GLUE
THEN, HE MAKES A HOPELESS MESS
YAAAAAAH!
THEN HE FREAKS OUT
CRASH!
© 1996 PAWS, INC. All Rights Reserved.

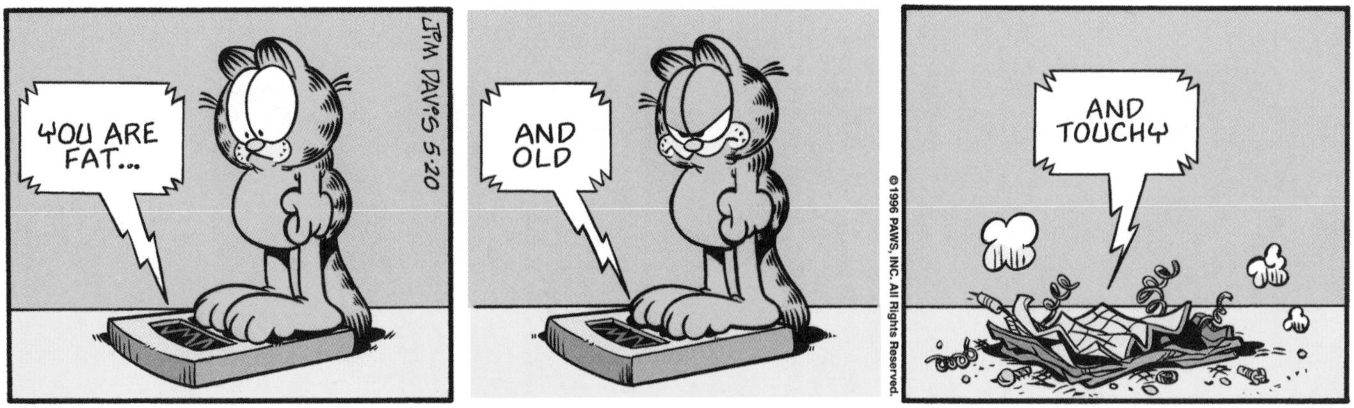
JIM DAVIS 5·20
YOU ARE FAT...
AND OLD
© 1996 PAWS, INC. All Rights Reserved.
AND TOUCHY

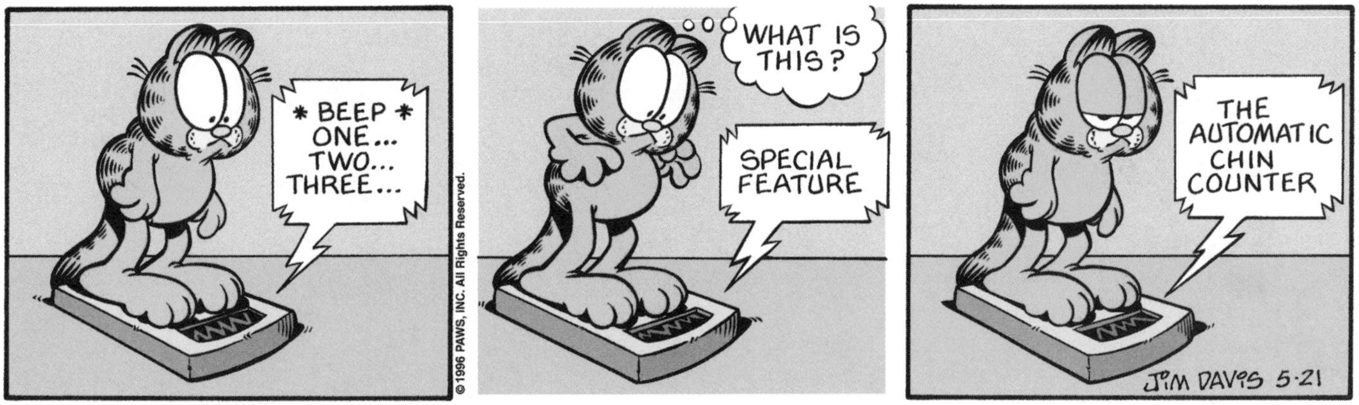
* BEEP * ONE... TWO... THREE...
© 1996 PAWS, INC. All Rights Reserved.
WHAT IS THIS?
SPECIAL FEATURE
THE AUTOMATIC CHIN COUNTER
JIM DAVIS 5·21

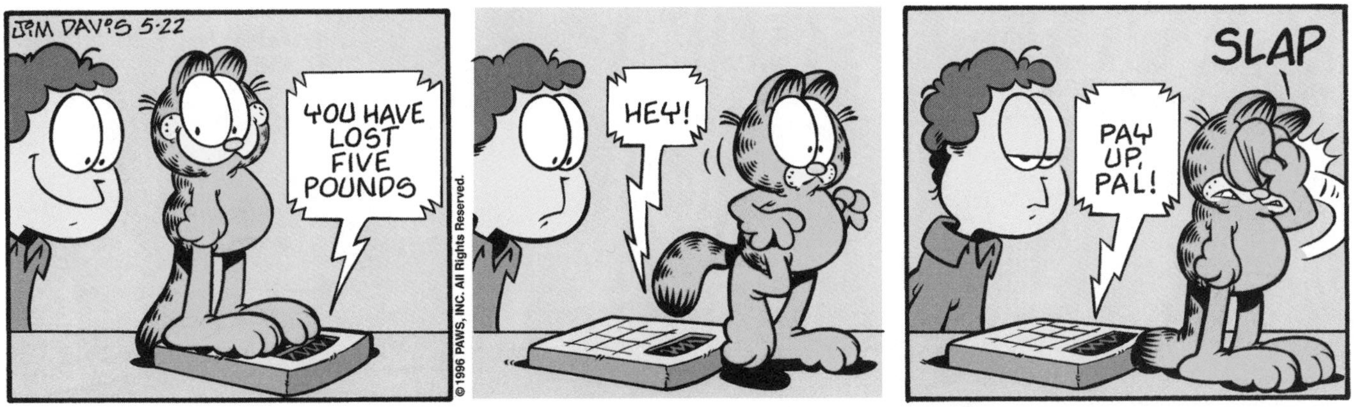
JIM DAVIS 5·22
YOU HAVE LOST FIVE POUNDS
© 1996 PAWS, INC. All Rights Reserved.
HEY!
SLAP
PAY UP, PAL!

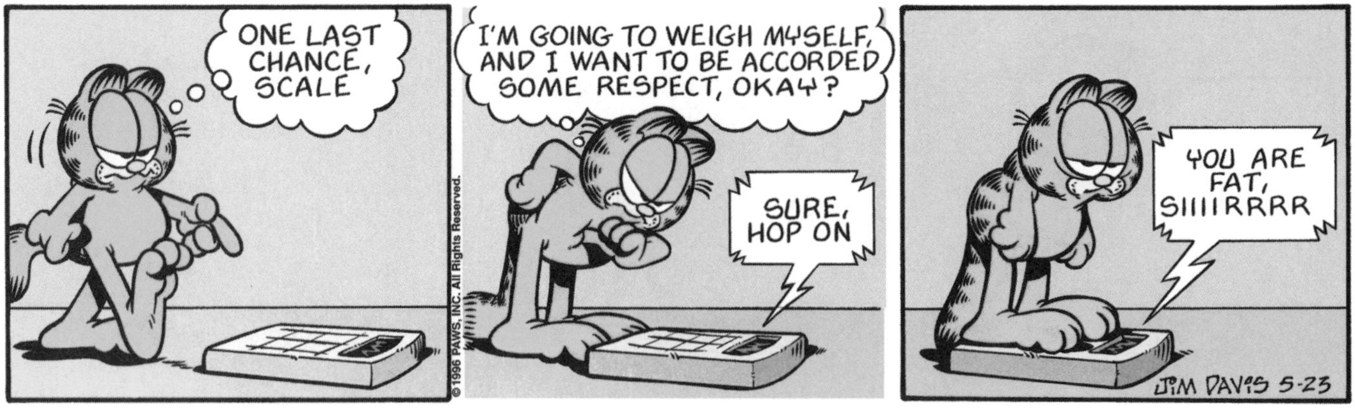
ONE LAST CHANCE, SCALE
I'M GOING TO WEIGH MYSELF, AND I WANT TO BE ACCORDED SOME RESPECT, OKAY?
SURE, HOP ON
YOU ARE FAT, SIIIIRRRR
JIM DAVIS 5-23
© 1996 PAWS, INC. All Rights Reserved.

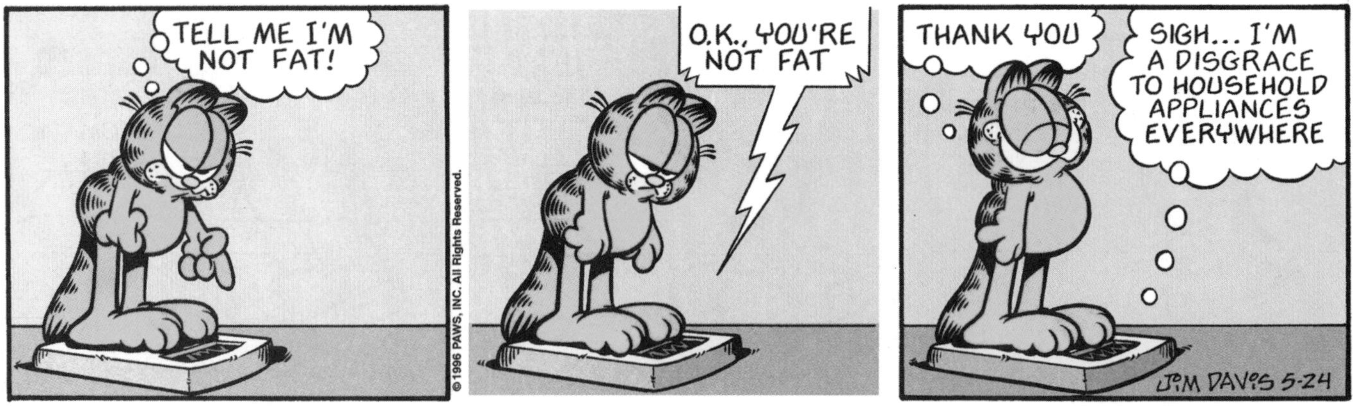
TELL ME I'M NOT FAT!
O.K., YOU'RE NOT FAT
THANK YOU
SIGH... I'M A DISGRACE TO HOUSEHOLD APPLIANCES EVERYWHERE
JIM DAVIS 5-24
© 1996 PAWS, INC. All Rights Reserved.

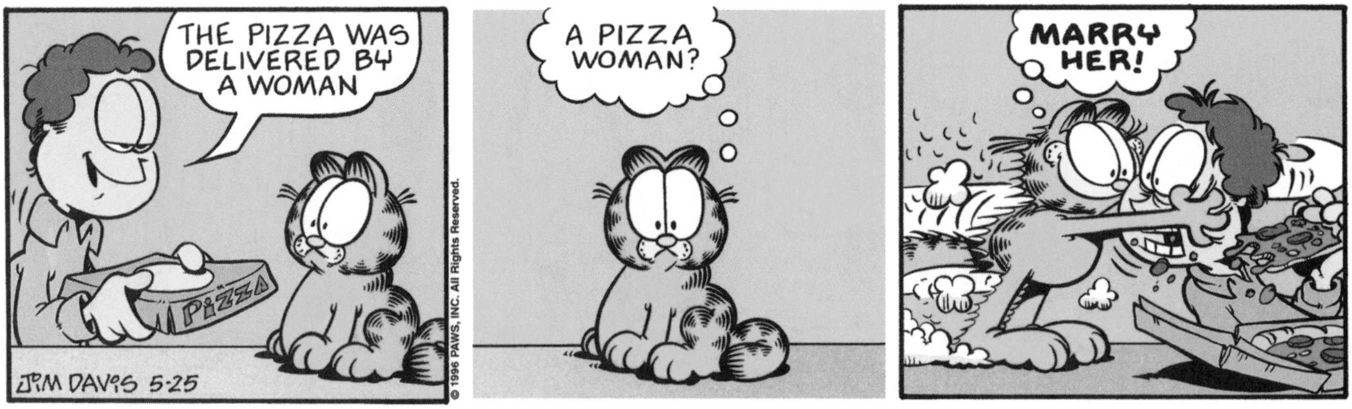
THE PIZZA WAS DELIVERED BY A WOMAN
PIZZA
A PIZZA WOMAN?
MARRY HER!
JIM DAVIS 5-25
© 1996 PAWS, INC. All Rights Reserved.

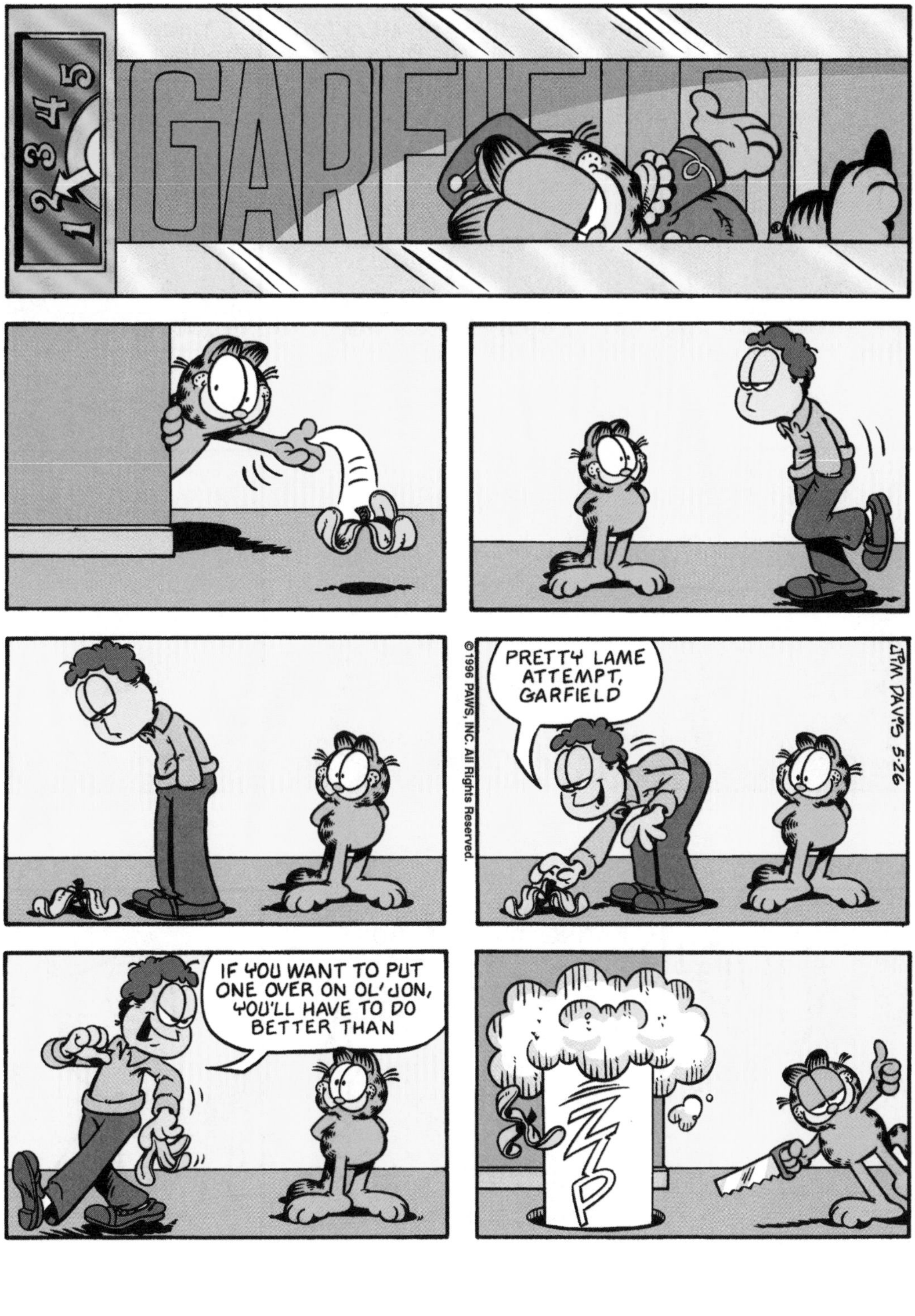
GARFIELD
1 2 3 4 5
© 1996 PAWS, INC. All Rights Reserved.
JPM DAVIS 5·26
PRETTY LAME ATTEMPT, GARFIELD
IF YOU WANT TO PUT ONE OVER ON OL' JON, YOU'LL HAVE TO DO BETTER THAN
ZZIP

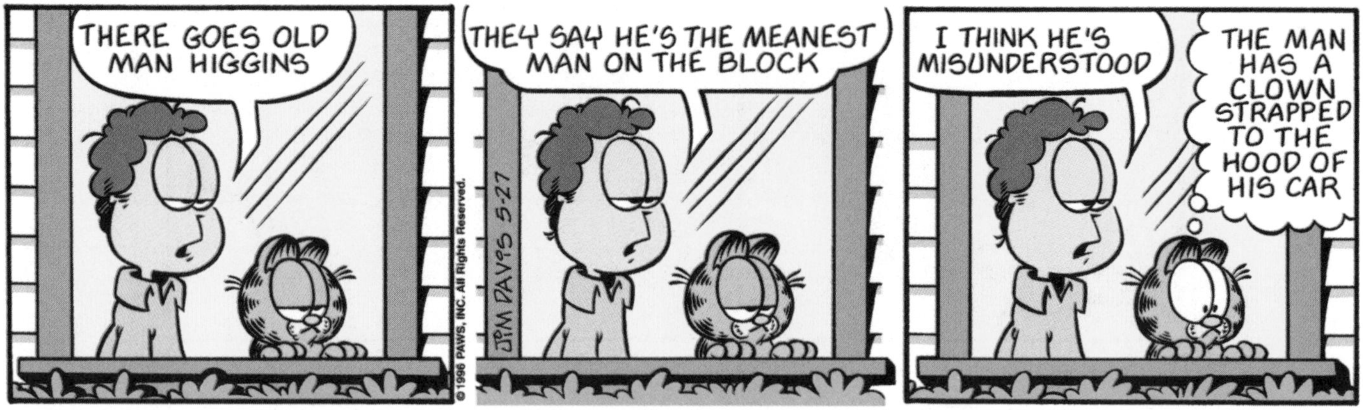
THERE GOES OLD MAN HIGGINS
THEY SAY HE'S THE MEANEST MAN ON THE BLOCK
I THINK HE'S MISUNDERSTOOD
THE MAN HAS A CLOWN STRAPPED TO THE HOOD OF HIS CAR
JIM DAVIS 5-27
© 1996 PAWS, INC. All Rights Reserved.

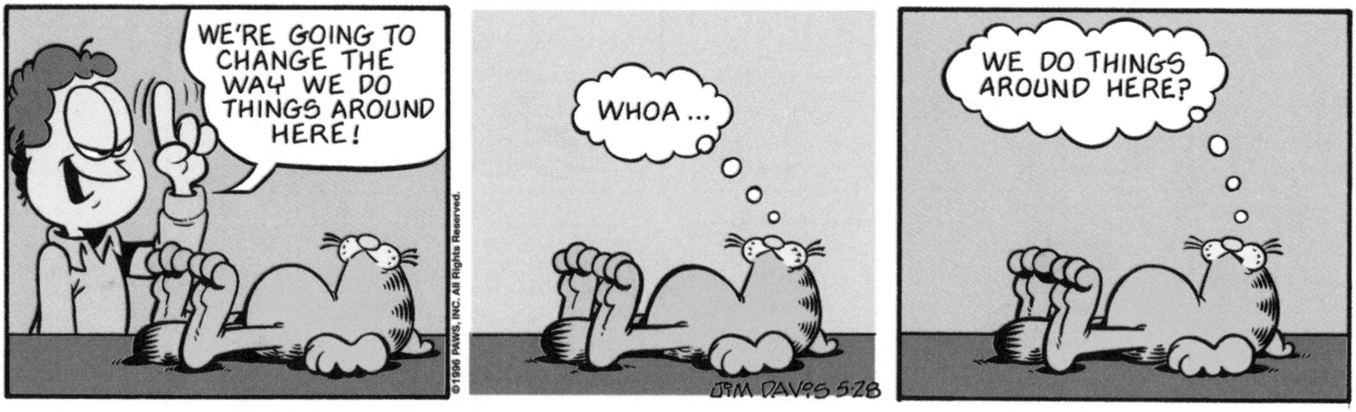
WE'RE GOING TO CHANGE THE WAY WE DO THINGS AROUND HERE!
WHOA ...
WE DO THINGS AROUND HERE?
JIM DAVIS 5-28
© 1996 PAWS, INC. All Rights Reserved.

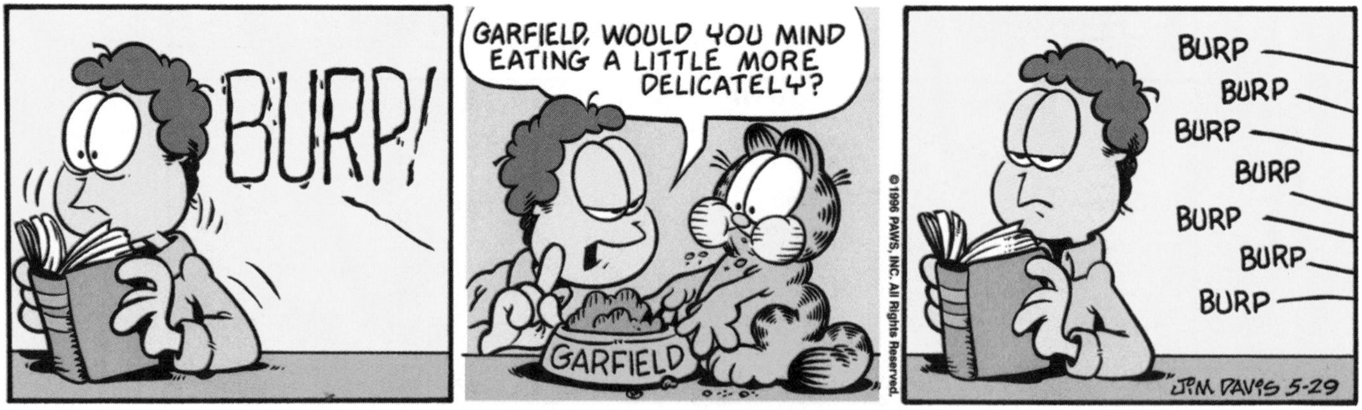
BURP!
GARFIELD, WOULD YOU MIND EATING A LITTLE MORE DELICATELY?
GARFIELD
BURP
BURP
BURP
BURP
BURP
BURP
BURP
JIM DAVIS 5-29
© 1996 PAWS, INC. All Rights Reserved.

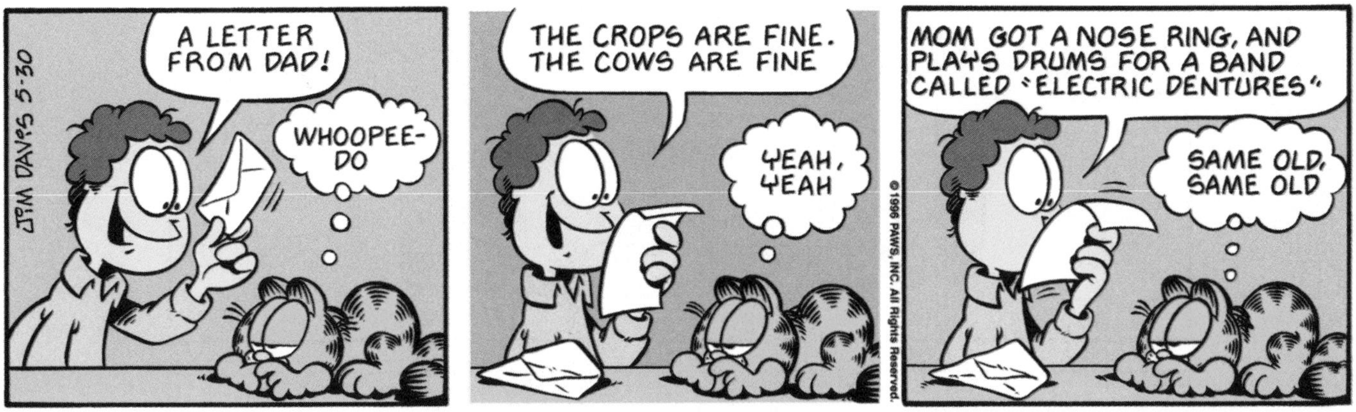
JIM DAVIS 5-30
A LETTER FROM DAD!
WHOOPEE-DO
THE CROPS ARE FINE. THE COWS ARE FINE
YEAH, YEAH
© 1996 PAWS, INC. All Rights Reserved.
MOM GOT A NOSE RING, AND PLAYS DRUMS FOR A BAND CALLED "ELECTRIC DENTURES"
SAME OLD, SAME OLD

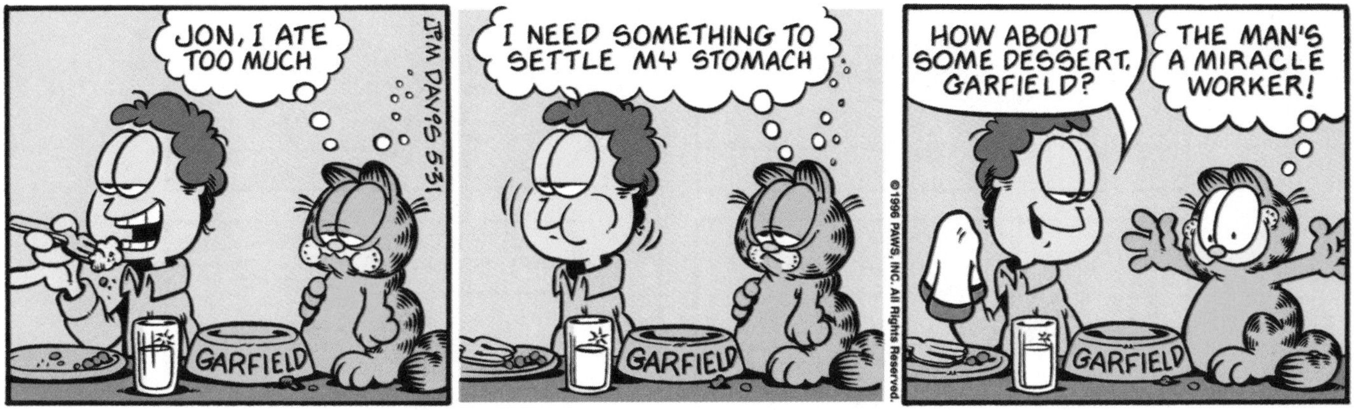
JON, I ATE TOO MUCH
JIM DAVIS 5-31
I NEED SOMETHING TO SETTLE MY STOMACH
GARFIELD
© 1996 PAWS, INC. All Rights Reserved.
HOW ABOUT SOME DESSERT, GARFIELD?
THE MAN'S A MIRACLE WORKER!

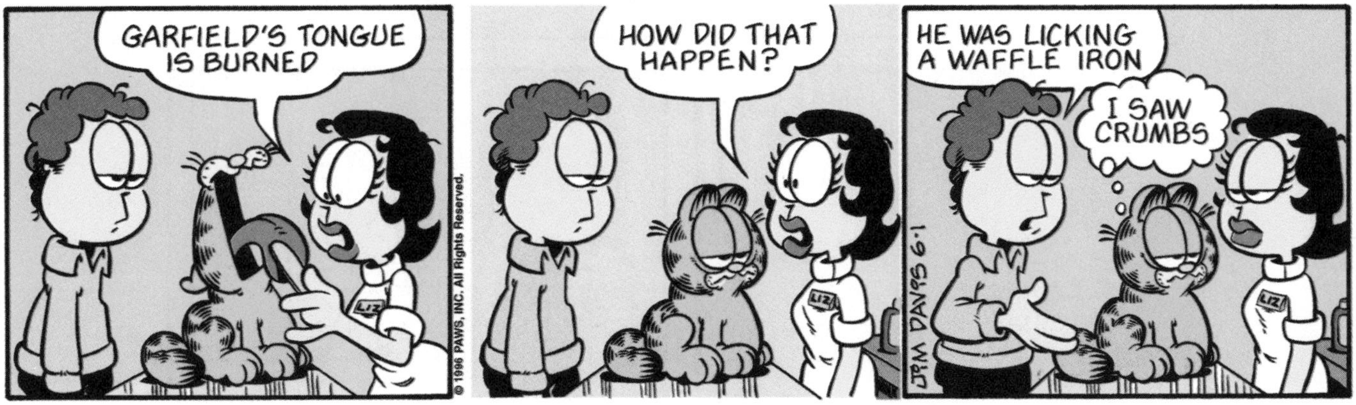
GARFIELD'S TONGUE IS BURNED
© 1996 PAWS, INC. All Rights Reserved.
HOW DID THAT HAPPEN?
HE WAS LICKING A WAFFLE IRON
I SAW CRUMBS
JIM DAVIS 6-1

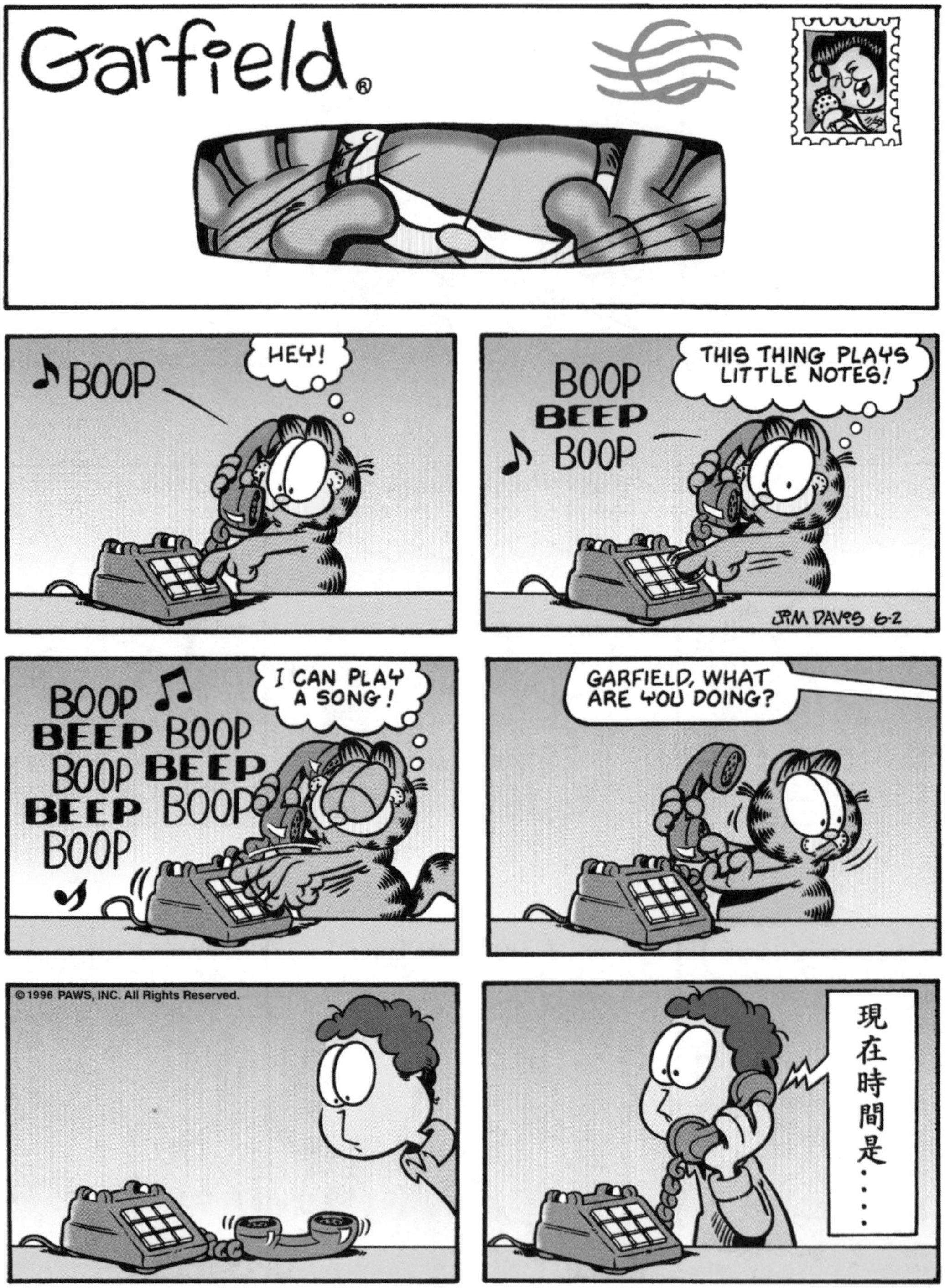
Garfield®
♪ BOOP
HEY!
BOOP BEEP BOOP ♪
THIS THING PLAYS LITTLE NOTES!
JIM DAVIS 6-2
BOOP BEEP BOOP BOOP BEEP BEEP BOOP BOOP
I CAN PLAY A SONG!
GARFIELD, WHAT ARE YOU DOING?
© 1996 PAWS, INC. All Rights Reserved.
現在時間是……

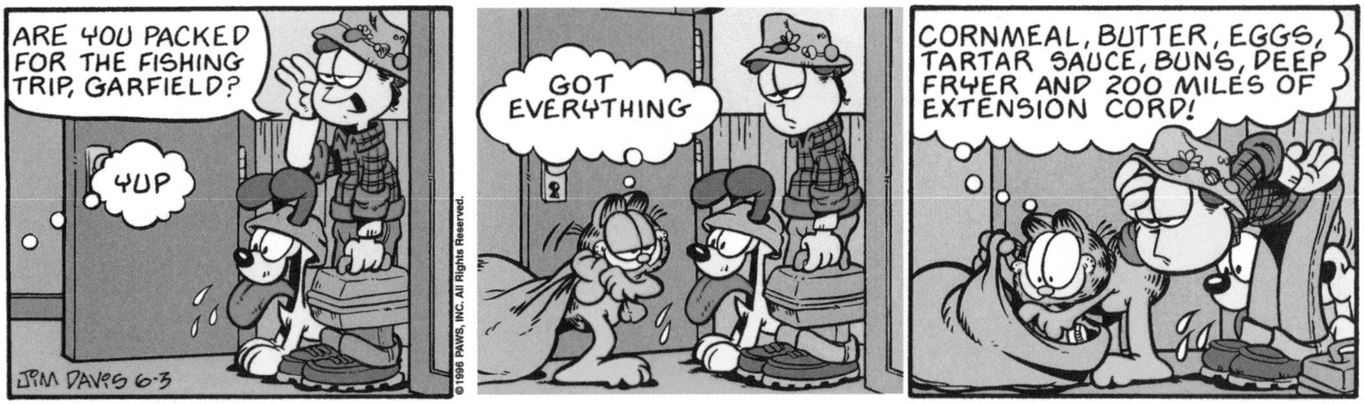
ARE YOU PACKED FOR THE FISHING TRIP, GARFIELD?
YUP
JIM DAVIS 6-3
©1996 PAWS, INC. All Rights Reserved.
GOT EVERYTHING
CORNMEAL, BUTTER, EGGS, TARTAR SAUCE, BUNS, DEEP FRYER AND 200 MILES OF EXTENSION CORD!

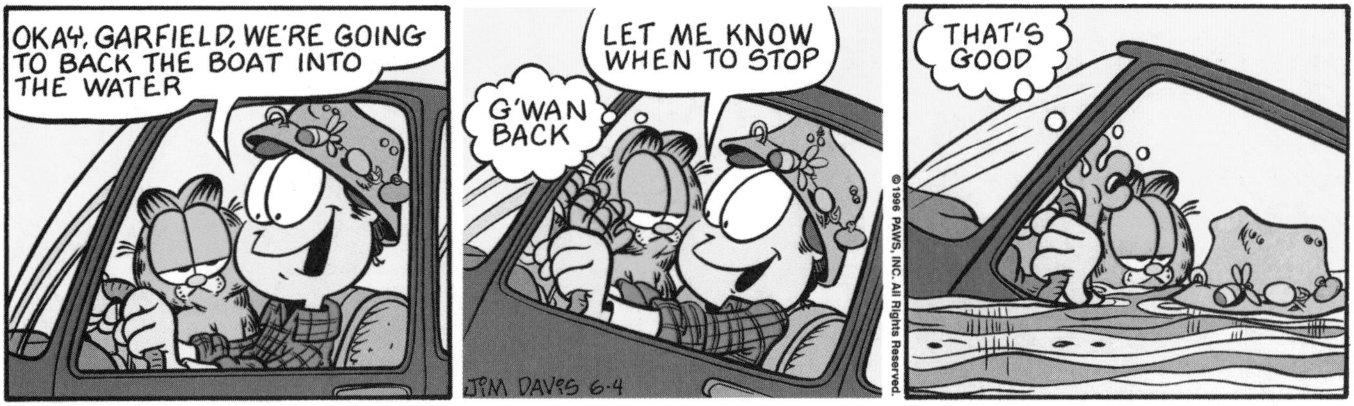
OKAY, GARFIELD, WE'RE GOING TO BACK THE BOAT INTO THE WATER
LET ME KNOW WHEN TO STOP
G'WAN BACK
JIM DAVIS 6-4
©1996 PAWS, INC. All Rights Reserved.
THAT'S GOOD

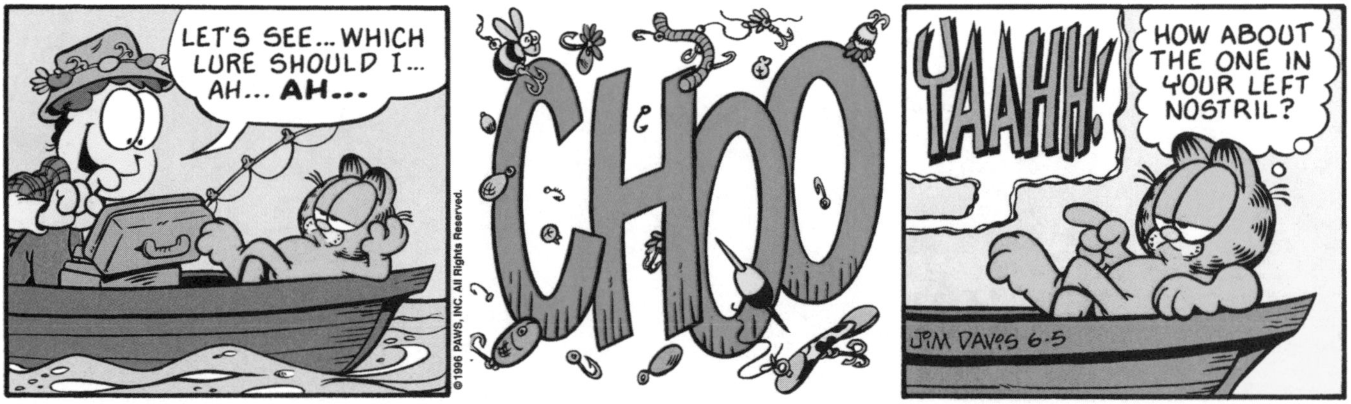
LET'S SEE... WHICH LURE SHOULD I... AH... **AH...**
©1996 PAWS, INC. All Rights Reserved.
CHOO
YAAHH!
HOW ABOUT THE ONE IN YOUR LEFT NOSTRIL?
JIM DAVIS 6-5

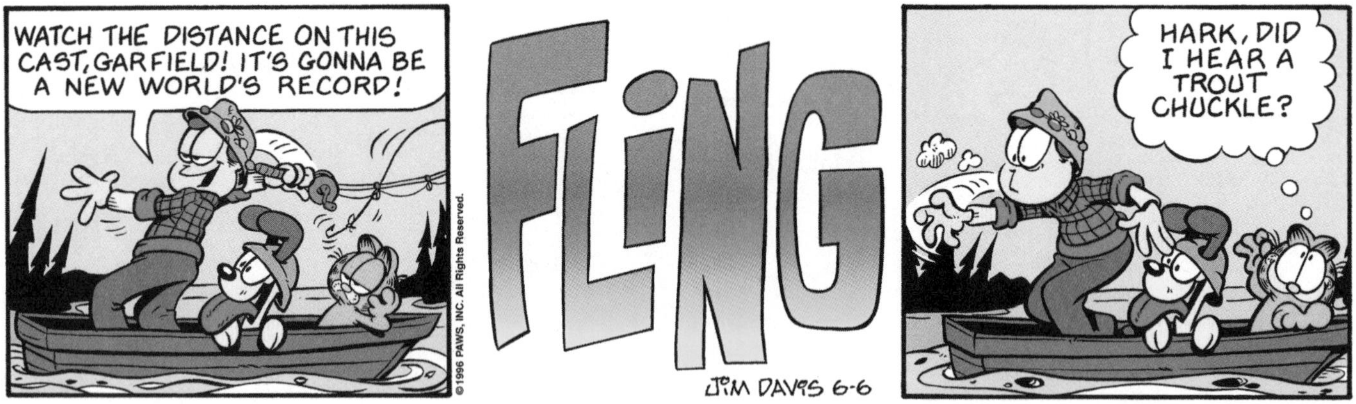
WATCH THE DISTANCE ON THIS CAST, GARFIELD! IT'S GONNA BE A NEW WORLD'S RECORD!
©1996 PAWS, INC. All Rights Reserved.
FLING
JIM DAVIS 6-6
HARK, DID I HEAR A TROUT CHUCKLE?

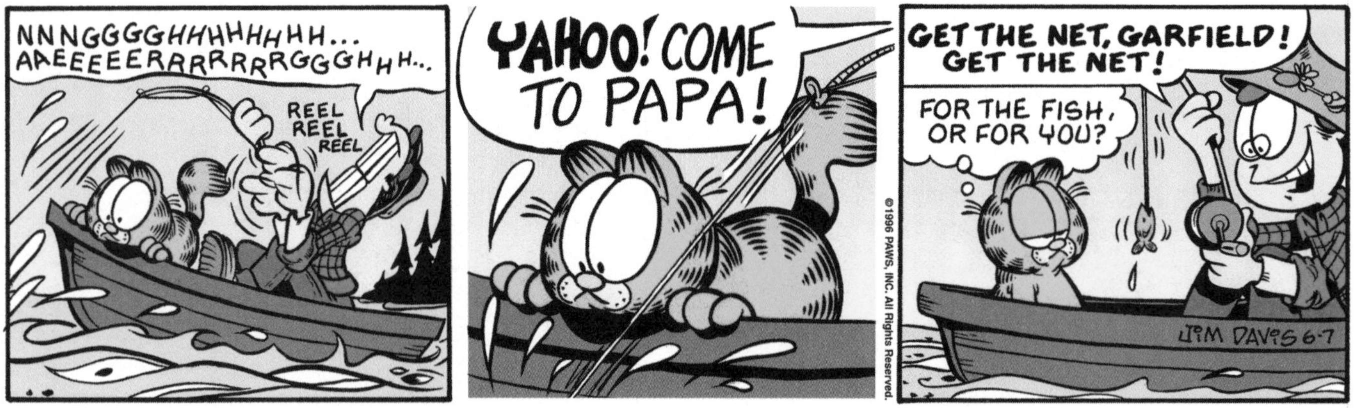
NNNGGGGHHHHHHHH... AAEEEEEERRRRRRRGGGHHH...
REEL REEL REEL
YAHOO! COME TO PAPA!
©1996 PAWS, INC. All Rights Reserved.
GET THE NET, GARFIELD! GET THE NET!
FOR THE FISH, OR FOR YOU?
JIM DAVIS 6-7

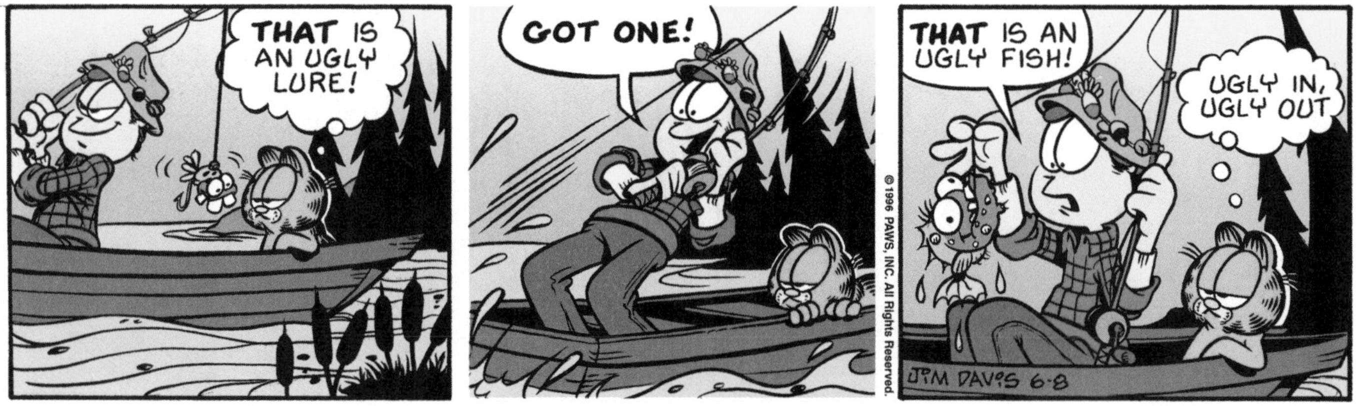
THAT IS AN UGLY LURE!
GOT ONE!
©1996 PAWS, INC. All Rights Reserved.
THAT IS AN UGLY FISH!
UGLY IN, UGLY OUT
JIM DAVIS 6-8

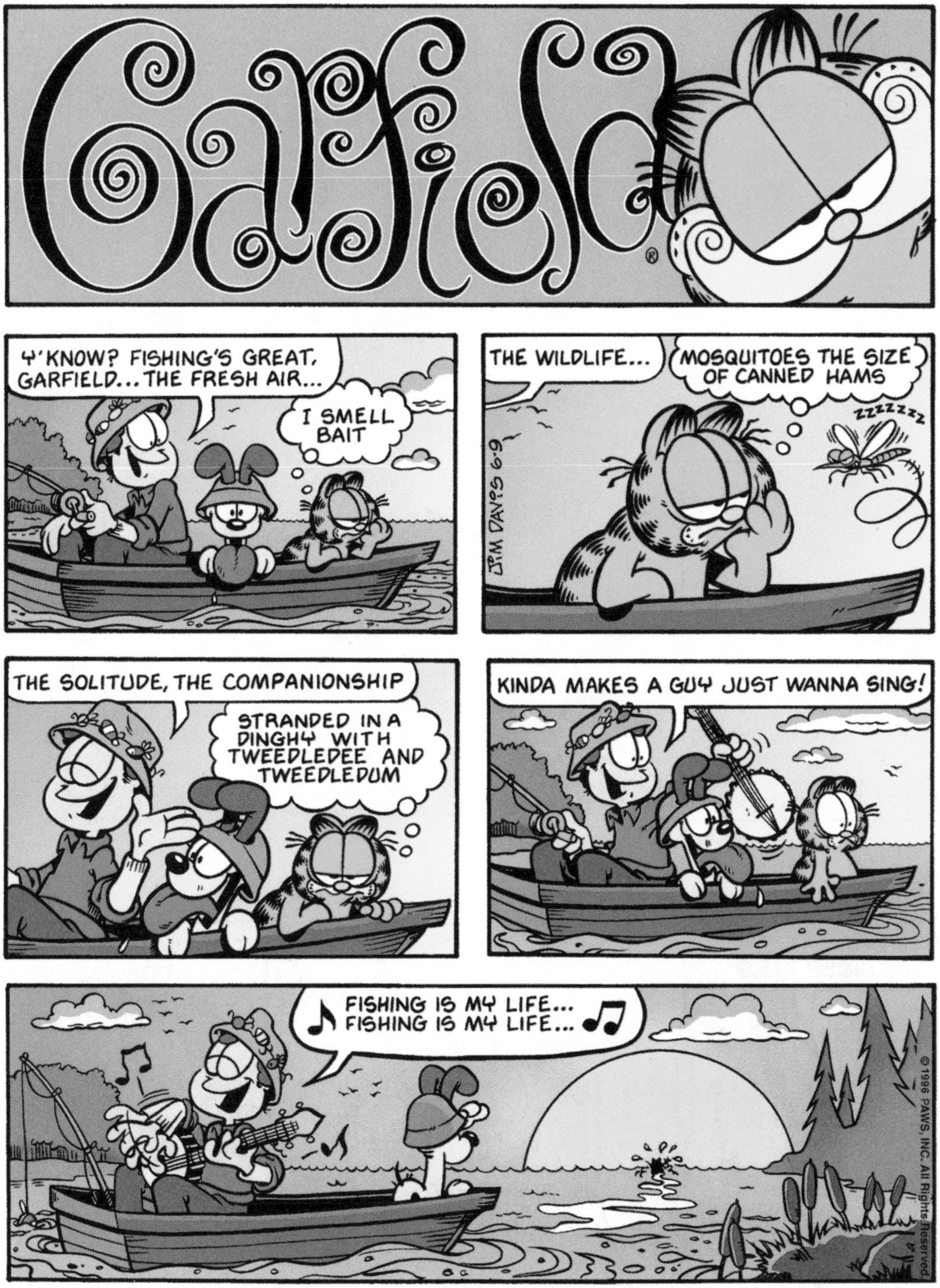
GARFIELD®
JIM DAVIS 6-9
Y'KNOW? FISHING'S GREAT, GARFIELD... THE FRESH AIR...
I SMELL BAIT
THE WILDLIFE...
MOSQUITOES THE SIZE OF CANNED HAMS
ZZZZZZZ
THE SOLITUDE, THE COMPANIONSHIP
STRANDED IN A DINGHY WITH TWEEDLEDEE AND TWEEDLEDUM
KINDA MAKES A GUY JUST WANNA SING!
♪ FISHING IS MY LIFE... FISHING IS MY LIFE... ♫
© 1996 PAWS, INC. All Rights Reserved.

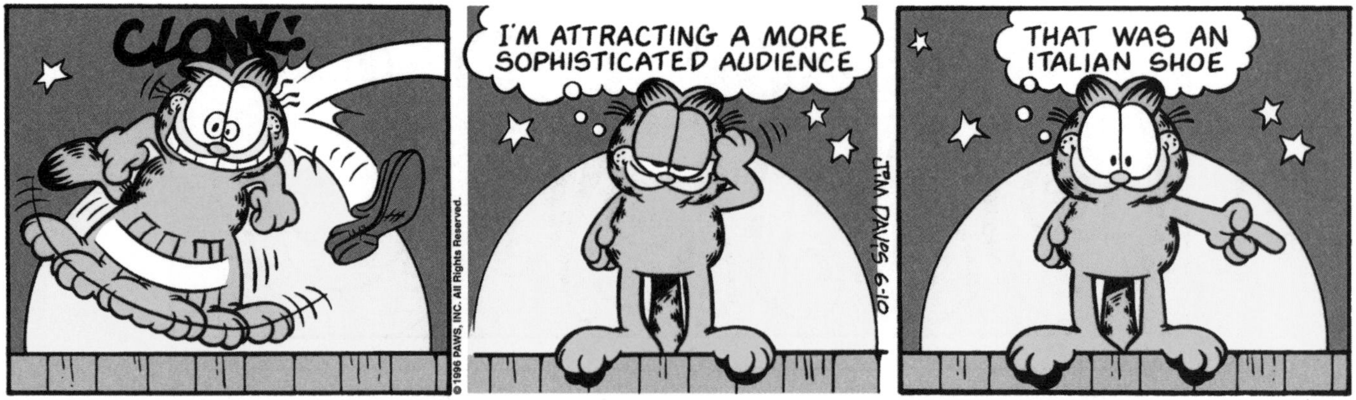
CLONK!
I'M ATTRACTING A MORE SOPHISTICATED AUDIENCE
THAT WAS AN ITALIAN SHOE
© 1996 PAWS, INC. All Rights Reserved.
JIM DAVIS 6-10

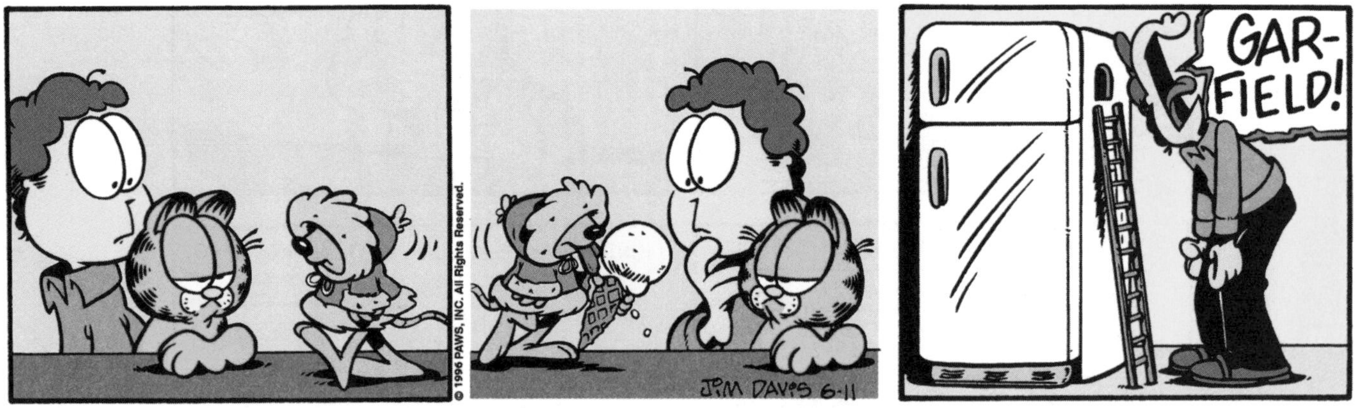
GAR-FIELD!
© 1996 PAWS, INC. All Rights Reserved.
JIM DAVIS 6-11

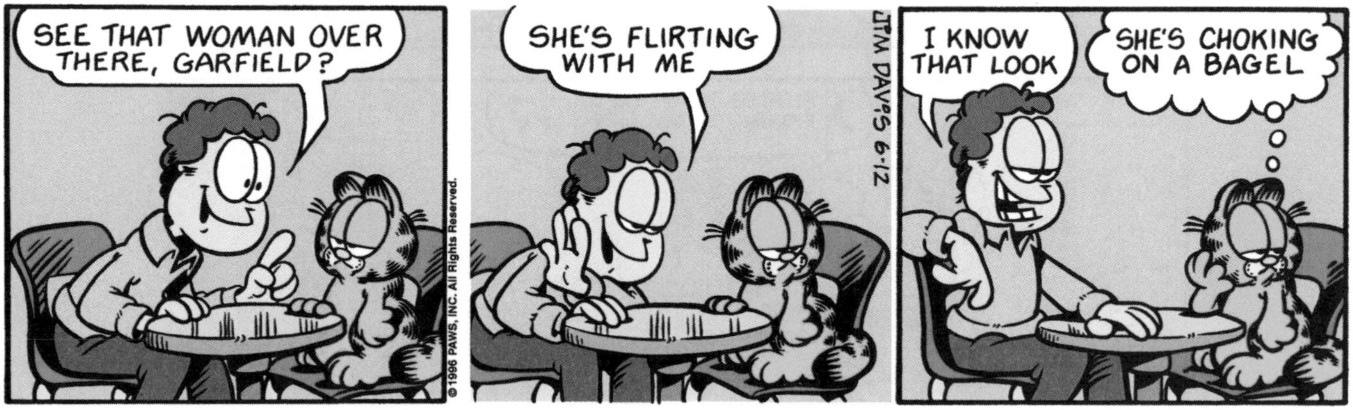
SEE THAT WOMAN OVER THERE, GARFIELD?
SHE'S FLIRTING WITH ME
I KNOW THAT LOOK
SHE'S CHOKING ON A BAGEL
© 1996 PAWS, INC. All Rights Reserved.
JIM DAVIS 6-12

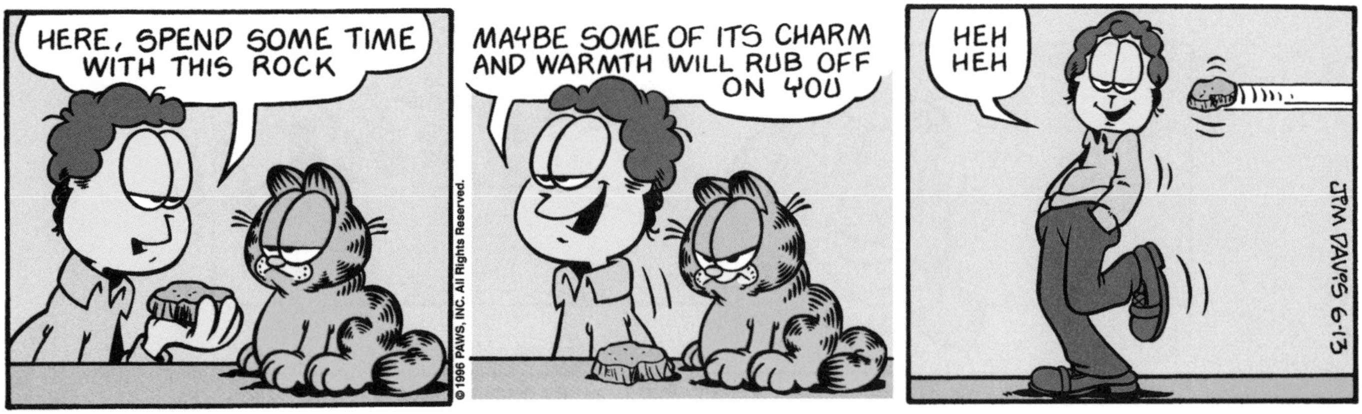
HERE, SPEND SOME TIME WITH THIS ROCK
MAYBE SOME OF ITS CHARM AND WARMTH WILL RUB OFF ON YOU
HEH HEH
© 1996 PAWS, INC. All Rights Reserved.
JIM DAVIS 6-13

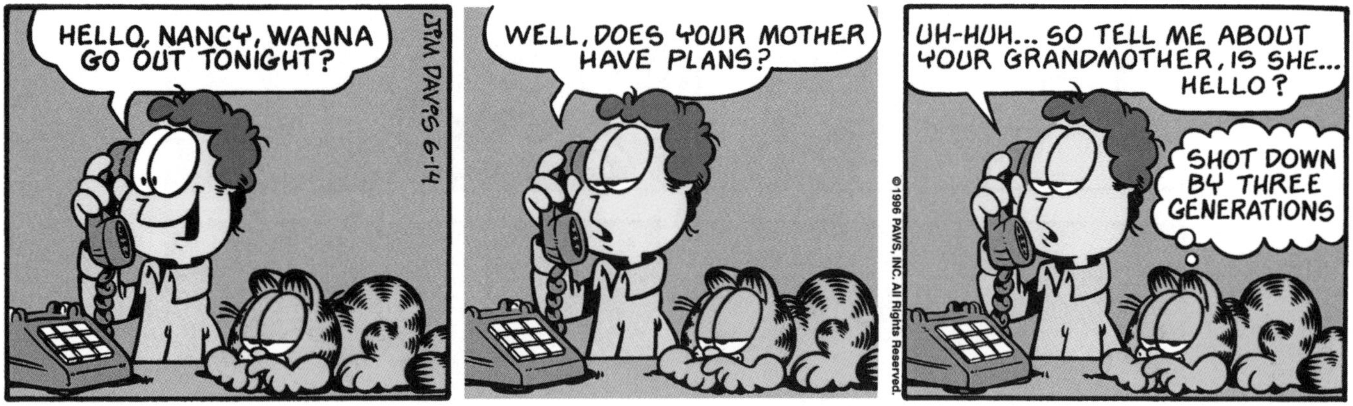
HELLO, NANCY, WANNA GO OUT TONIGHT?
WELL, DOES YOUR MOTHER HAVE PLANS?
UH-HUH... SO TELL ME ABOUT YOUR GRANDMOTHER, IS SHE... HELLO?
SHOT DOWN BY THREE GENERATIONS
JIM DAVIS 6-14
© 1996 PAWS, INC. All Rights Reserved.

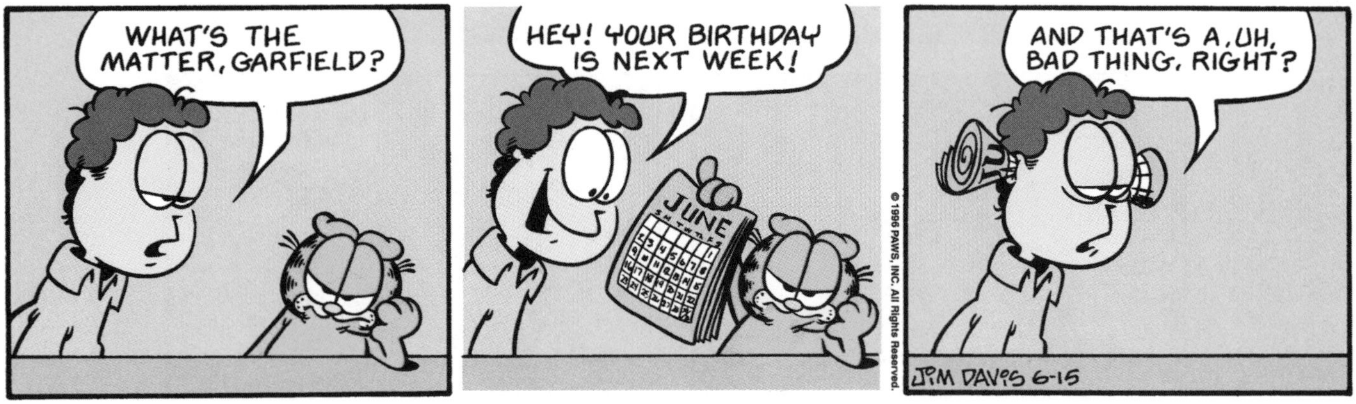
WHAT'S THE MATTER, GARFIELD?
HEY! YOUR BIRTHDAY IS NEXT WEEK!
JUNE
AND THAT'S A, UH, BAD THING, RIGHT?
© 1996 PAWS, INC. All Rights Reserved.
JIM DAVIS 6-15

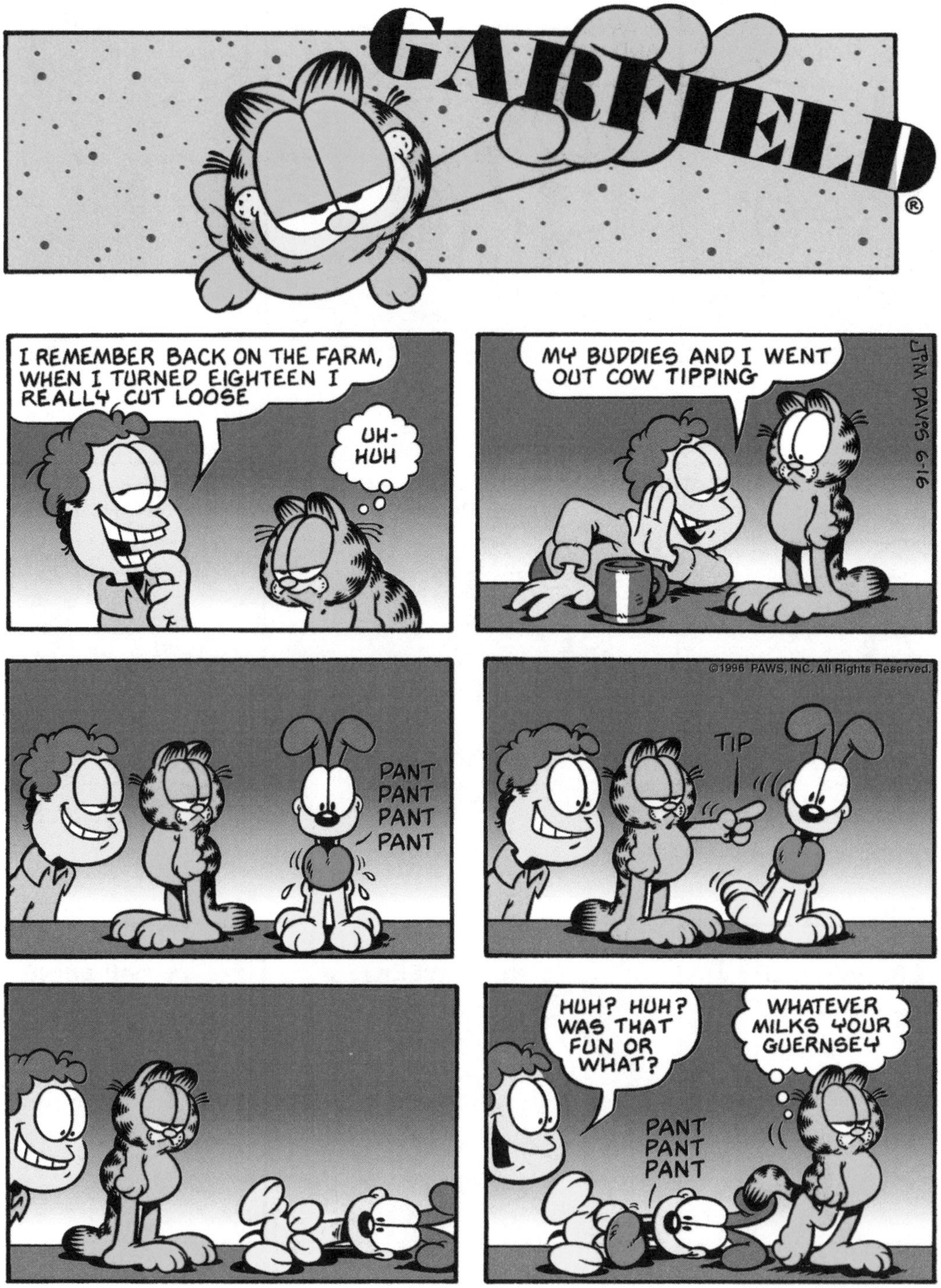
GARFIELD®
I REMEMBER BACK ON THE FARM, WHEN I TURNED EIGHTEEN I REALLY CUT LOOSE
UH-HUH
MY BUDDIES AND I WENT OUT COW TIPPING
JIM DAVIS 6-16
©1996 PAWS, INC. All Rights Reserved.
PANT PANT PANT PANT
TIP
HUH? HUH? WAS THAT FUN OR WHAT?
WHATEVER MILKS YOUR GUERNSEY
PANT PANT PANT

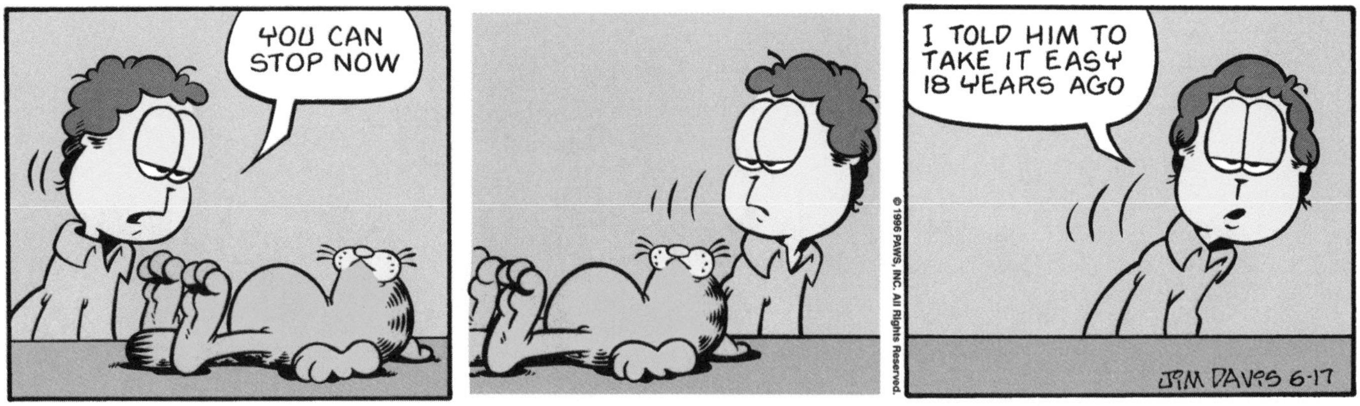
YOU CAN STOP NOW
I TOLD HIM TO TAKE IT EASY 18 YEARS AGO
© 1996 PAWS, INC. All Rights Reserved.
JIM DAVIS 6-17

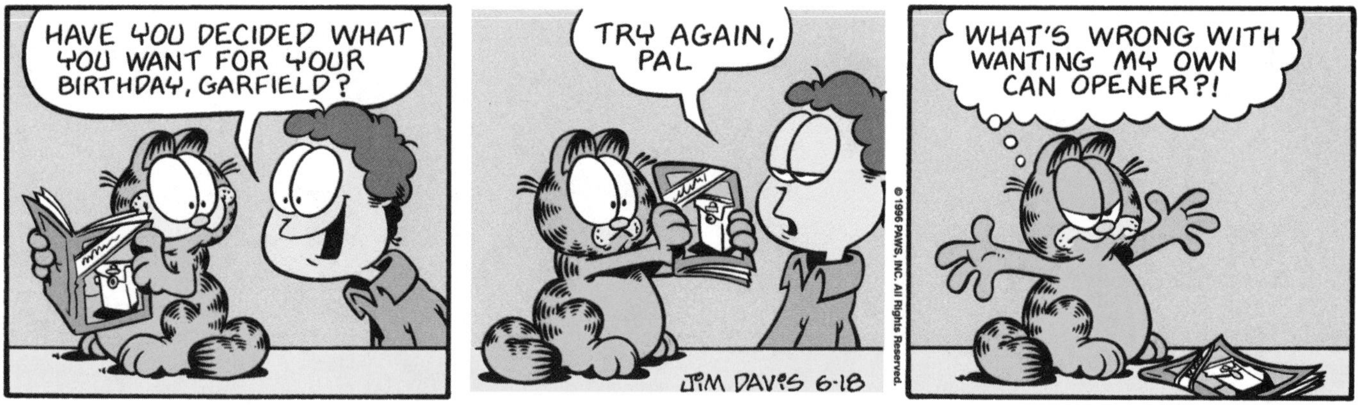
HAVE YOU DECIDED WHAT YOU WANT FOR YOUR BIRTHDAY, GARFIELD?
TRY AGAIN, PAL
WHAT'S WRONG WITH WANTING MY OWN CAN OPENER?!
© 1996 PAWS, INC. All Rights Reserved.
JIM DAVIS 6-18

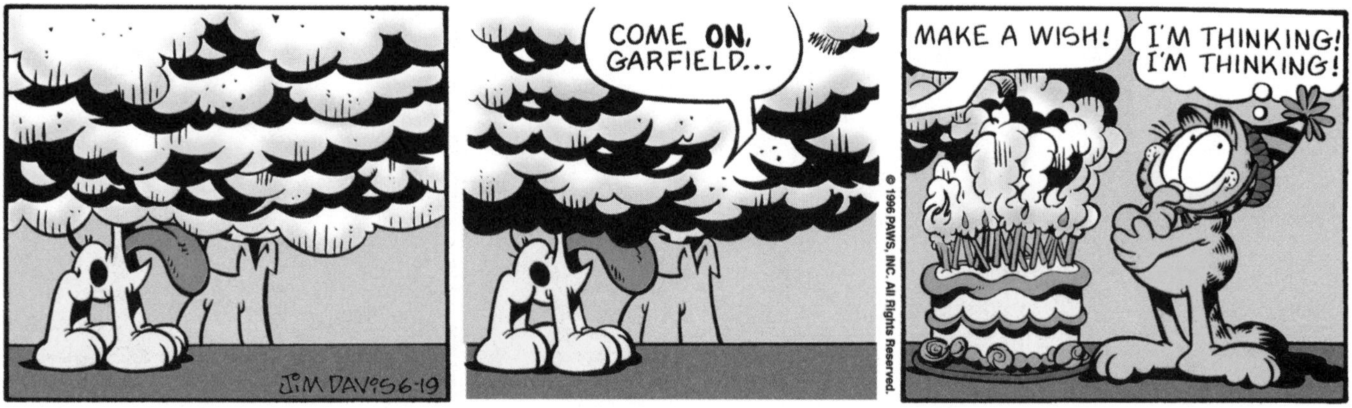
COME **ON**, GARFIELD...
MAKE A WISH!
I'M THINKING! I'M THINKING!
© 1996 PAWS, INC. All Rights Reserved.
JIM DAVIS 6-19

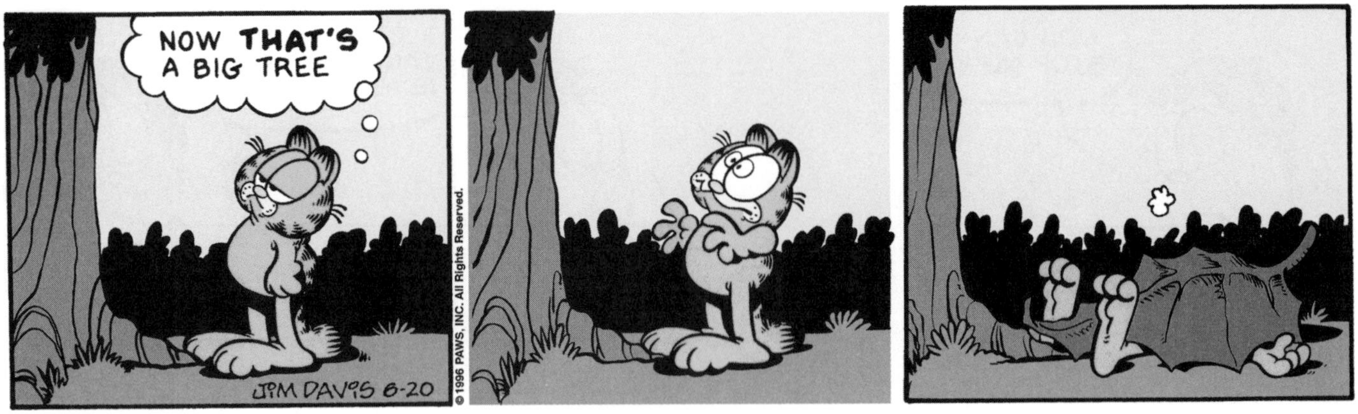
NOW THAT'S A BIG TREE
© 1996 PAWS, INC. All Rights Reserved.
JIM DAVIS 6-20

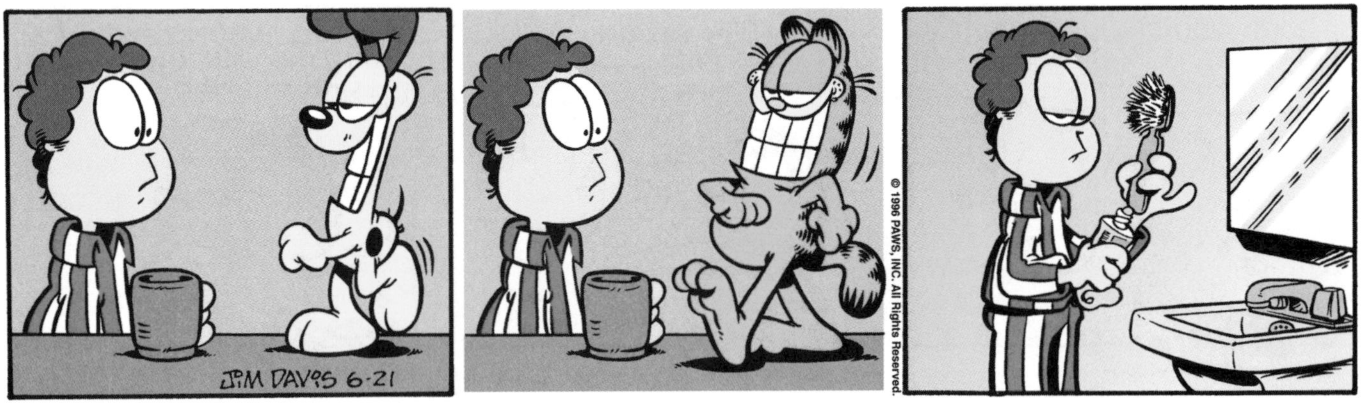
JIM DAVIS 6-21
© 1996 PAWS, INC. All Rights Reserved.

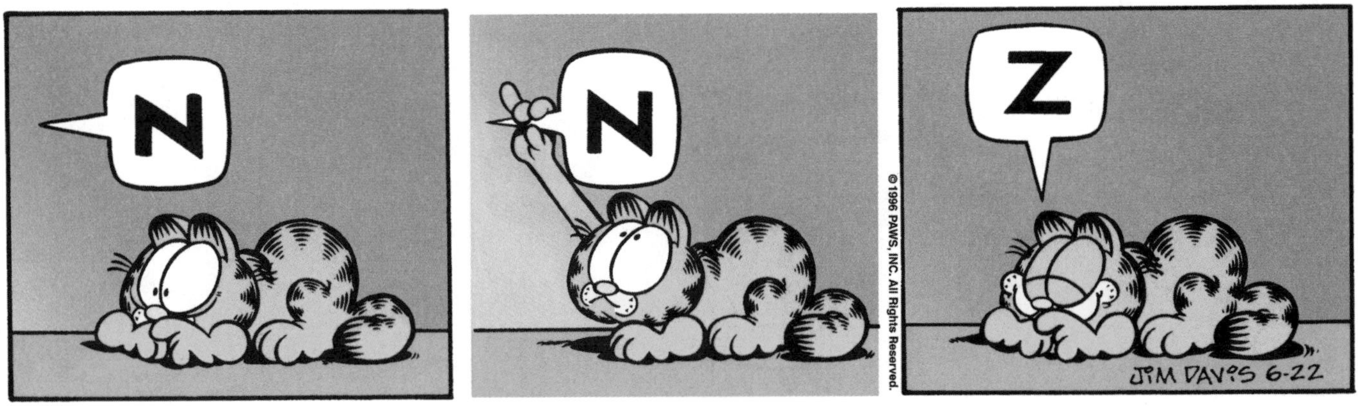
N
N
Z
© 1996 PAWS, INC. All Rights Reserved.
JIM DAVIS 6-22

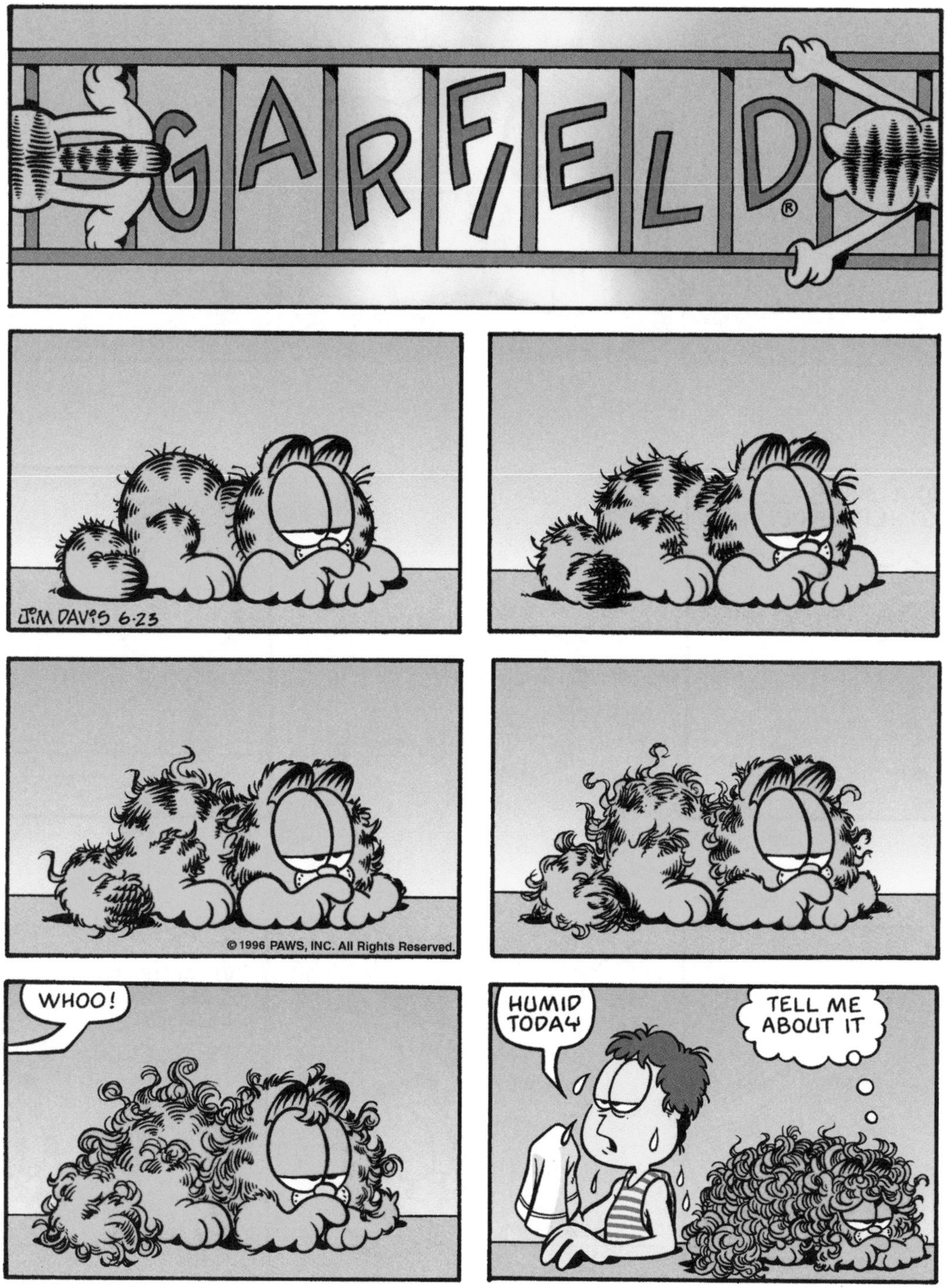
GARFIELD®
JIM DAVIS 6-23
© 1996 PAWS, INC. All Rights Reserved.
WHOO!
HUMID TODAY
TELL ME ABOUT IT

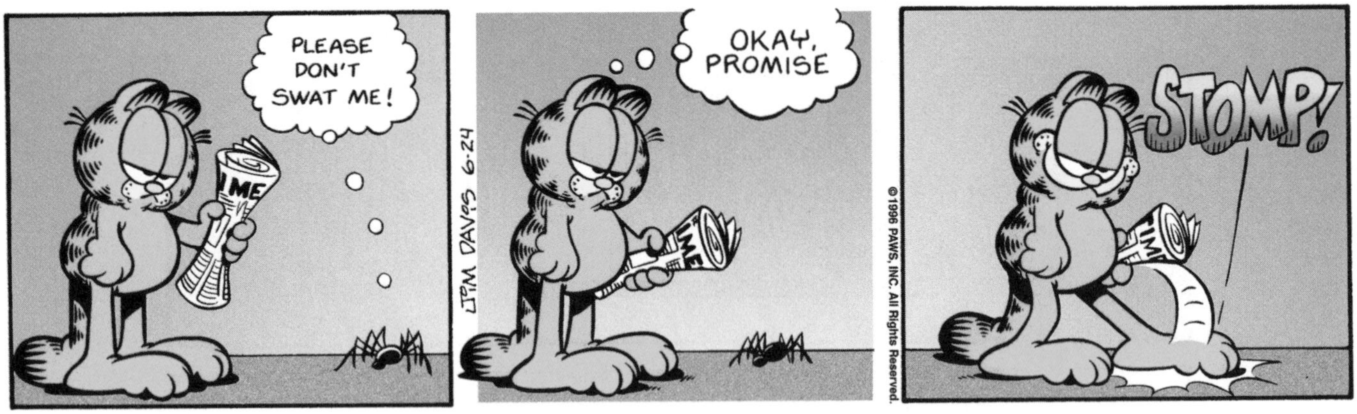
PLEASE DON'T SWAT ME!
OKAY, PROMISE
JIM DAVIS 6-24
STOMP!
© 1996 PAWS, INC. All Rights Reserved.

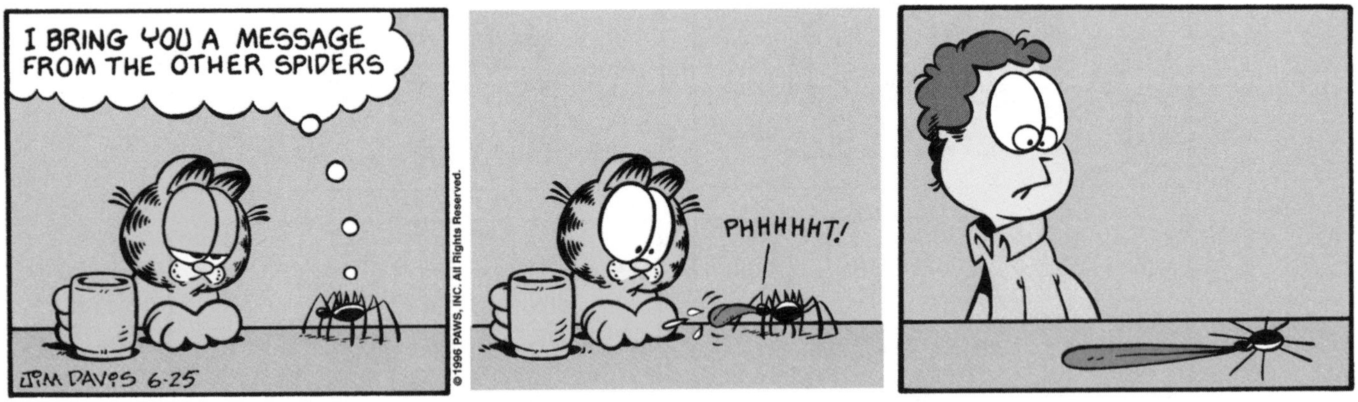
I BRING YOU A MESSAGE FROM THE OTHER SPIDERS
JIM DAVIS 6-25
© 1996 PAWS, INC. All Rights Reserved.
PHHHHHT!

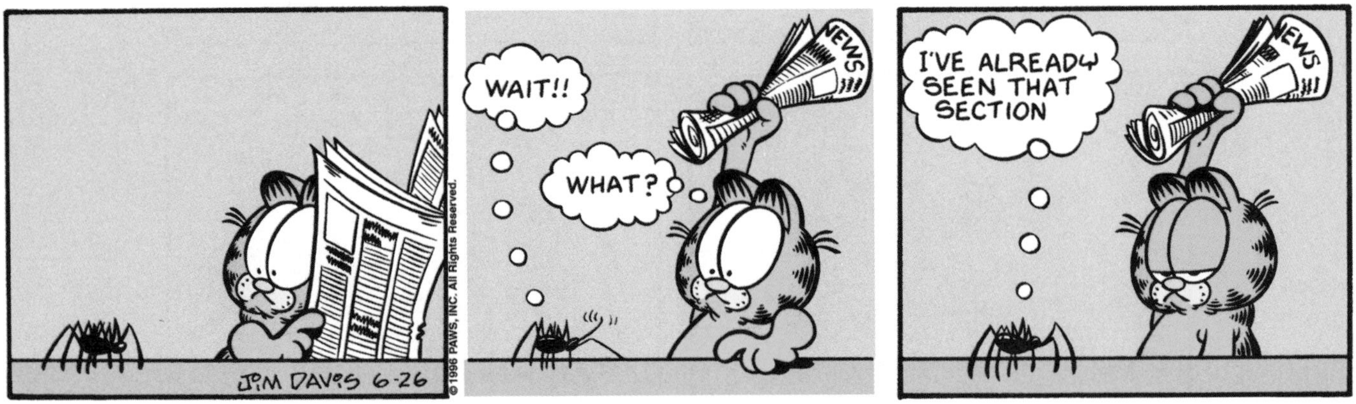
JIM DAVIS 6-26
© 1996 PAWS, INC. All Rights Reserved.
WAIT!!
WHAT?
NEWS
I'VE ALREADY SEEN THAT SECTION

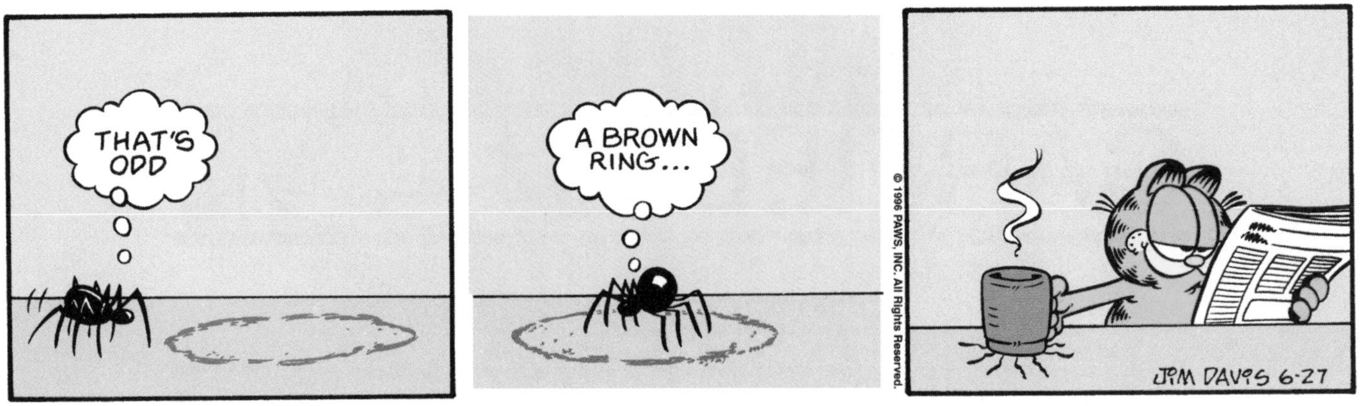
THAT'S ODD
A BROWN RING...
© 1996 PAWS, INC. All Rights Reserved.
JIM DAVIS 6-27

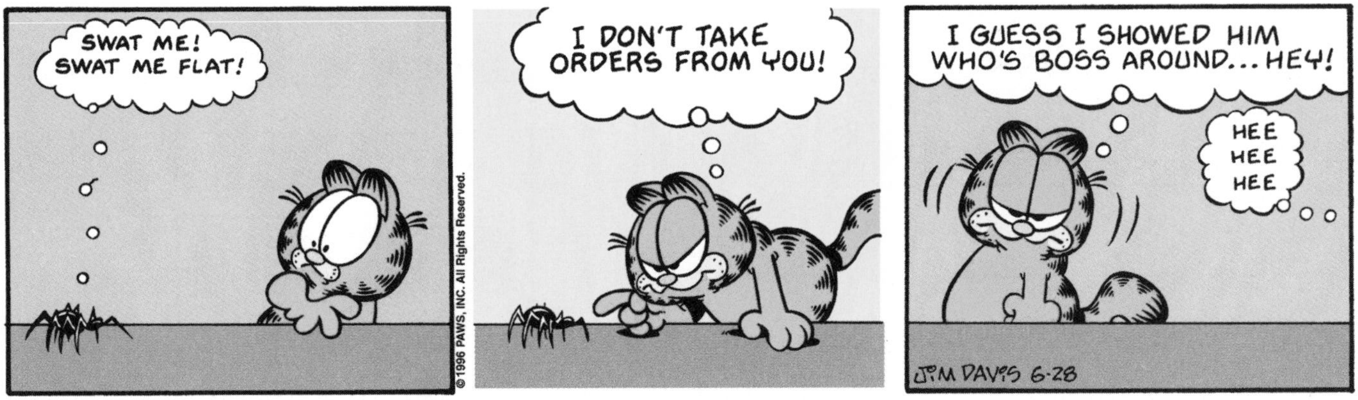
SWAT ME! SWAT ME FLAT!
© 1996 PAWS, INC. All Rights Reserved.
I DON'T TAKE ORDERS FROM YOU!
I GUESS I SHOWED HIM WHO'S BOSS AROUND... HEY!
HEE HEE HEE
JIM DAVIS 6-28

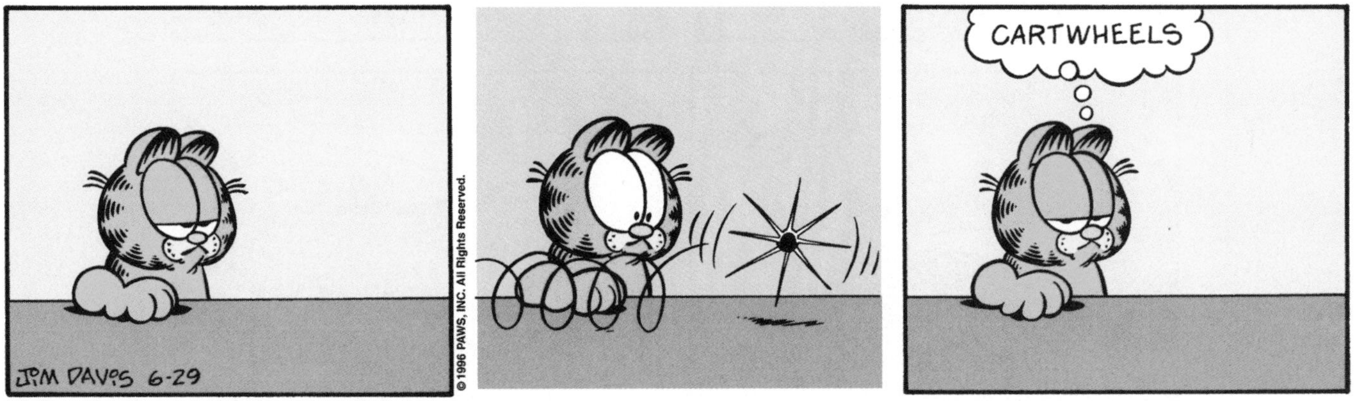
JIM DAVIS 6-29
© 1996 PAWS, INC. All Rights Reserved.
CARTWHEELS

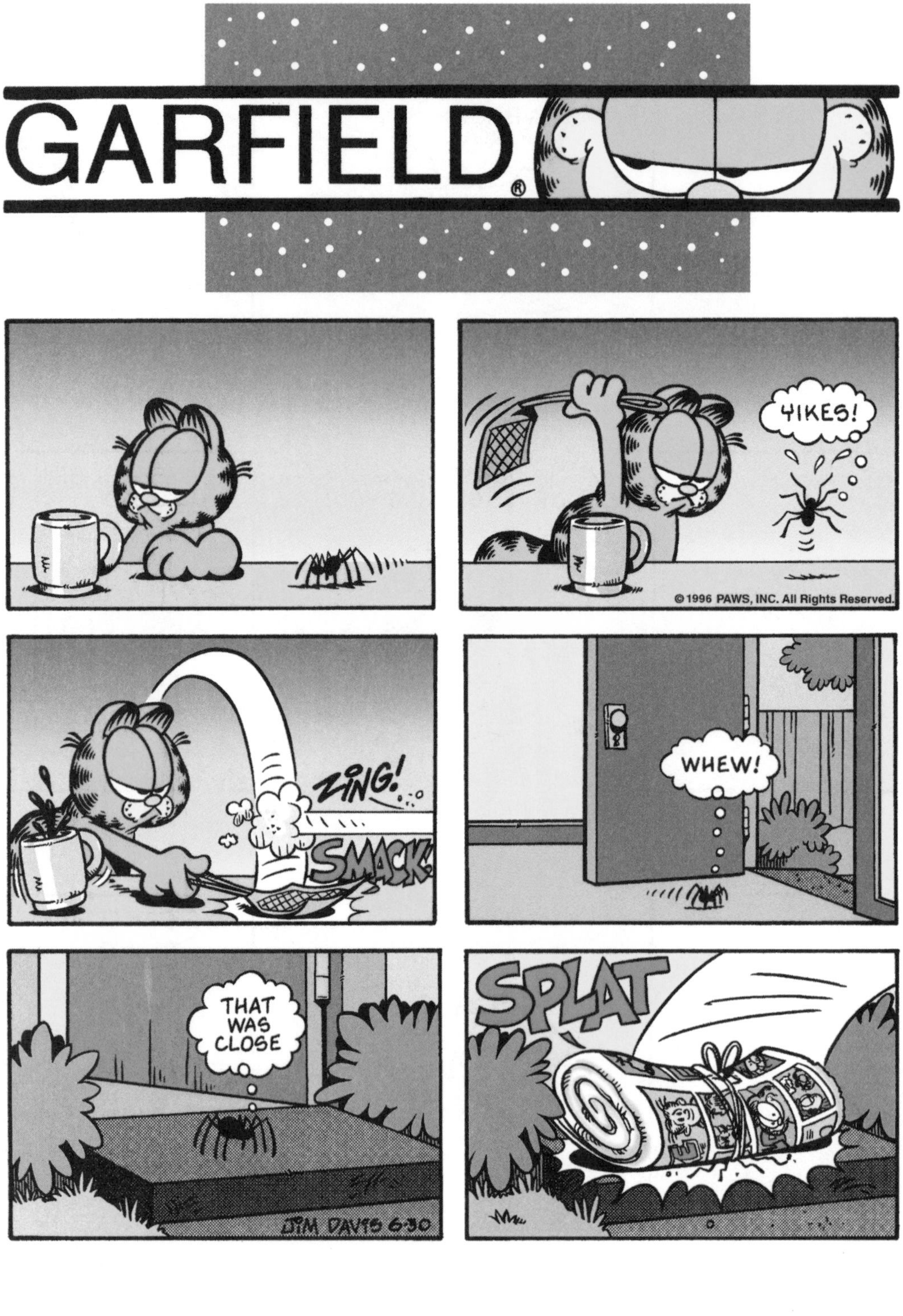
GARFIELD®
YIKES!
© 1996 PAWS, INC. All Rights Reserved.
ZING!
SMACK!
WHEW!
THAT WAS CLOSE
JIM DAVIS 6-30
SPLAT

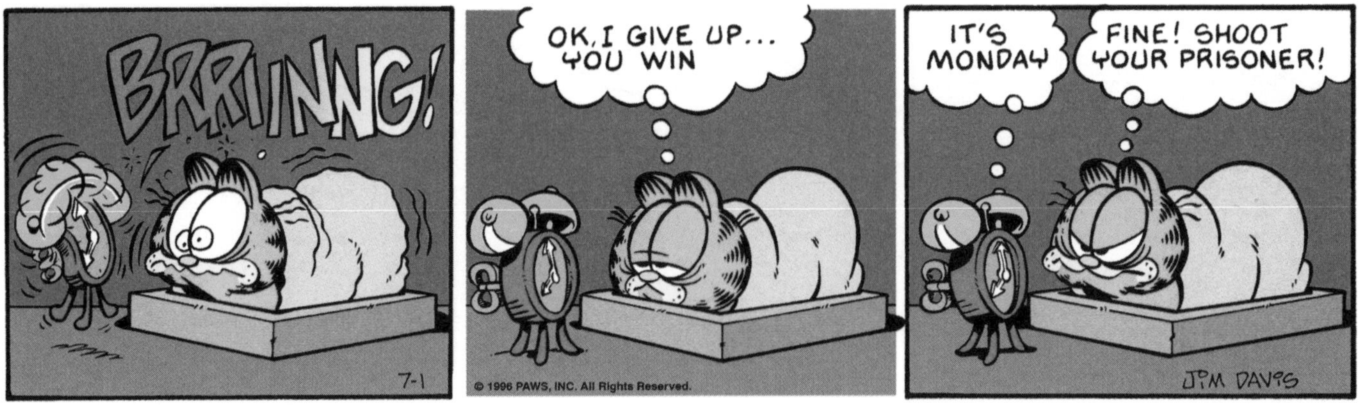
BRRIINNG!
7-1
OK, I GIVE UP... YOU WIN
© 1996 PAWS, INC. All Rights Reserved.
IT'S MONDAY
FINE! SHOOT YOUR PRISONER!
JIM DAVIS

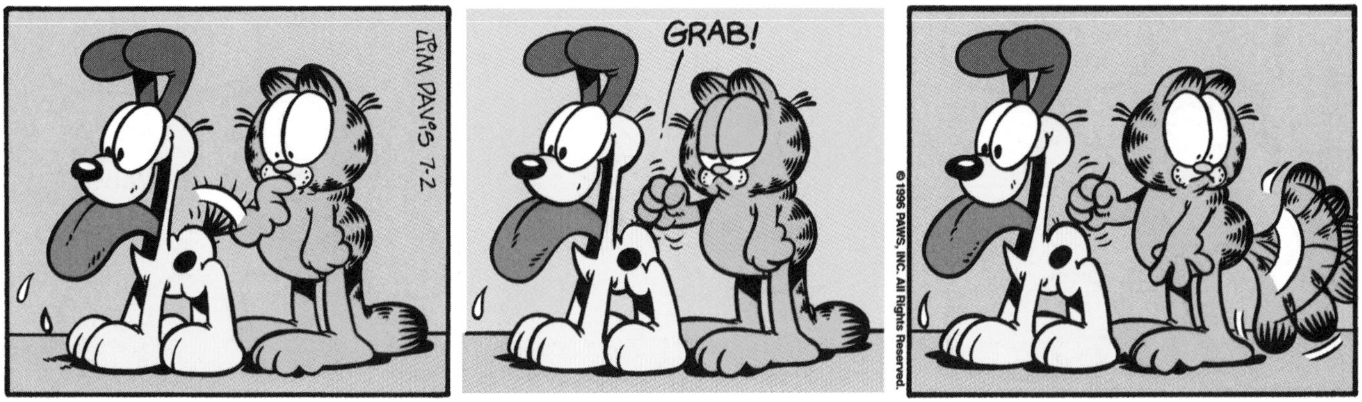
JIM DAVIS 7-2
GRAB!
© 1996 PAWS, INC. All Rights Reserved.

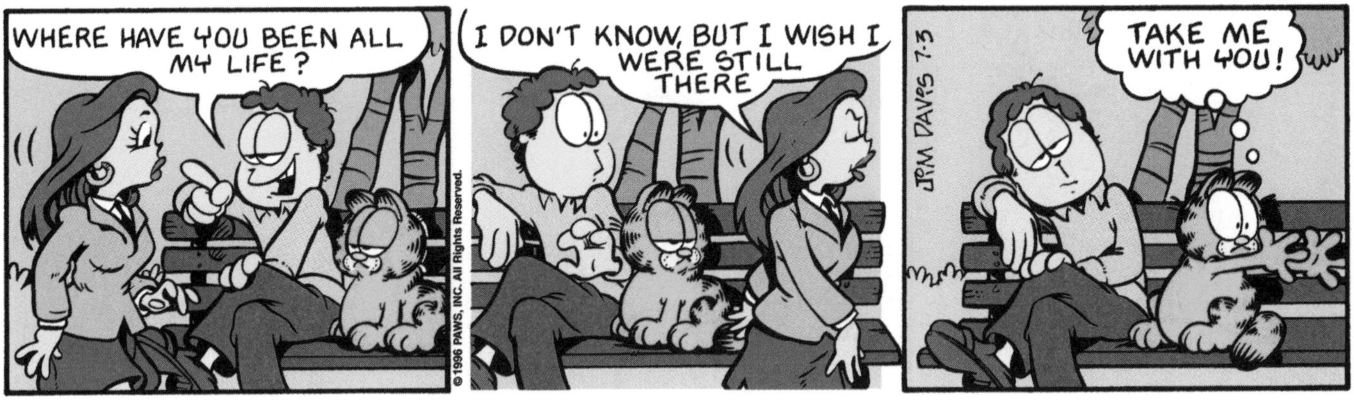
WHERE HAVE YOU BEEN ALL MY LIFE?
© 1996 PAWS, INC. All Rights Reserved.
I DON'T KNOW, BUT I WISH I WERE STILL THERE
JIM DAVIS 7-3
TAKE ME WITH YOU!

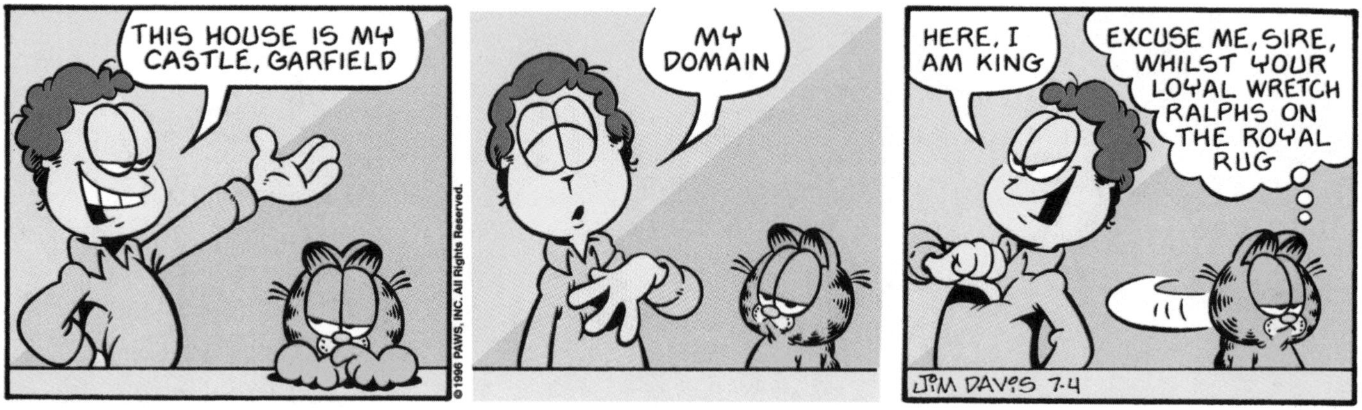
THIS HOUSE IS MY CASTLE, GARFIELD
MY DOMAIN
HERE, I AM KING
EXCUSE ME, SIRE, WHILST YOUR LOYAL WRETCH RALPHS ON THE ROYAL RUG
©1996 PAWS, INC. All Rights Reserved.
JIM DAVIS 7-4

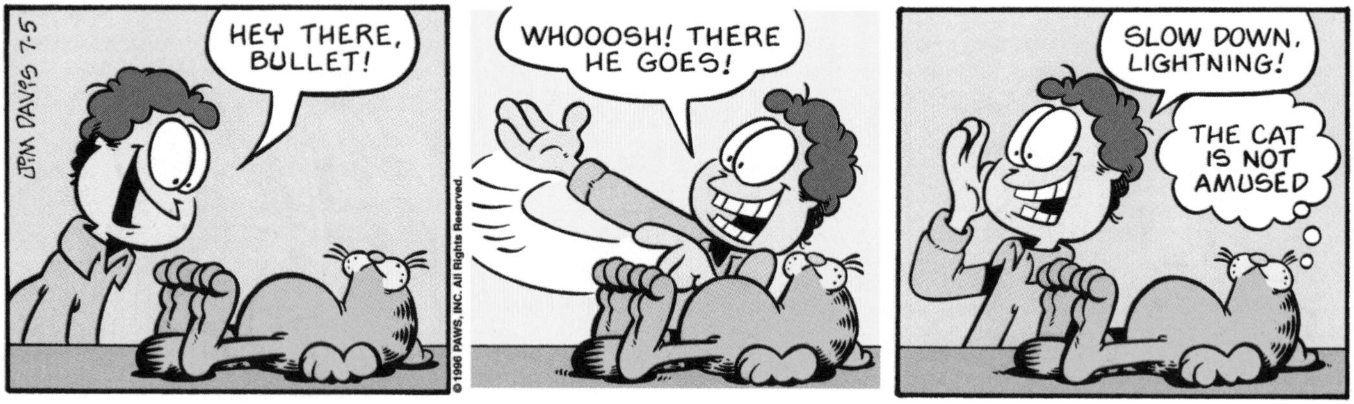
JIM DAVIS 7-5
HEY THERE, BULLET!
WHOOOSH! THERE HE GOES!
SLOW DOWN, LIGHTNING!
THE CAT IS NOT AMUSED
©1996 PAWS, INC. All Rights Reserved.

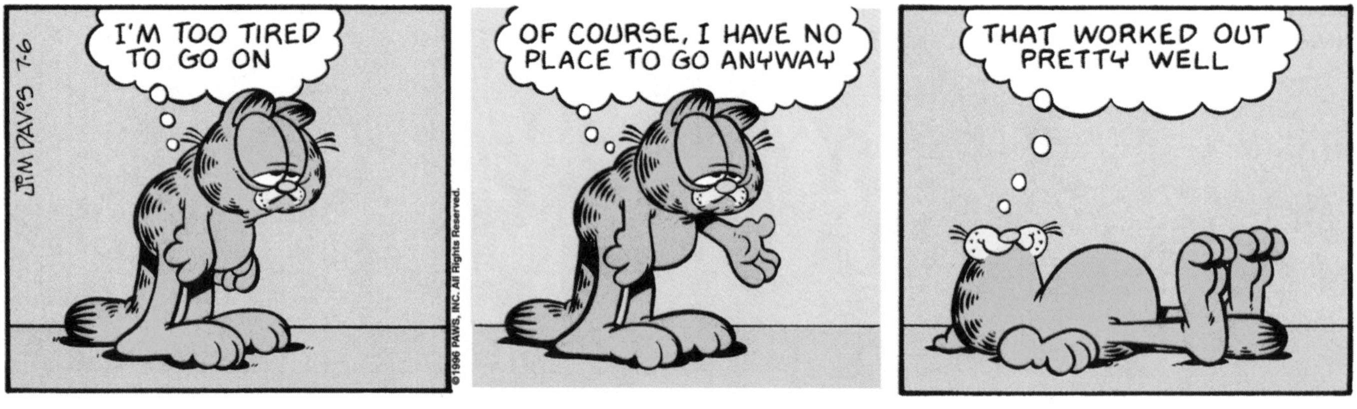
JIM DAVIS 7-6
I'M TOO TIRED TO GO ON
OF COURSE, I HAVE NO PLACE TO GO ANYWAY
THAT WORKED OUT PRETTY WELL
©1996 PAWS, INC. All Rights Reserved.

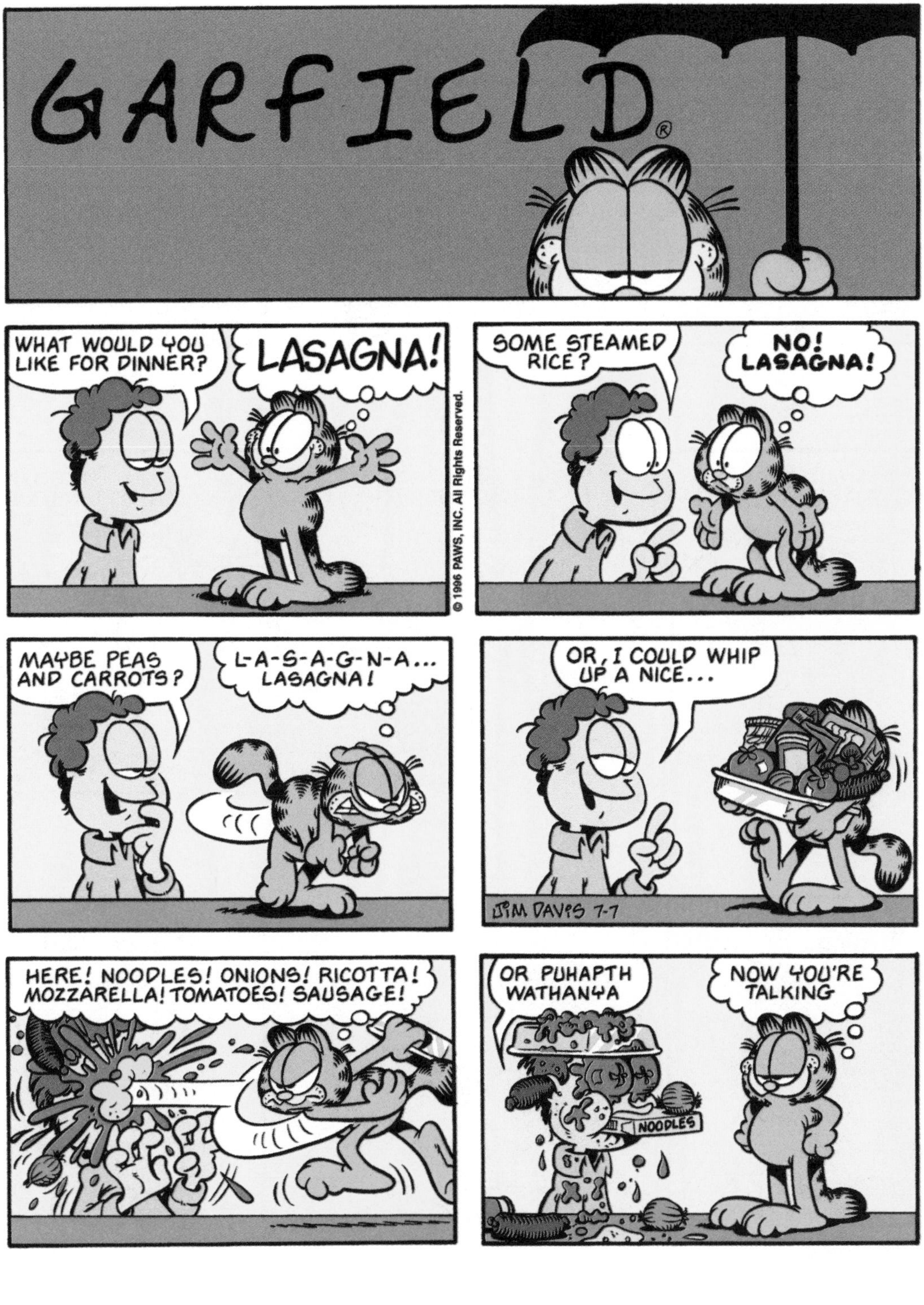

GARFIELD®
WHAT WOULD YOU LIKE FOR DINNER?
LASAGNA!
© 1996 PAWS, INC. All Rights Reserved.
SOME STEAMED RICE?
NO! LASAGNA!
MAYBE PEAS AND CARROTS?
L-A-S-A-G-N-A... LASAGNA!
OR, I COULD WHIP UP A NICE...
JIM DAVIS 7-7
HERE! NOODLES! ONIONS! RICOTTA! MOZZARELLA! TOMATOES! SAUSAGE!
OR PUHAPTH WATHANYA
NOODLES
NOW YOU'RE TALKING

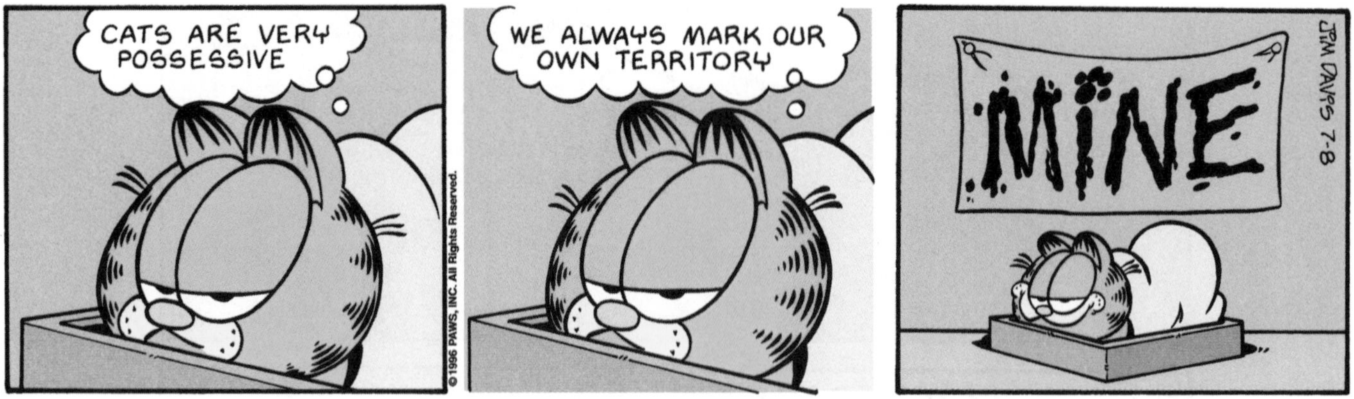
CATS ARE VERY POSSESSIVE
WE ALWAYS MARK OUR OWN TERRITORY
MINE
JIM DAVIS 7-8
© 1996 PAWS, INC. All Rights Reserved.

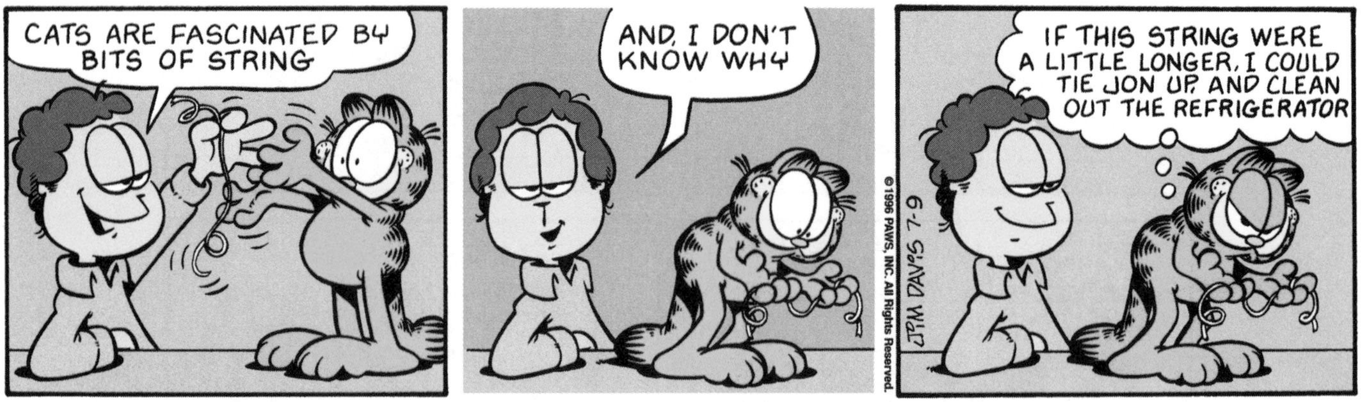
CATS ARE FASCINATED BY BITS OF STRING
AND, I DON'T KNOW WHY
IF THIS STRING WERE A LITTLE LONGER, I COULD TIE JON UP, AND CLEAN OUT THE REFRIGERATOR
JIM DAVIS 7-9
© 1996 PAWS, INC. All Rights Reserved.

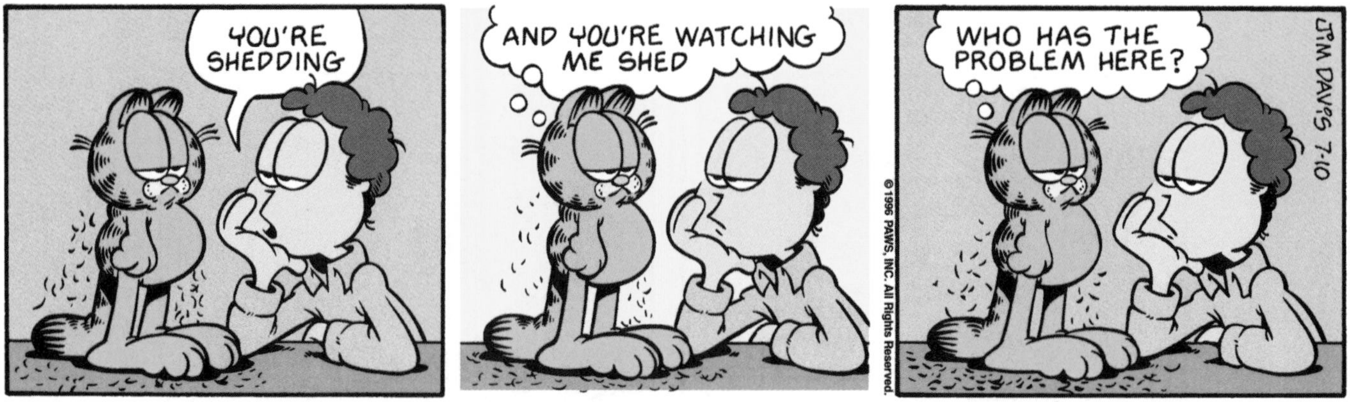
YOU'RE SHEDDING
AND YOU'RE WATCHING ME SHED
WHO HAS THE PROBLEM HERE?
JIM DAVIS 7-10
© 1996 PAWS, INC. All Rights Reserved.

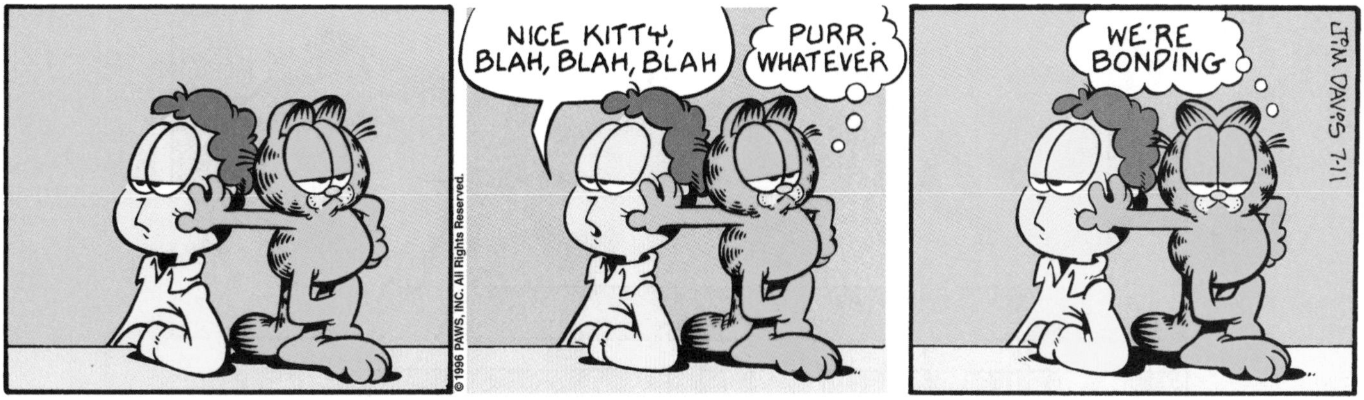
© 1996 PAWS, INC. All Rights Reserved.
NICE KITTY, BLAH, BLAH, BLAH
PURR. WHATEVER
WE'RE BONDING
JIM DAVIS 7-11

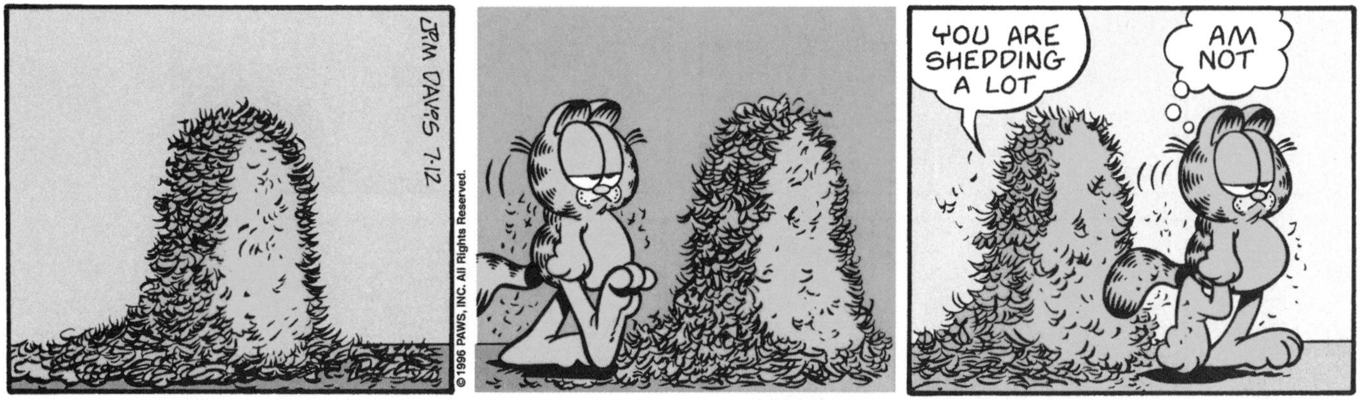
JIM DAVIS 7-12
© 1996 PAWS, INC. All Rights Reserved.
YOU ARE SHEDDING A LOT
AM NOT

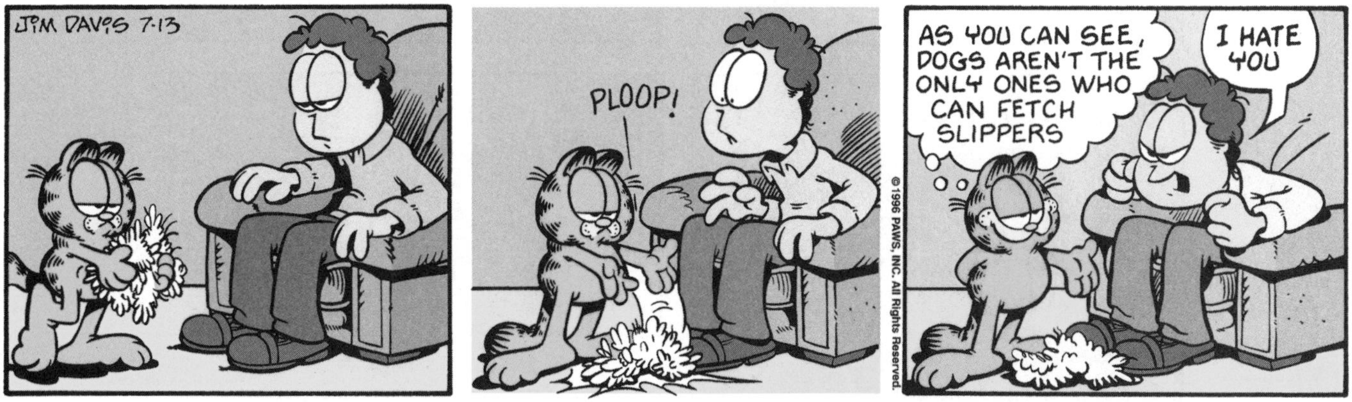
JIM DAVIS 7-13
PLOOP!
© 1996 PAWS, INC. All Rights Reserved.
AS YOU CAN SEE, DOGS AREN'T THE ONLY ONES WHO CAN FETCH SLIPPERS
I HATE YOU

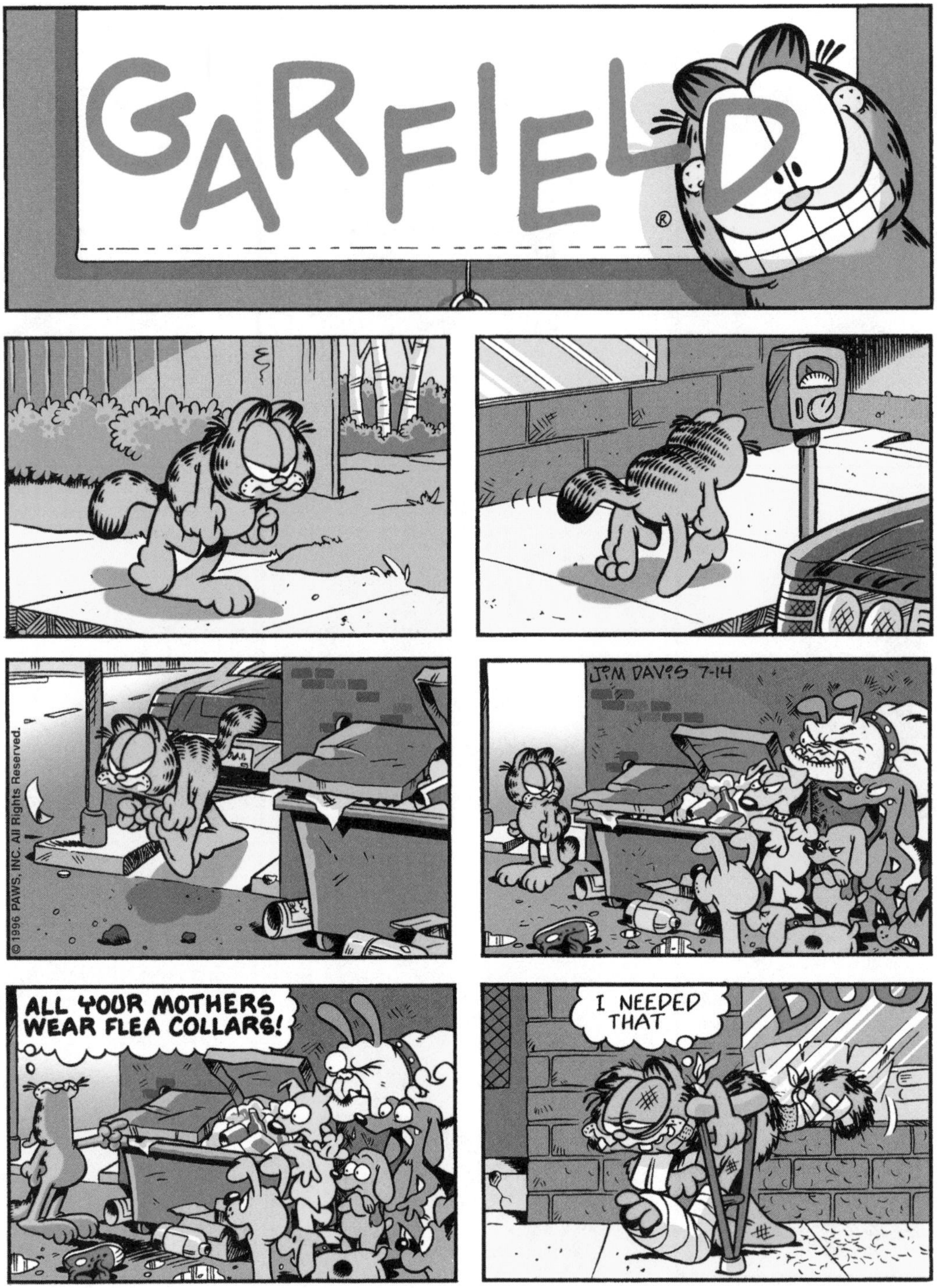
GARFIELD®
JIM DAVIS 7-14
© 1996 PAWS, INC. All Rights Reserved.
ALL YOUR MOTHERS WEAR FLEA COLLARS!
I NEEDED THAT

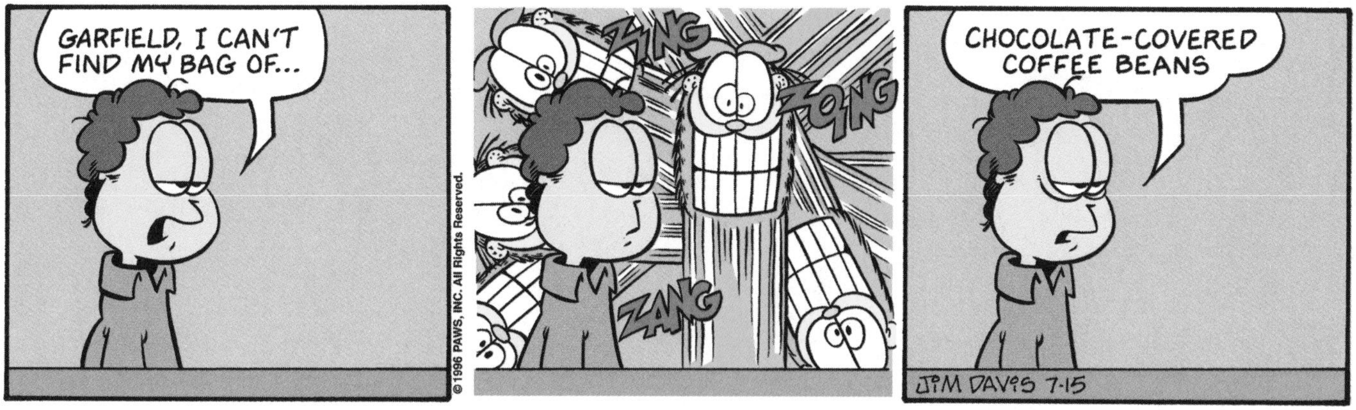
GARFIELD, I CAN'T FIND MY BAG OF...
ZING
ZOING
ZANG
CHOCOLATE-COVERED COFFEE BEANS
JIM DAVIS 7-15
© 1996 PAWS, INC. All Rights Reserved.

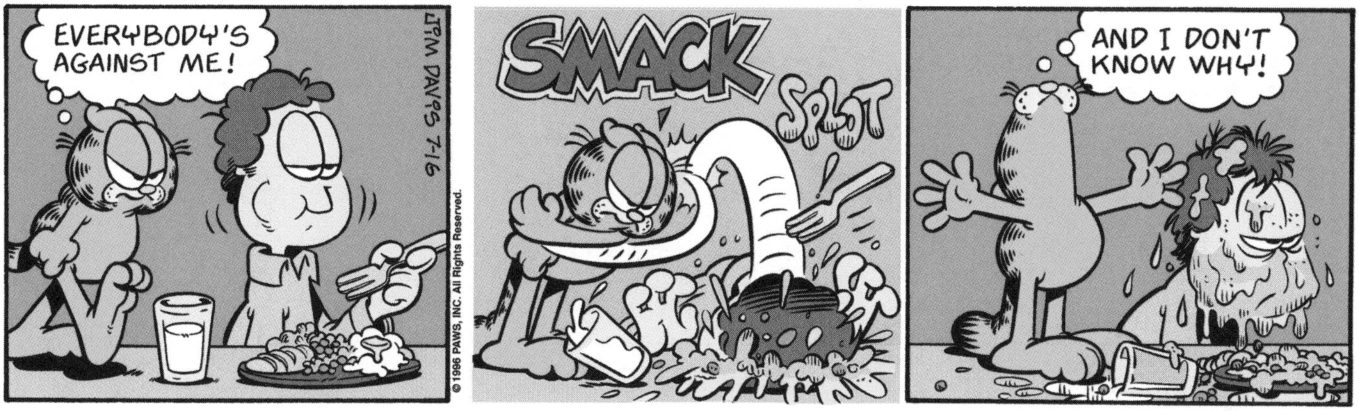
EVERYBODY'S AGAINST ME!
JIM DAVIS 7-16
SMACK
SPLOT
AND I DON'T KNOW WHY!
© 1996 PAWS, INC. All Rights Reserved.

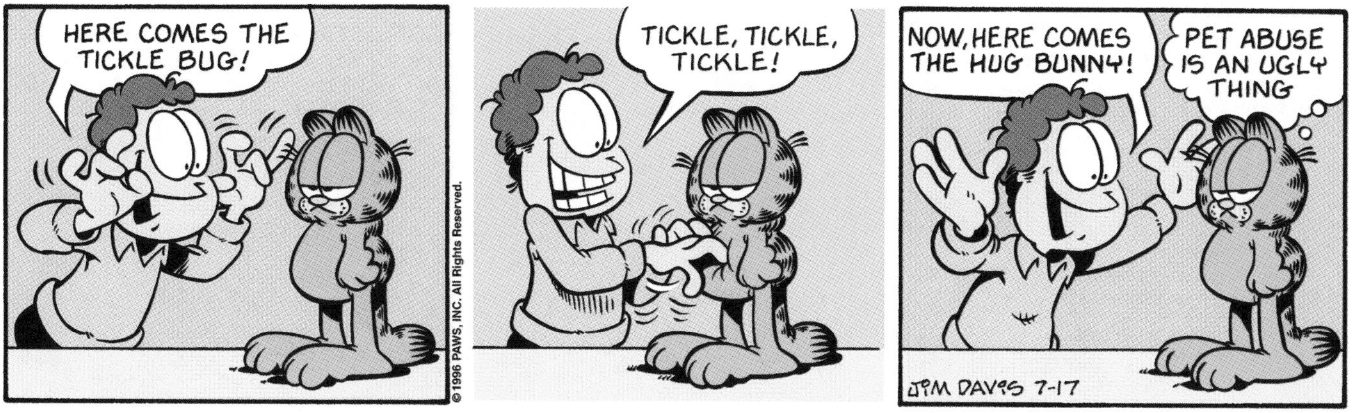
HERE COMES THE TICKLE BUG!
TICKLE, TICKLE, TICKLE!
NOW, HERE COMES THE HUG BUNNY!
PET ABUSE IS AN UGLY THING
JIM DAVIS 7-17
© 1996 PAWS, INC. All Rights Reserved.

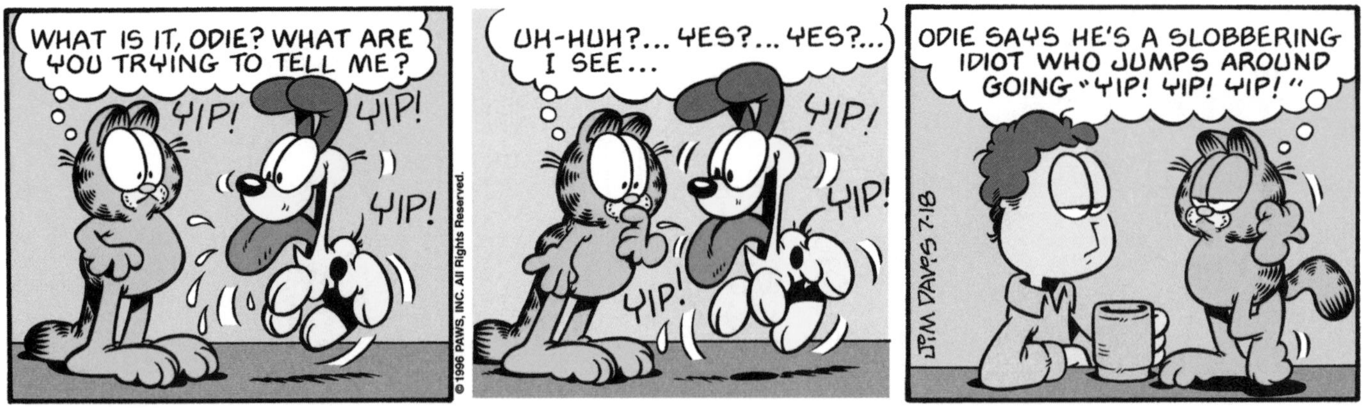
WHAT IS IT, ODIE? WHAT ARE YOU TRYING TO TELL ME?
YIP! YIP! YIP!
© 1996 PAWS, INC. All Rights Reserved.
UH-HUH?... YES?... YES?... I SEE...
YIP! YIP! YIP!
ODIE SAYS HE'S A SLOBBERING IDIOT WHO JUMPS AROUND GOING "YIP! YIP! YIP!"
JIM DAVIS 7-18

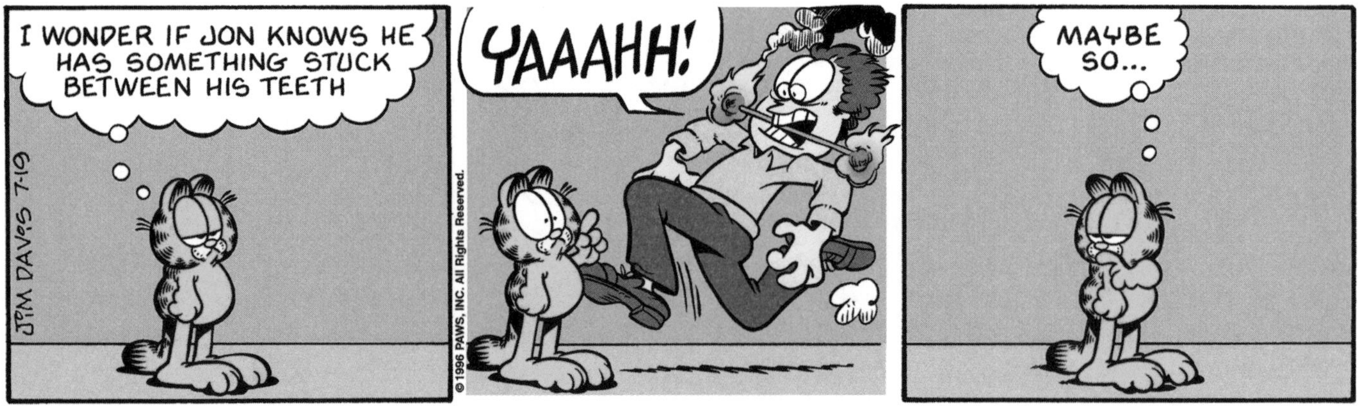
I WONDER IF JON KNOWS HE HAS SOMETHING STUCK BETWEEN HIS TEETH
JIM DAVIS 7-19
© 1996 PAWS, INC. All Rights Reserved.
YAAAHH!
MAYBE SO...

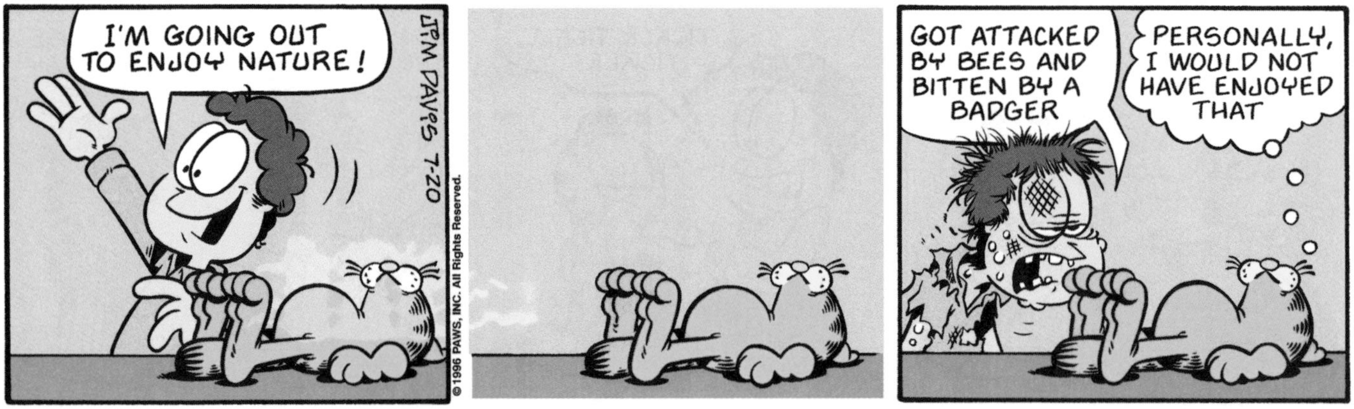
I'M GOING OUT TO ENJOY NATURE!
JIM DAVIS 7-20
© 1996 PAWS, INC. All Rights Reserved.
GOT ATTACKED BY BEES AND BITTEN BY A BADGER
PERSONALLY, I WOULD NOT HAVE ENJOYED THAT

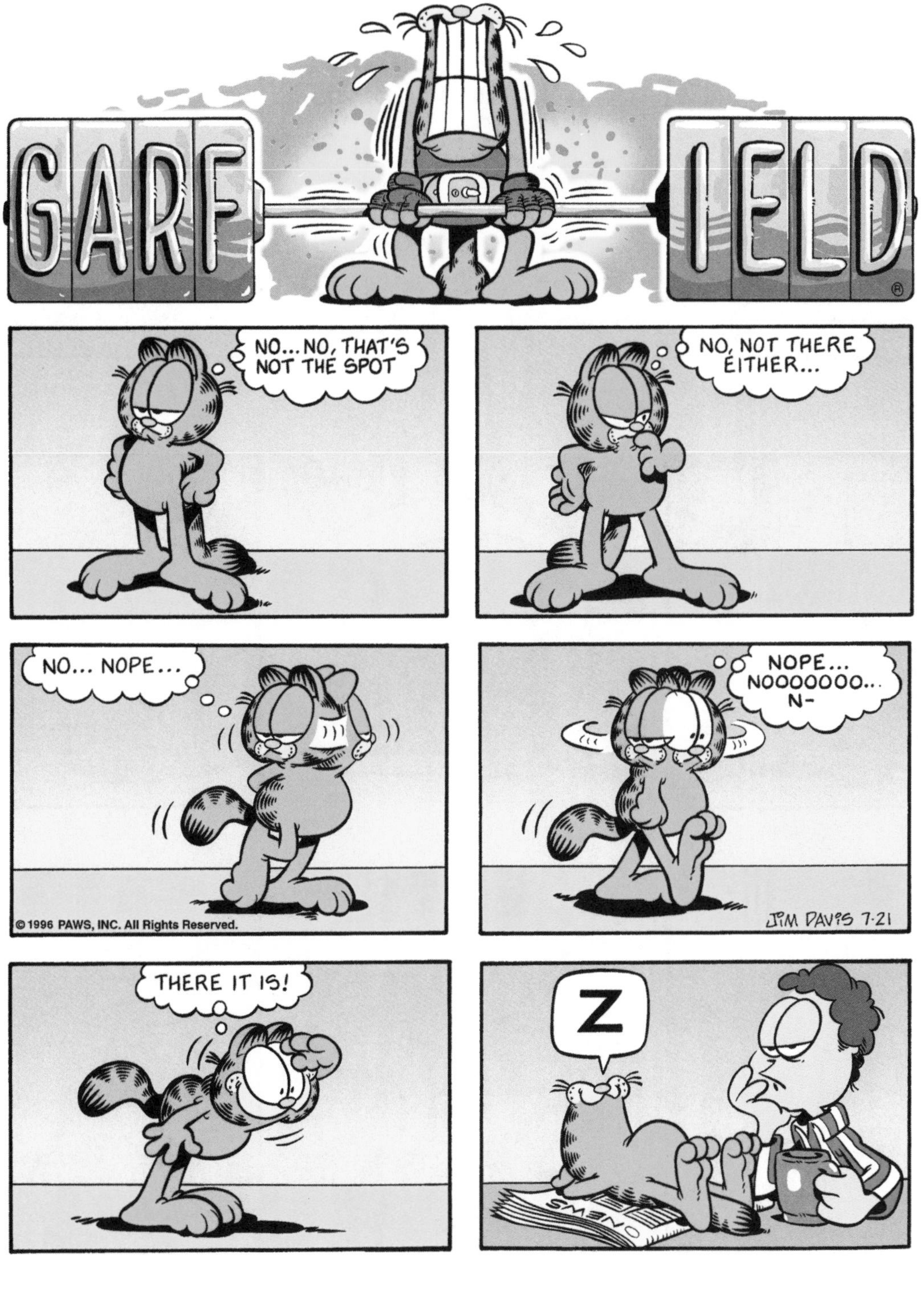
GARFIELD ®
NO... NO, THAT'S NOT THE SPOT
NO, NOT THERE EITHER...
NO... NOPE...
NOPE... NOOOOOOO... N-
THERE IT IS!
Z
NEWS
JIM DAVIS 7·21

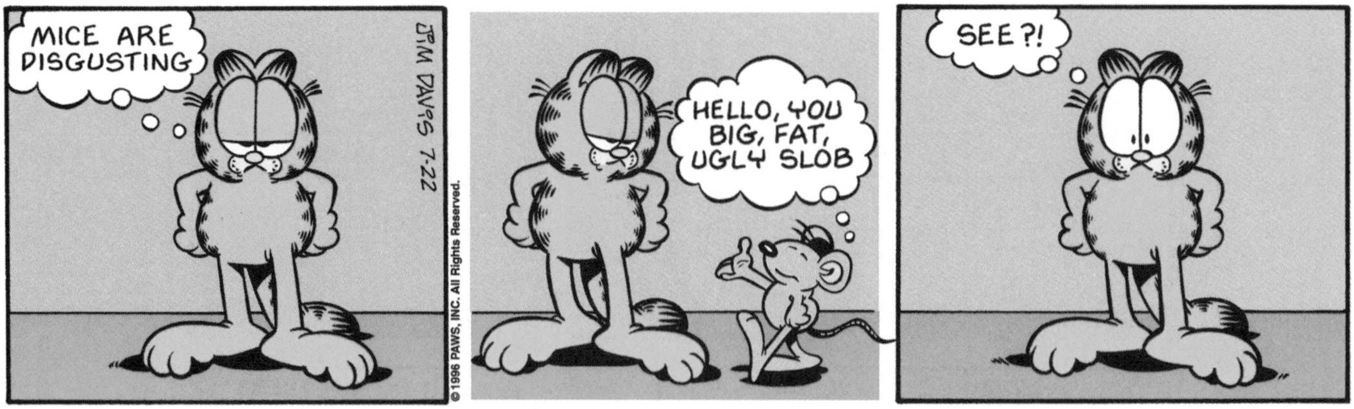
MICE ARE DISGUSTING
JIM DAVIS 7-22
© 1996 PAWS, INC. All Rights Reserved.
HELLO, YOU BIG, FAT, UGLY SLOB
SEE?!

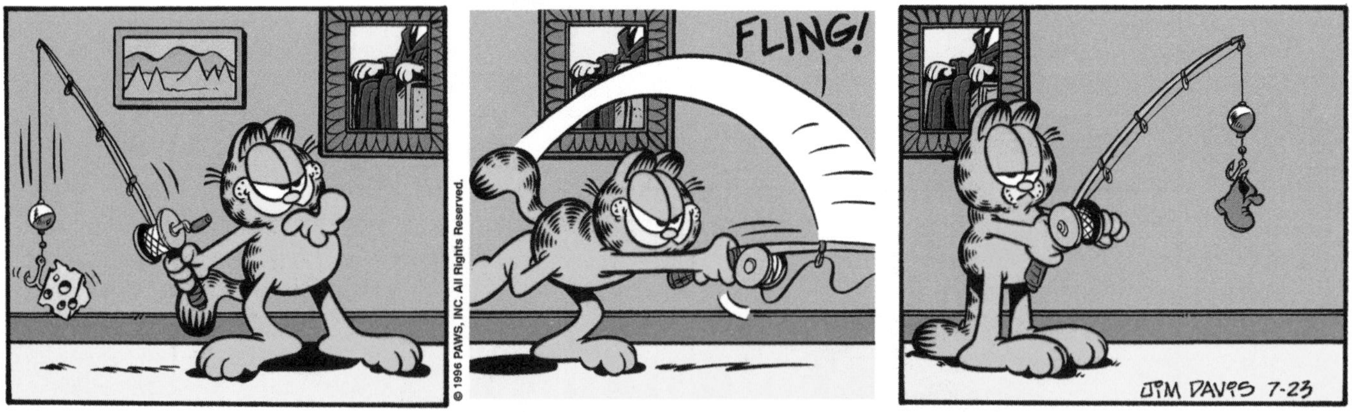
© 1996 PAWS, INC. All Rights Reserved.
FLING!
JIM DAVIS 7-23

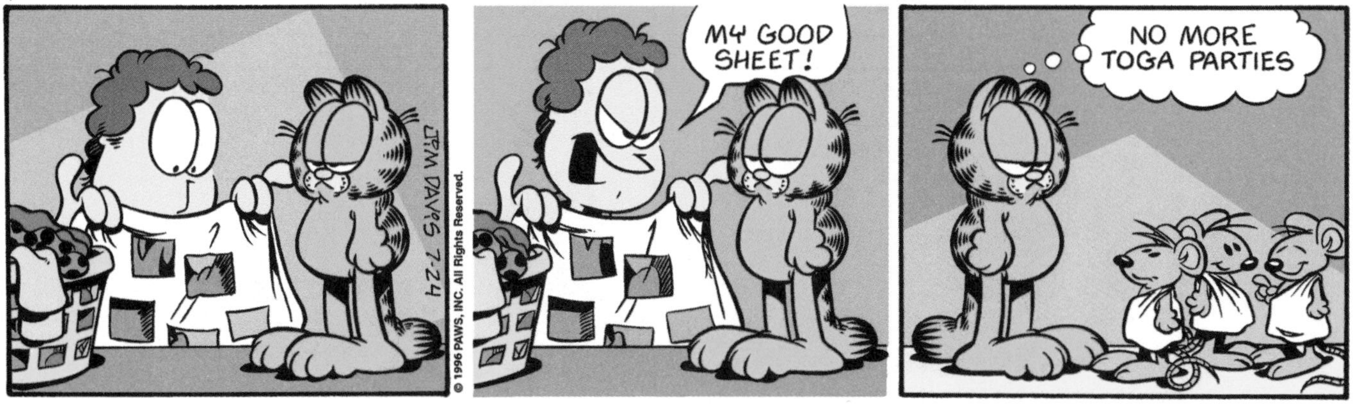
JIM DAVIS 7-24
© 1996 PAWS, INC. All Rights Reserved.
MY GOOD SHEET!
NO MORE TOGA PARTIES

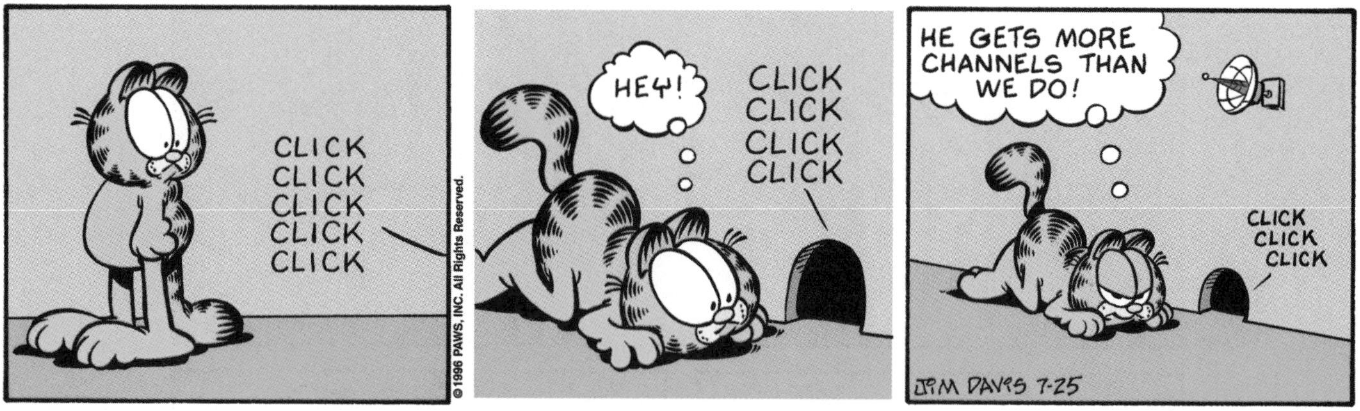
CLICK
CLICK
CLICK
CLICK
CLICK
© 1996 PAWS, INC. All Rights Reserved.
HEY!
CLICK
CLICK
CLICK
CLICK
HE GETS MORE CHANNELS THAN WE DO!
CLICK
CLICK
CLICK
JIM DAVIS 7-25

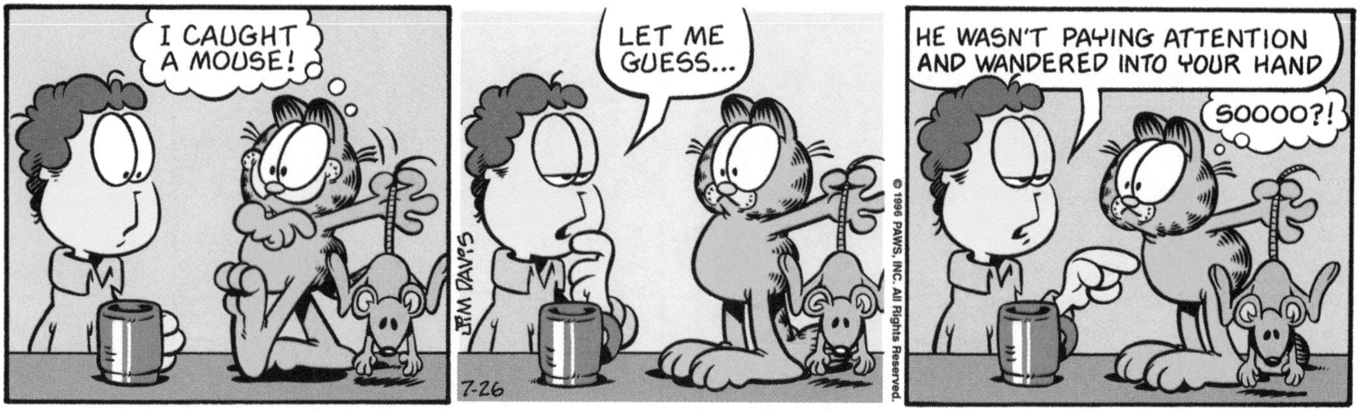
I CAUGHT A MOUSE!
JIM DAVIS
7-26
LET ME GUESS...
© 1996 PAWS, INC. All Rights Reserved.
HE WASN'T PAYING ATTENTION AND WANDERED INTO YOUR HAND
SOOOO?!

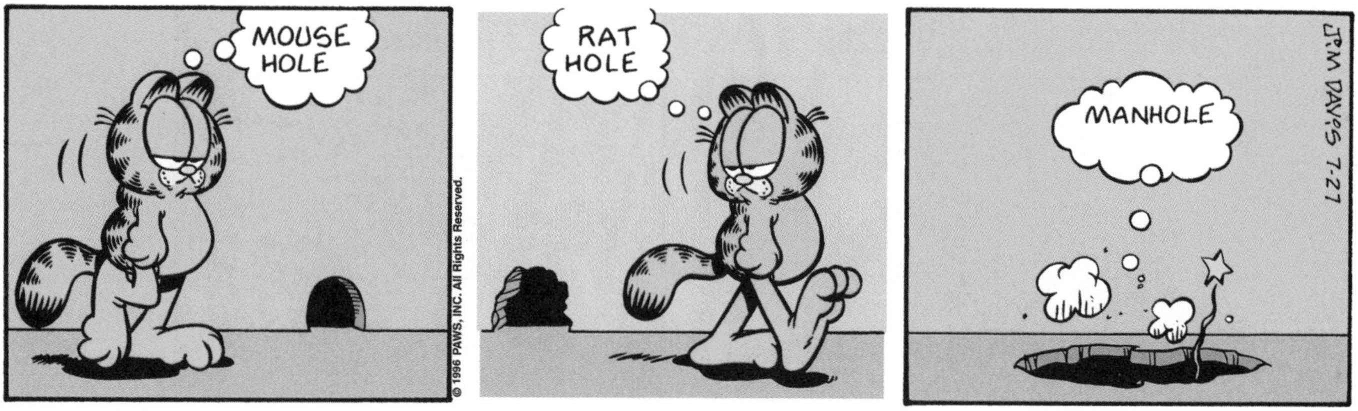
MOUSE HOLE
© 1996 PAWS, INC. All Rights Reserved.
RAT HOLE
JIM DAVIS 7-27
MANHOLE

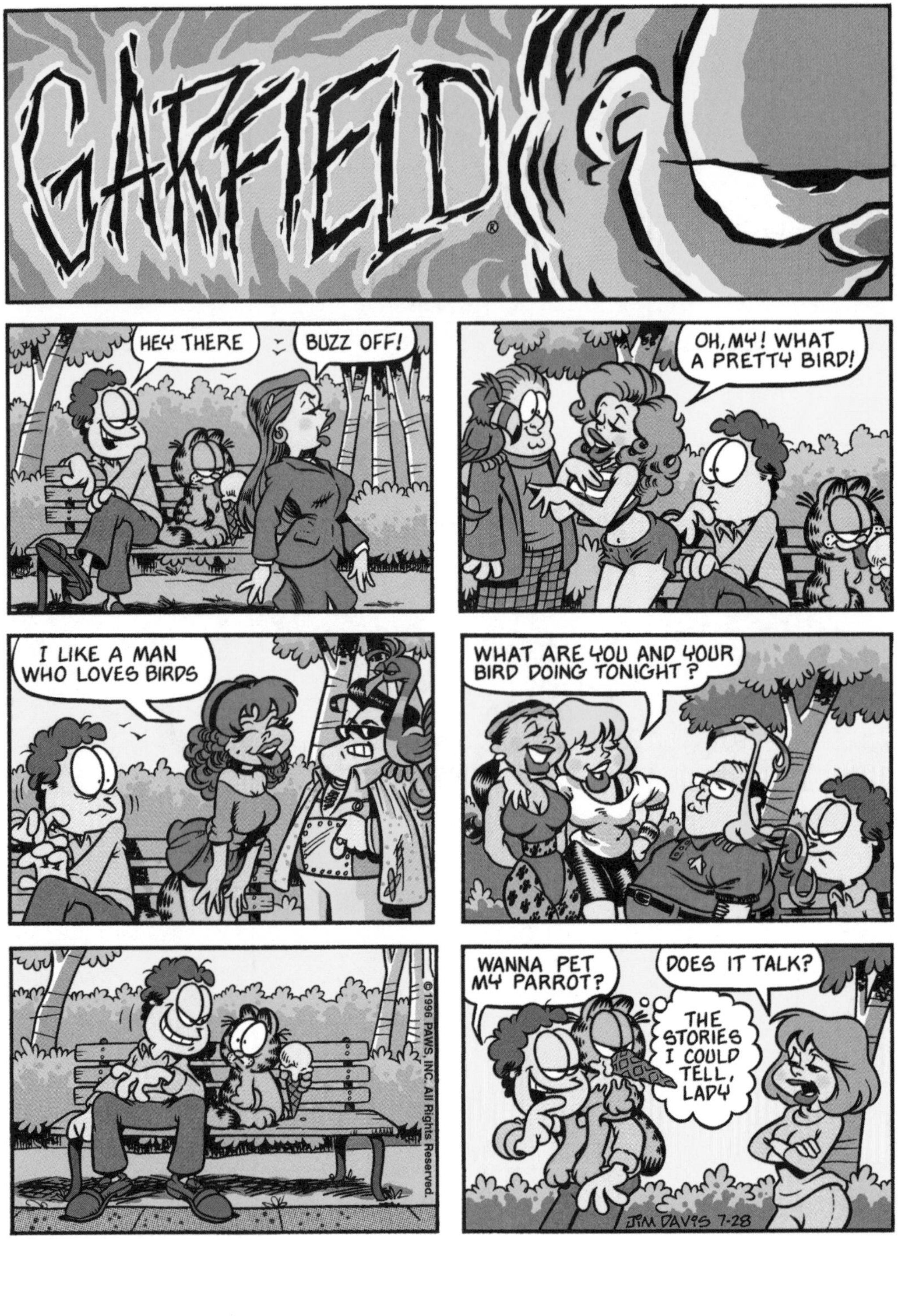

GARFIELD®
HEY THERE
BUZZ OFF!
OH, MY! WHAT A PRETTY BIRD!
I LIKE A MAN WHO LOVES BIRDS
WHAT ARE YOU AND YOUR BIRD DOING TONIGHT?
© 1996 PAWS, INC. All Rights Reserved.
WANNA PET MY PARROT?
DOES IT TALK?
THE STORIES I COULD TELL, LADY
JIM DAVIS 7-28

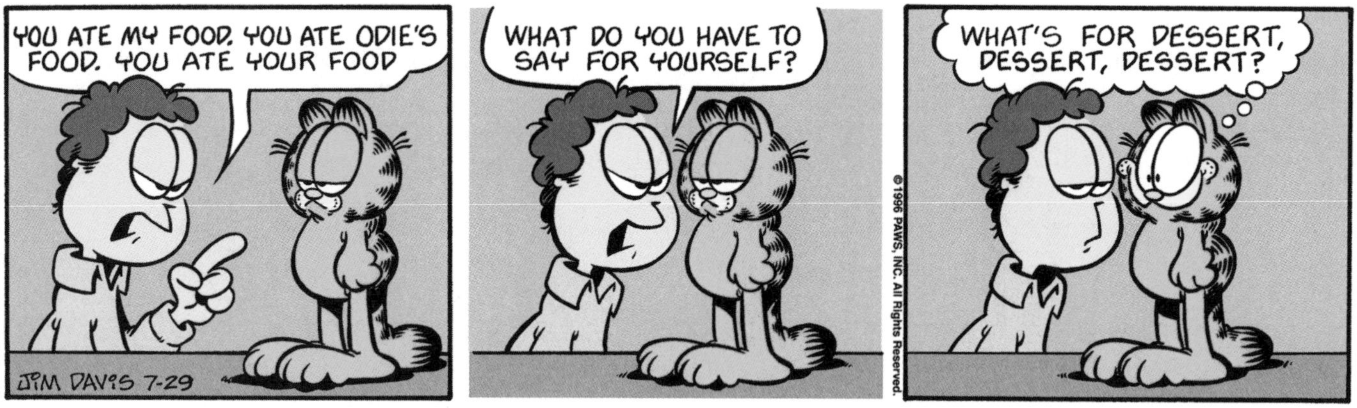

YOU ATE MY FOOD. YOU ATE ODIE'S FOOD. YOU ATE YOUR FOOD
WHAT DO YOU HAVE TO SAY FOR YOURSELF?
WHAT'S FOR DESSERT, DESSERT, DESSERT?
JIM DAVIS 7-29
©1996 PAWS, INC. All Rights Reserved.

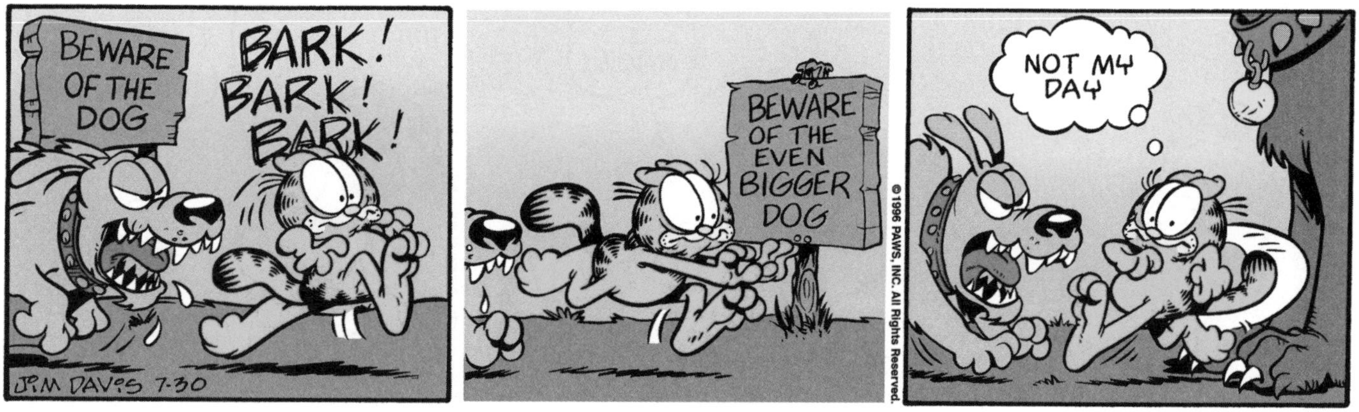

BEWARE OF THE DOG
BARK! BARK! BARK!
BEWARE OF THE EVEN BIGGER DOG
NOT MY DAY
JIM DAVIS 7-30
©1996 PAWS, INC. All Rights Reserved.

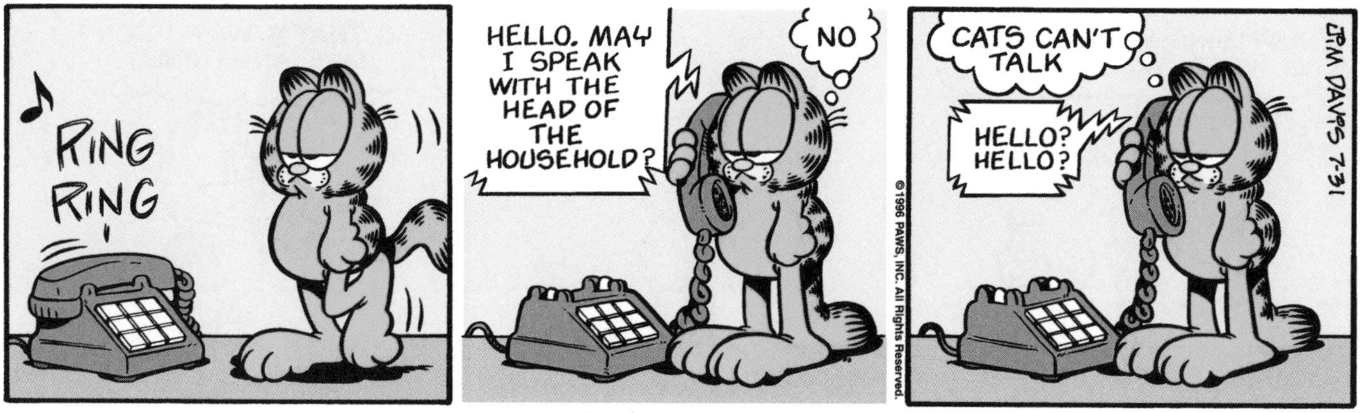

RING RING
HELLO. MAY I SPEAK WITH THE HEAD OF THE HOUSEHOLD?
NO
CATS CAN'T TALK
HELLO? HELLO?
JIM DAVIS 7-31
©1996 PAWS, INC. All Rights Reserved.

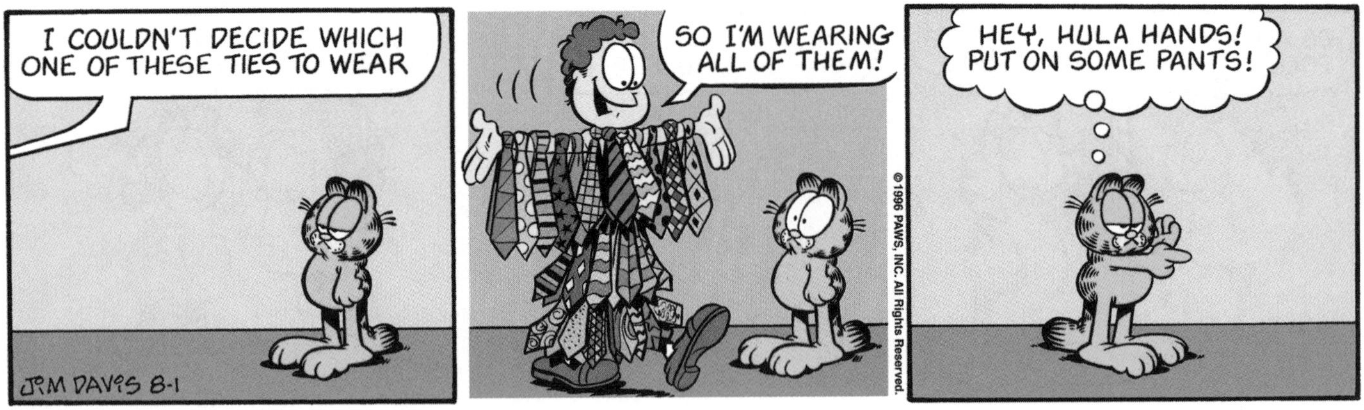
I COULDN'T DECIDE WHICH ONE OF THESE TIES TO WEAR
JIM DAVIS 8-1
SO I'M WEARING ALL OF THEM!
© 1996 PAWS, INC. All Rights Reserved.
HEY, HULA HANDS! PUT ON SOME PANTS!

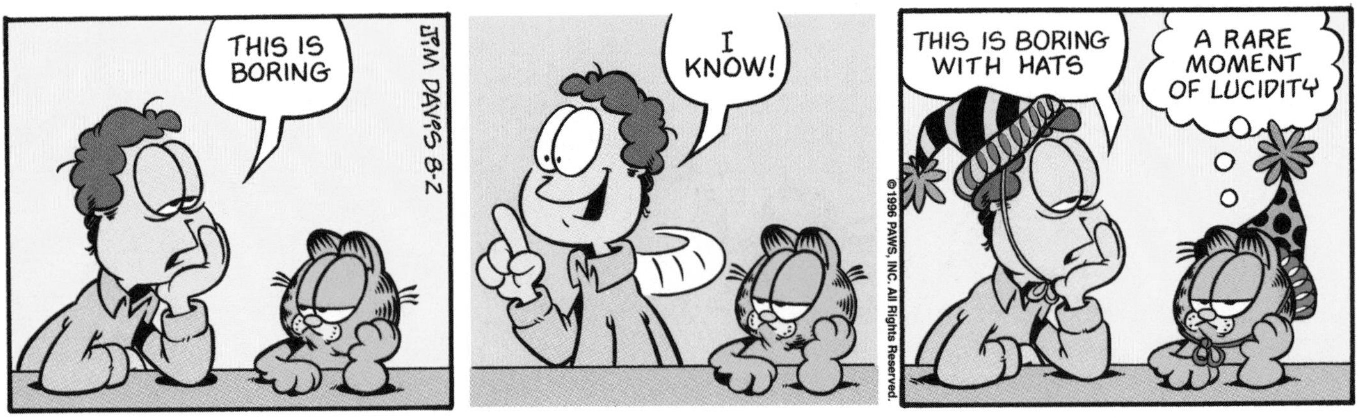
THIS IS BORING
JIM DAVIS 8-2
I KNOW!
© 1996 PAWS, INC. All Rights Reserved.
THIS IS BORING WITH HATS
A RARE MOMENT OF LUCIDITY

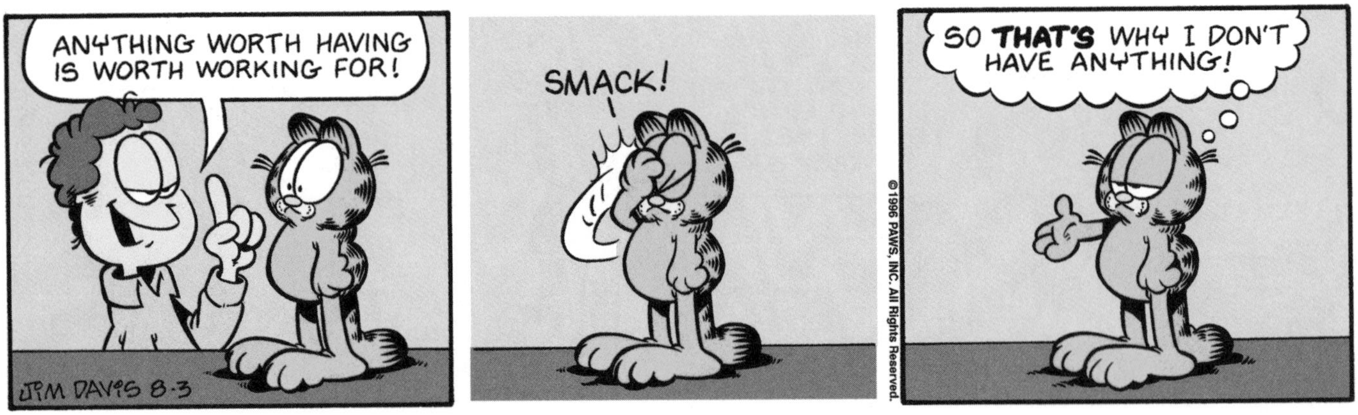
ANYTHING WORTH HAVING IS WORTH WORKING FOR!
JIM DAVIS 8-3
SMACK!
© 1996 PAWS, INC. All Rights Reserved.
SO **THAT'S** WHY I DON'T HAVE ANYTHING!

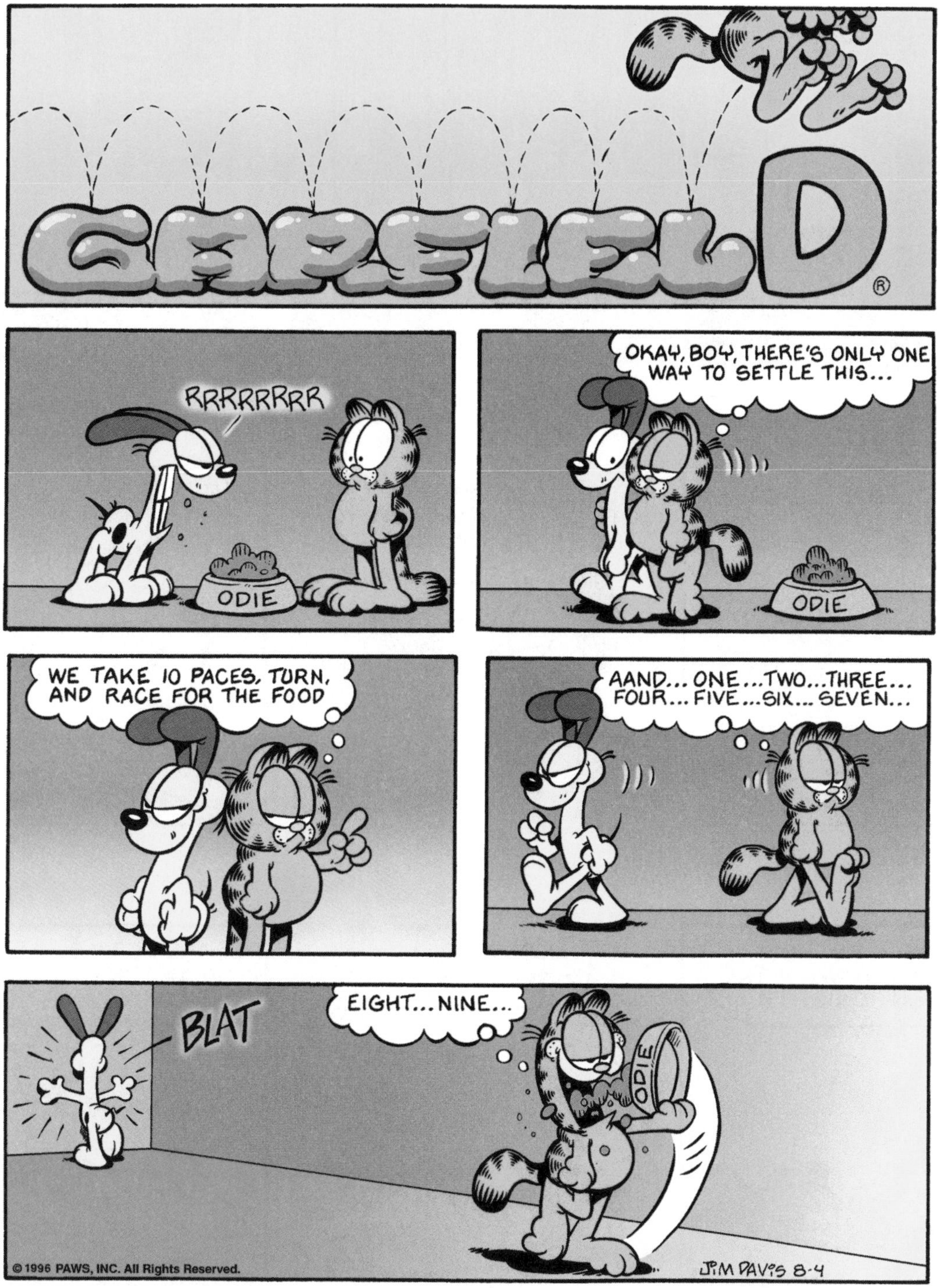
GARFIELD
RRRRRRRR
OKAY, BOY, THERE'S ONLY ONE WAY TO SETTLE THIS...
ODIE
WE TAKE 10 PACES, TURN, AND RACE FOR THE FOOD
AAND... ONE... TWO... THREE... FOUR... FIVE... SIX... SEVEN...
EIGHT... NINE...
BLAT
ODIE
JIM DAVIS 8-4

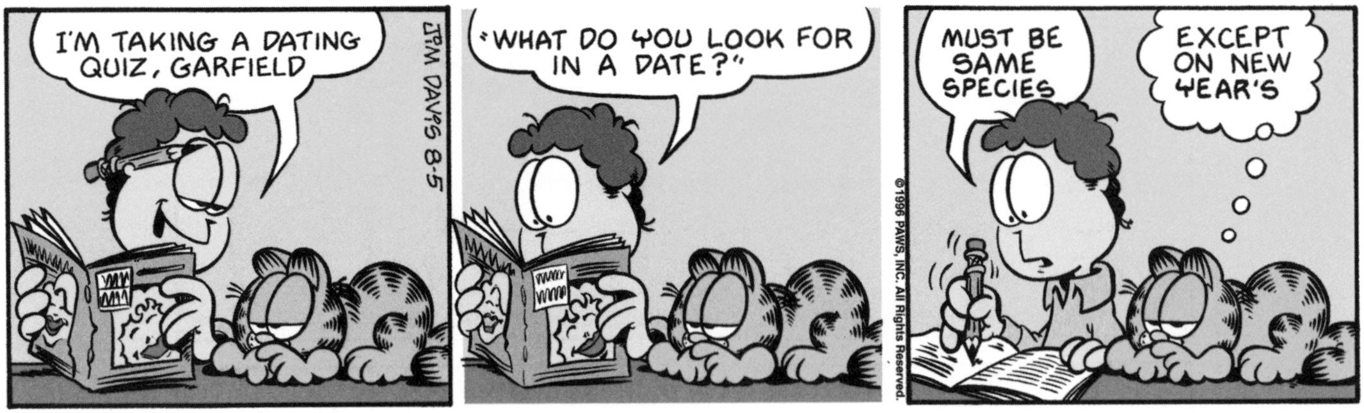
I'M TAKING A DATING QUIZ, GARFIELD
JIM DAVIS 8-5
"WHAT DO YOU LOOK FOR IN A DATE?"
© 1996 PAWS, INC. All Rights Reserved.
MUST BE SAME SPECIES
EXCEPT ON NEW YEAR'S

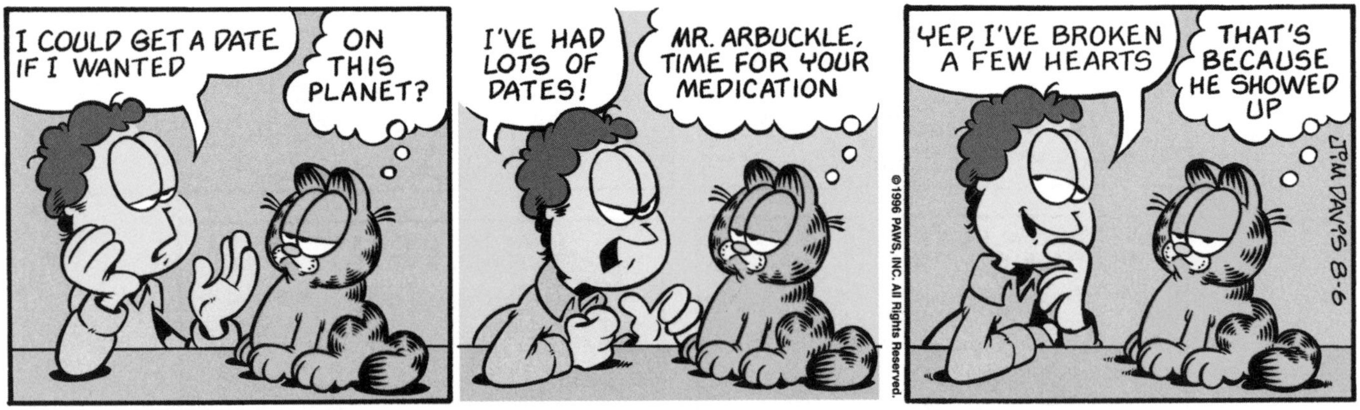
I COULD GET A DATE IF I WANTED
ON THIS PLANET?
I'VE HAD LOTS OF DATES!
MR. ARBUCKLE, TIME FOR YOUR MEDICATION
© 1996 PAWS, INC. All Rights Reserved.
YEP, I'VE BROKEN A FEW HEARTS
THAT'S BECAUSE HE SHOWED UP
JIM DAVIS 8-6

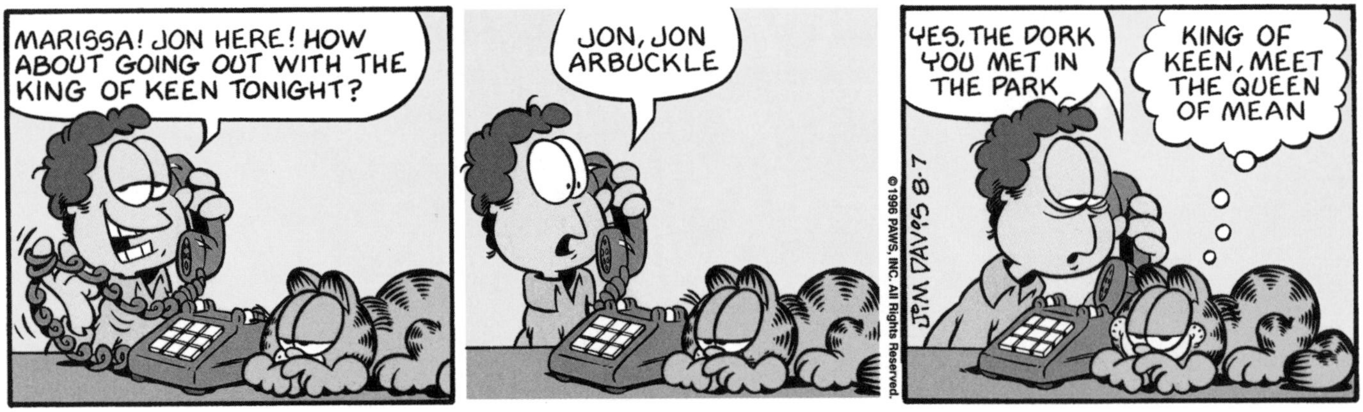
MARISSA! JON HERE! HOW ABOUT GOING OUT WITH THE KING OF KEEN TONIGHT?
JON, JON ARBUCKLE
© 1996 PAWS, INC. All Rights Reserved.
JIM DAVIS 8-7
YES, THE DORK YOU MET IN THE PARK
KING OF KEEN, MEET THE QUEEN OF MEAN

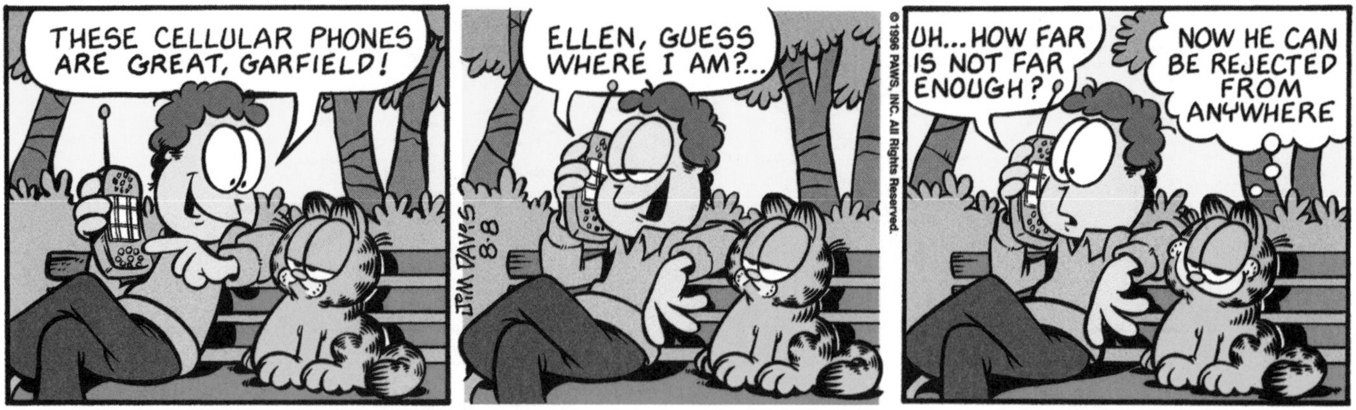
THESE CELLULAR PHONES ARE GREAT, GARFIELD!
ELLEN, GUESS WHERE I AM?...
JIM DAVIS 8-8
© 1996 PAWS, INC. All Rights Reserved.
UH... HOW FAR IS NOT FAR ENOUGH?
NOW HE CAN BE REJECTED FROM ANYWHERE

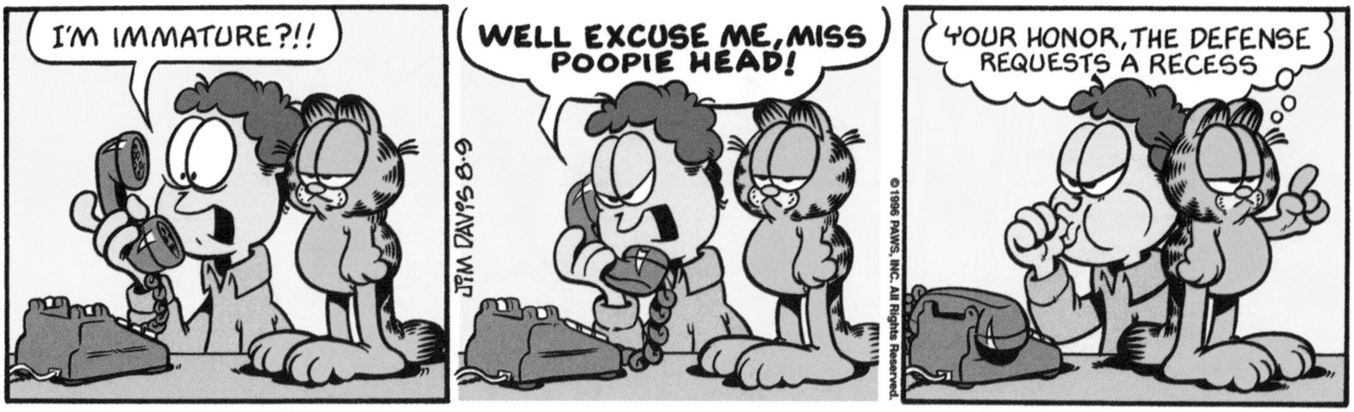
I'M IMMATURE?!!
JIM DAVIS 8-9
WELL EXCUSE ME, MISS POOPIE HEAD!
© 1996 PAWS, INC. All Rights Reserved.
YOUR HONOR, THE DEFENSE REQUESTS A RECESS

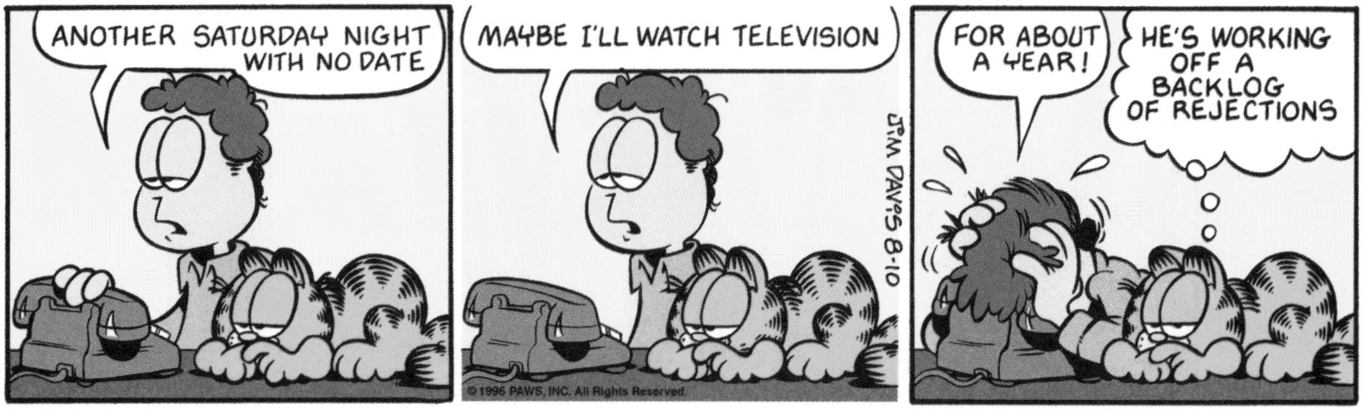
ANOTHER SATURDAY NIGHT WITH NO DATE
MAYBE I'LL WATCH TELEVISION
JIM DAVIS 8-10
© 1996 PAWS, INC. All Rights Reserved.
FOR ABOUT A YEAR!
HE'S WORKING OFF A BACKLOG OF REJECTIONS

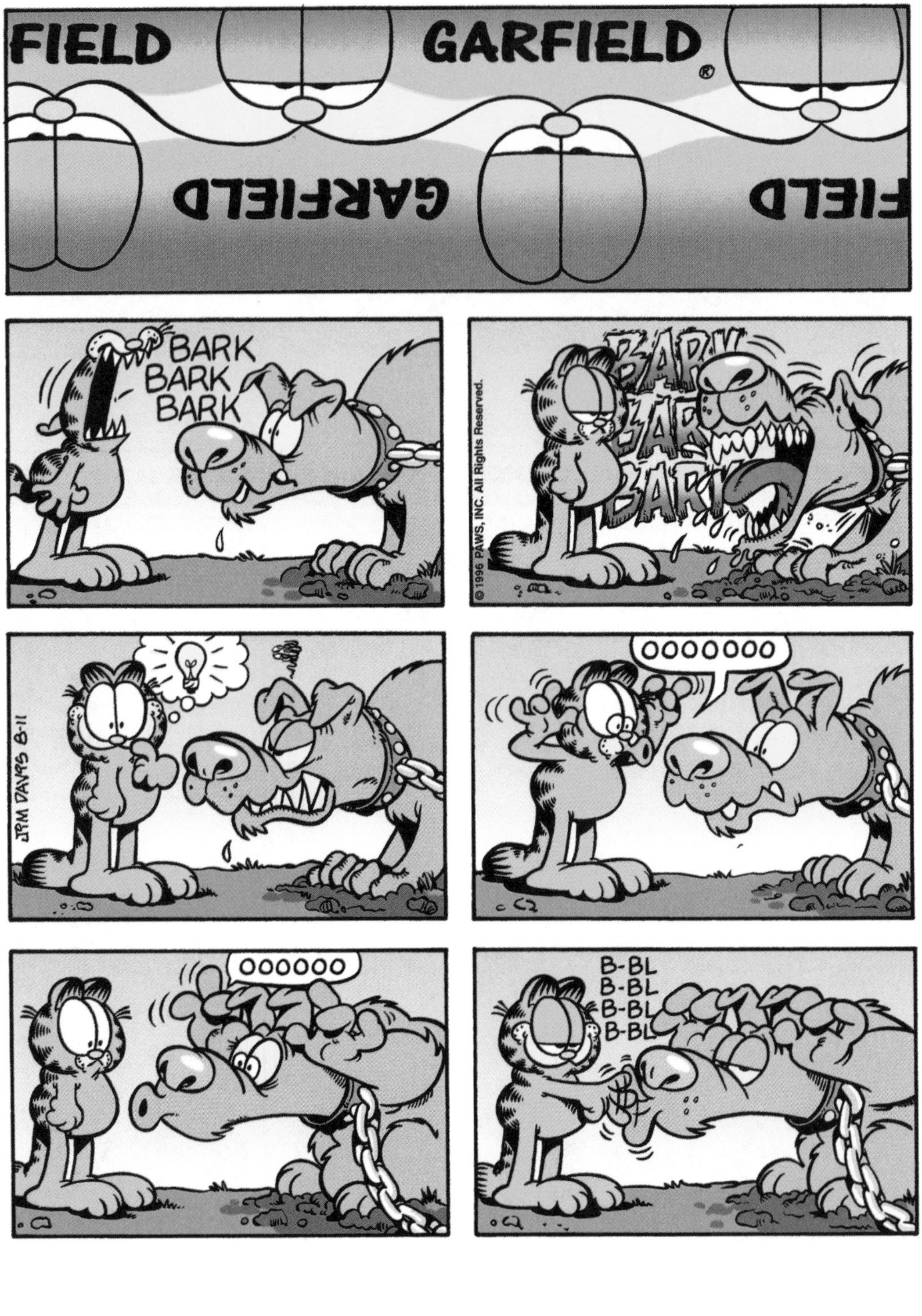
GARFIELD
BARK
BARK
BARK
© 1996 PAWS, INC. All Rights Reserved.
JIM DAVIS 8-11
OOOOOOO
OOOOOO
B-BL
B-BL
B-BL
B-BL

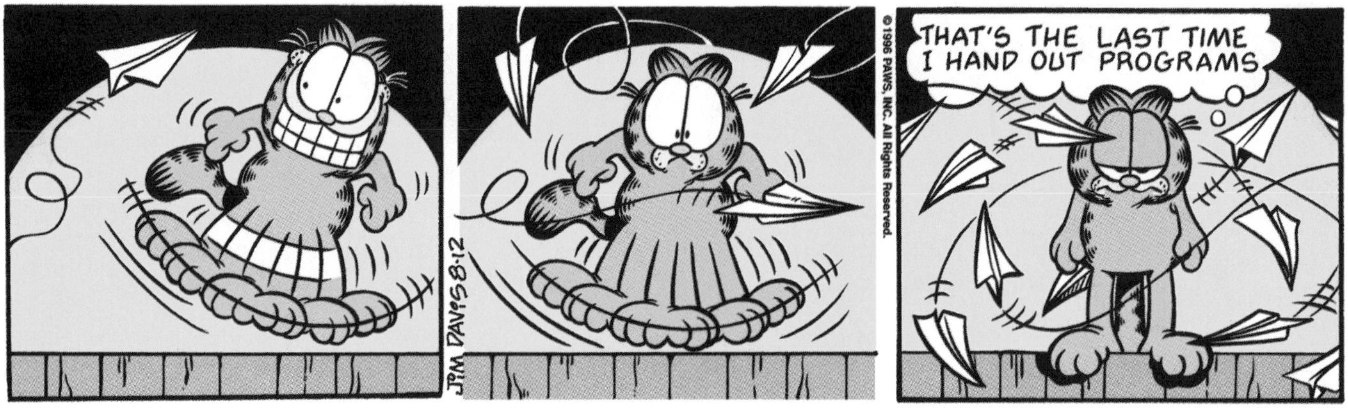
JIM DAVIS 8·12
© 1996 PAWS, INC. All Rights Reserved.
THAT'S THE LAST TIME I HAND OUT PROGRAMS

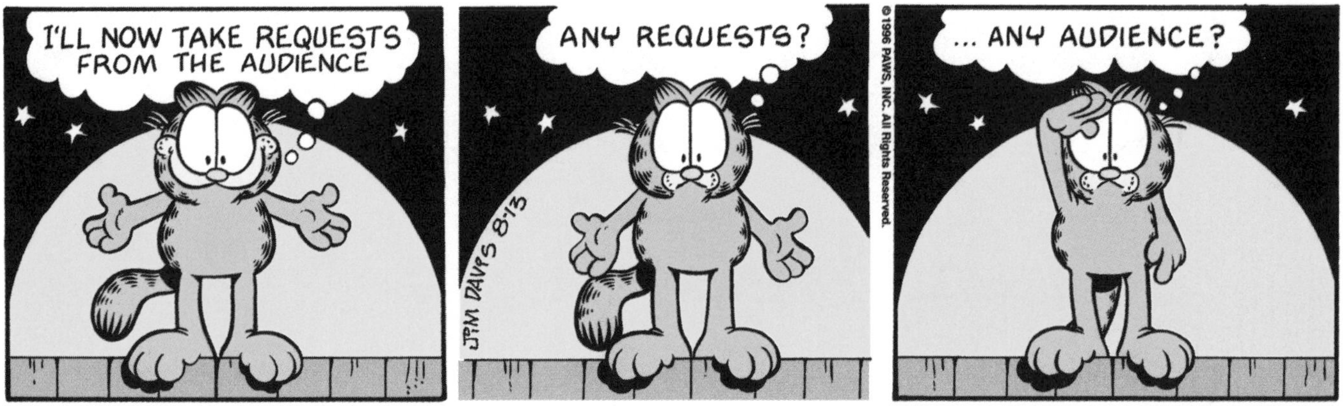
I'LL NOW TAKE REQUESTS FROM THE AUDIENCE
JIM DAVIS 8·13
ANY REQUESTS?
© 1996 PAWS, INC. All Rights Reserved.
... ANY AUDIENCE?

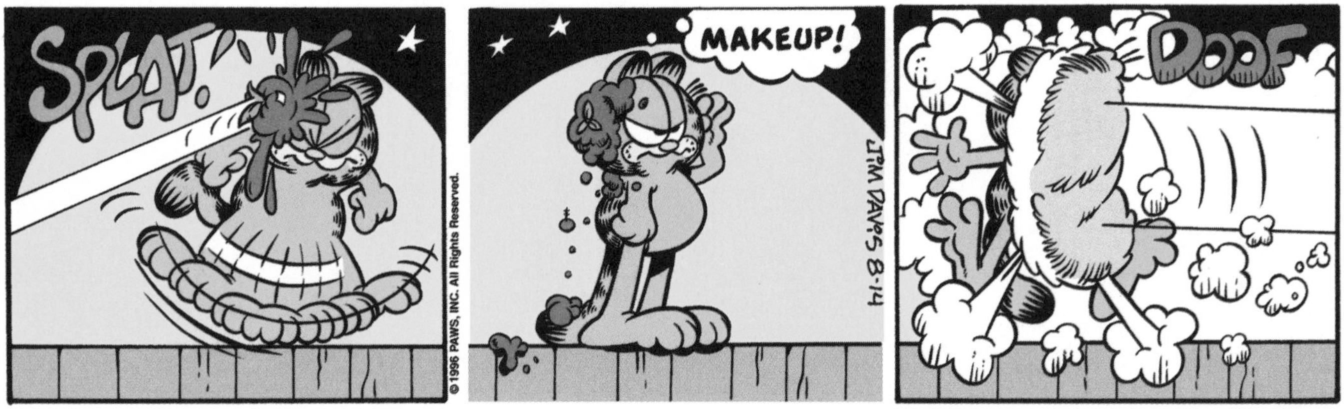
SPLAT!
© 1996 PAWS, INC. All Rights Reserved.
MAKEUP!
JIM DAVIS 8·14
DOOF

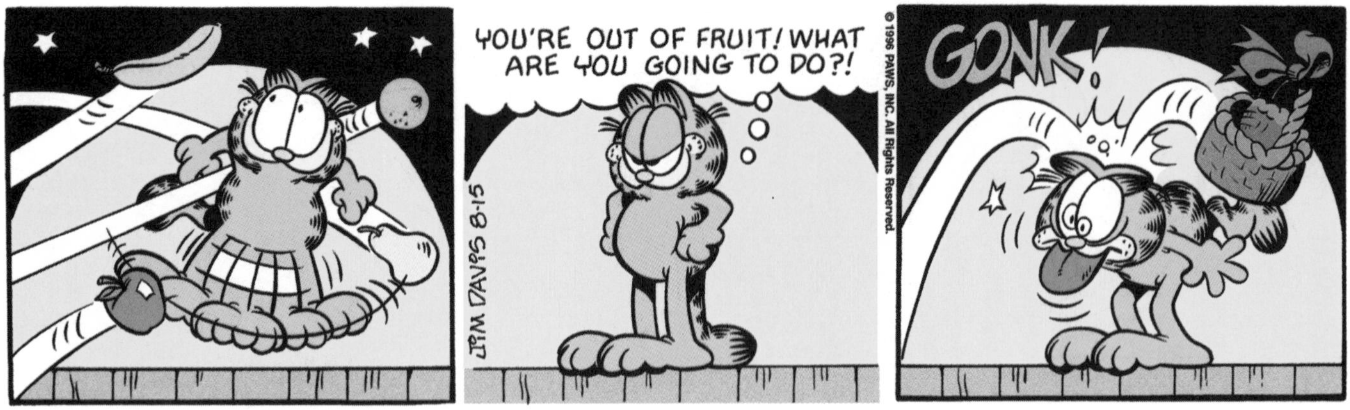
JIM DAVIS 8-15
YOU'RE OUT OF FRUIT! WHAT ARE YOU GOING TO DO?!
© 1996 PAWS, INC. All Rights Reserved.
GONK!

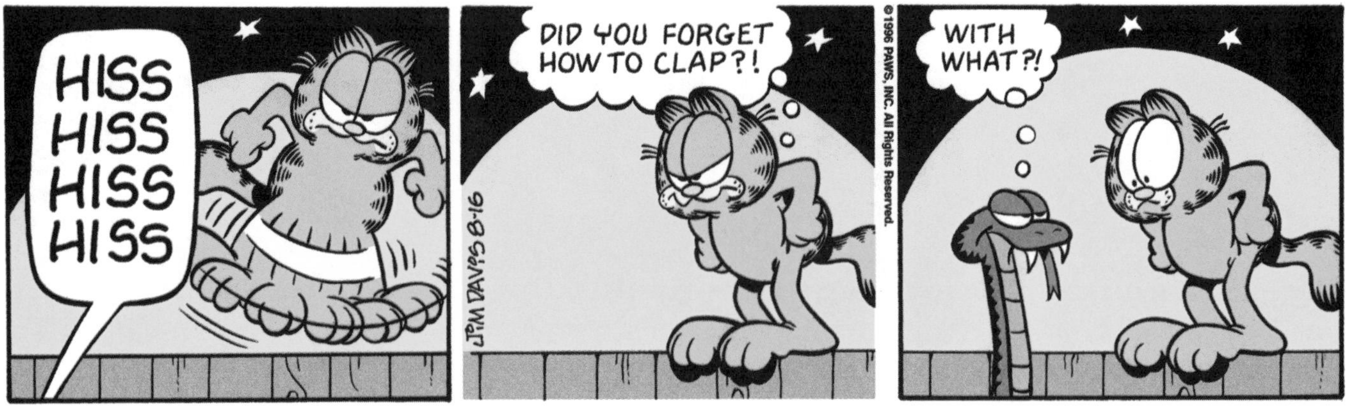
HISS HISS HISS HISS
JIM DAVIS 8-16
DID YOU FORGET HOW TO CLAP?!
© 1996 PAWS, INC. All Rights Reserved.
WITH WHAT?!

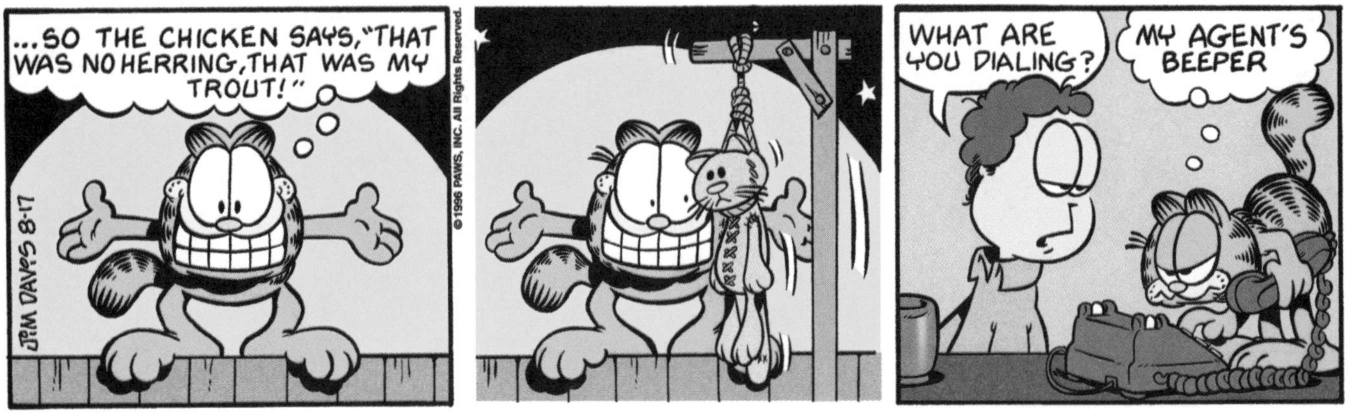
...SO THE CHICKEN SAYS, "THAT WAS NO HERRING, THAT WAS MY TROUT!"
JIM DAVIS 8-17
© 1996 PAWS, INC. All Rights Reserved.
WHAT ARE YOU DIALING?
MY AGENT'S BEEPER

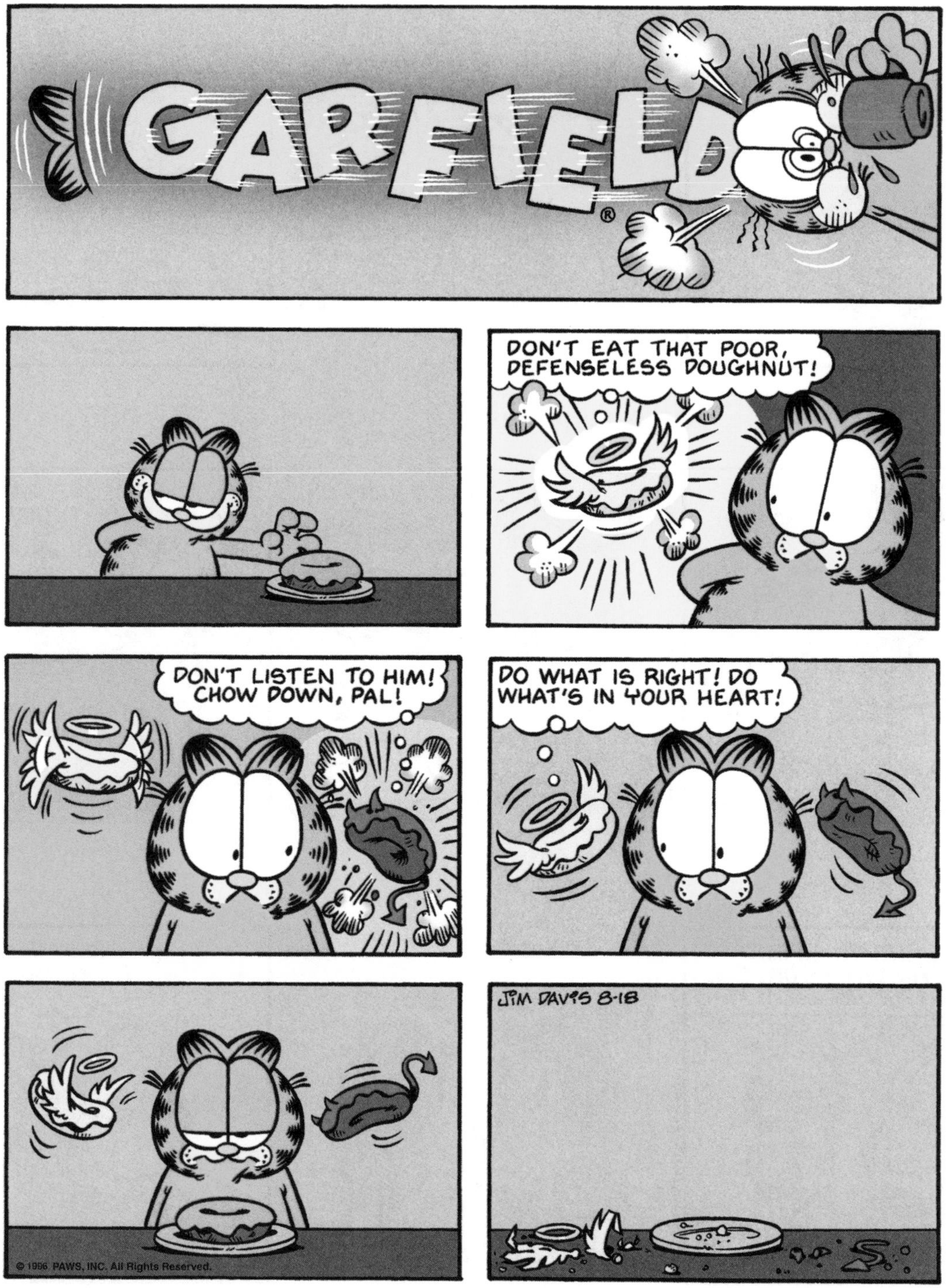
GARFIELD®
DON'T EAT THAT POOR, DEFENSELESS DOUGHNUT!
DON'T LISTEN TO HIM! CHOW DOWN, PAL!
DO WHAT IS RIGHT! DO WHAT'S IN YOUR HEART!
JIM DAVIS 8-18
© 1996 PAWS, INC. All Rights Reserved.

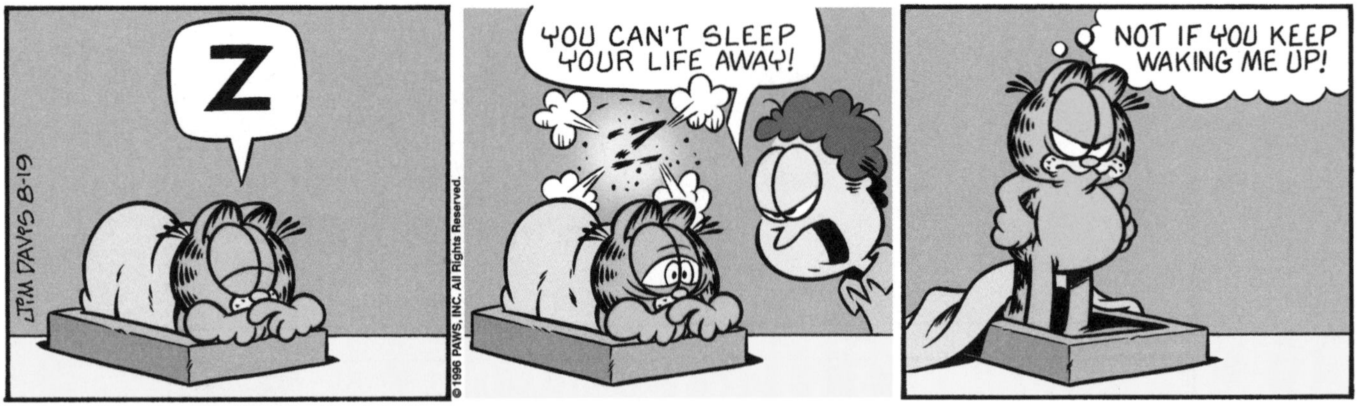
Z
YOU CAN'T SLEEP YOUR LIFE AWAY!
NOT IF YOU KEEP WAKING ME UP!
JIM DAVIS 8-19
© 1996 PAWS, INC. All Rights Reserved.

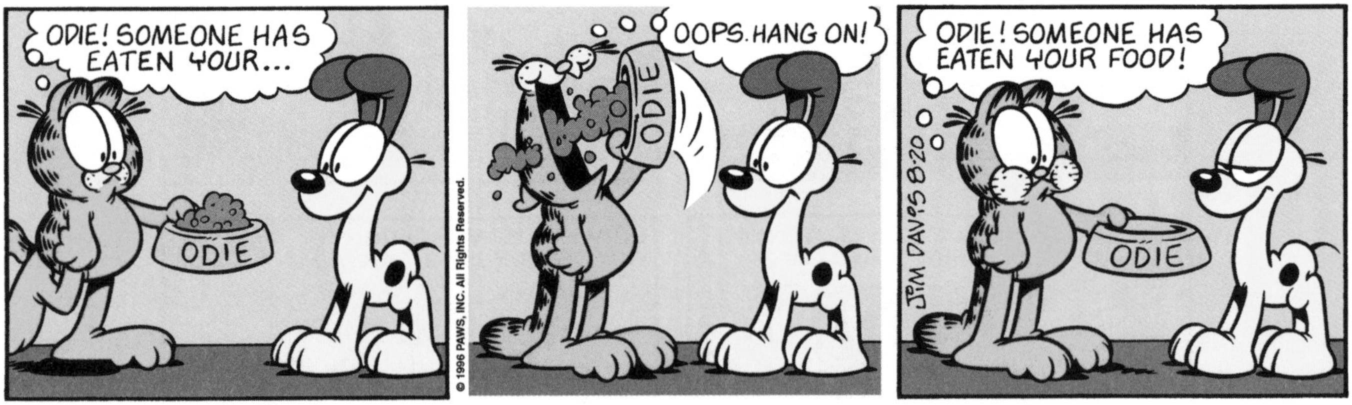
ODIE! SOMEONE HAS EATEN YOUR...
ODIE
OOPS. HANG ON!
ODIE
ODIE! SOMEONE HAS EATEN YOUR FOOD!
ODIE
JIM DAVIS 8-20
© 1996 PAWS, INC. All Rights Reserved.

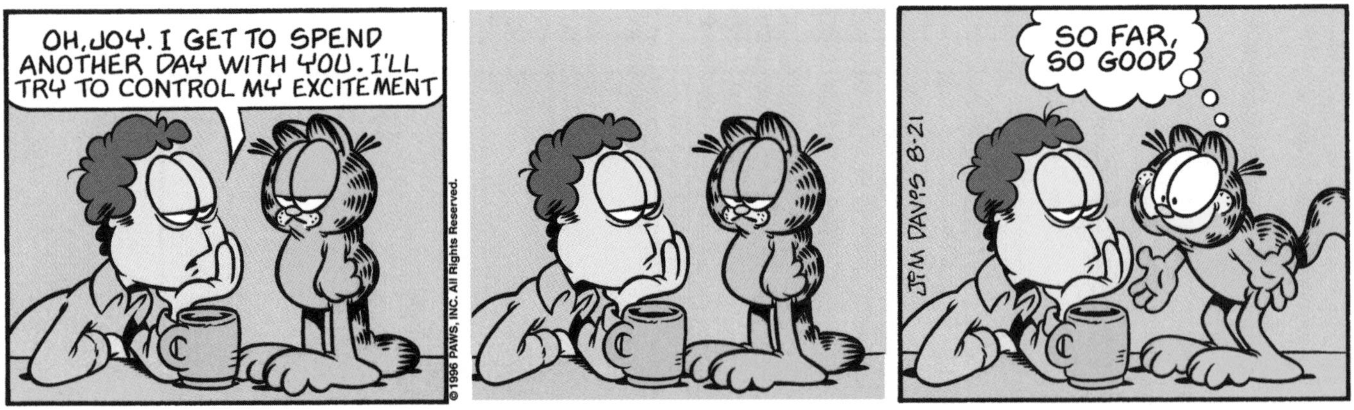
OH, JOY. I GET TO SPEND ANOTHER DAY WITH YOU. I'LL TRY TO CONTROL MY EXCITEMENT
SO FAR, SO GOOD
JIM DAVIS 8-21
© 1996 PAWS, INC. All Rights Reserved.

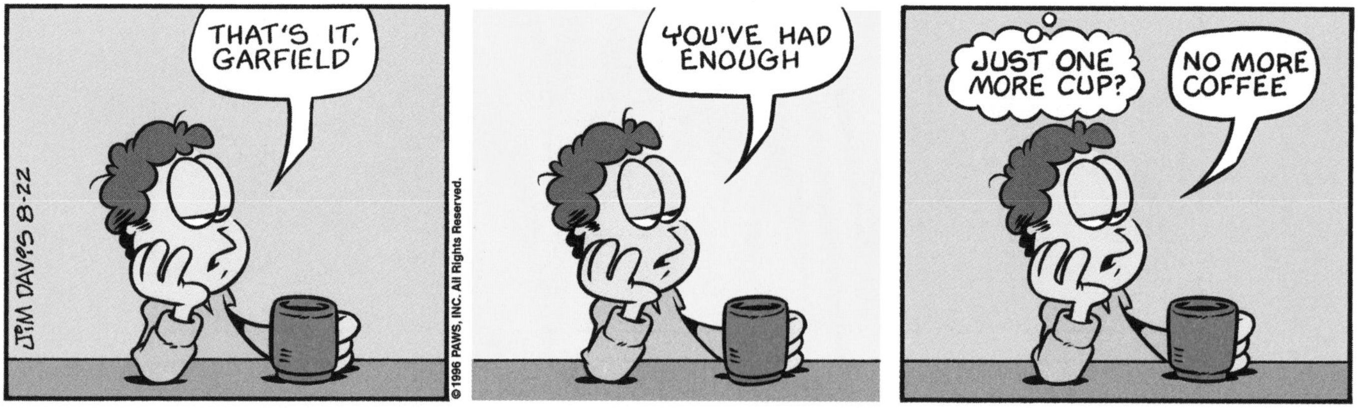
JIM DAVIS 8-22
THAT'S IT, GARFIELD
YOU'VE HAD ENOUGH
JUST ONE MORE CUP?
NO MORE COFFEE
© 1996 PAWS, INC. All Rights Reserved.

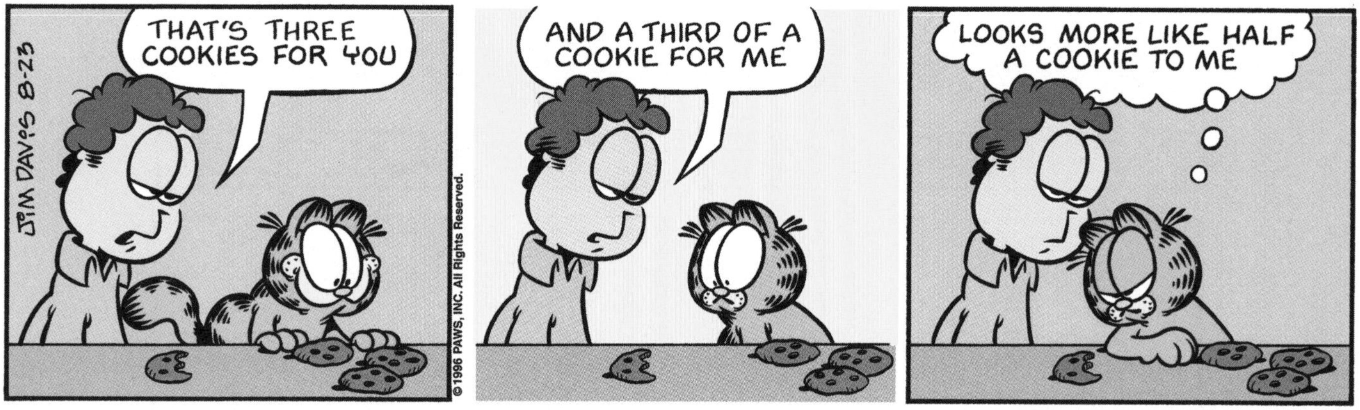
JIM DAVIS 8-23
THAT'S THREE COOKIES FOR YOU
AND A THIRD OF A COOKIE FOR ME
LOOKS MORE LIKE HALF A COOKIE TO ME
© 1996 PAWS, INC. All Rights Reserved.

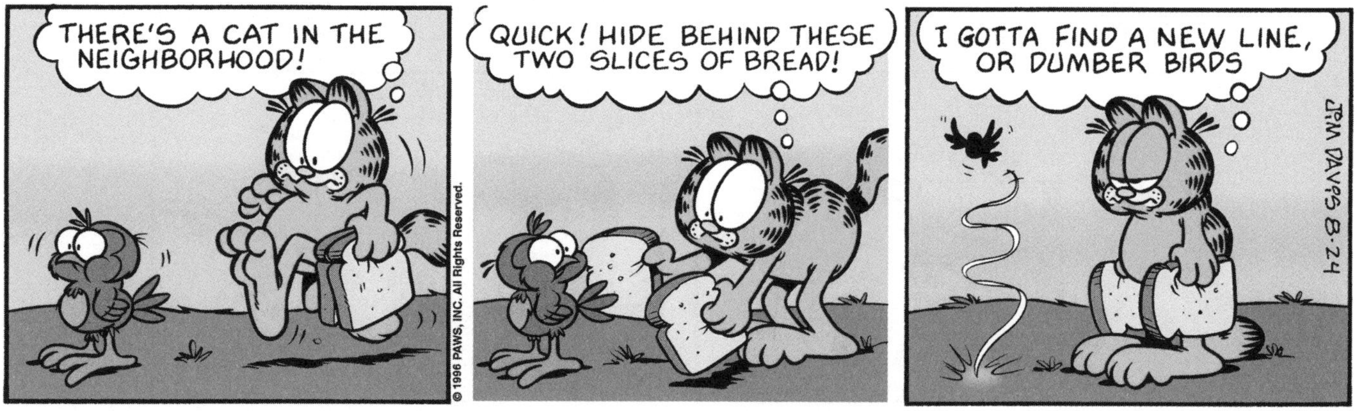
THERE'S A CAT IN THE NEIGHBORHOOD!
QUICK! HIDE BEHIND THESE TWO SLICES OF BREAD!
I GOTTA FIND A NEW LINE, OR DUMBER BIRDS
JIM DAVIS 8-24
© 1996 PAWS, INC. All Rights Reserved.

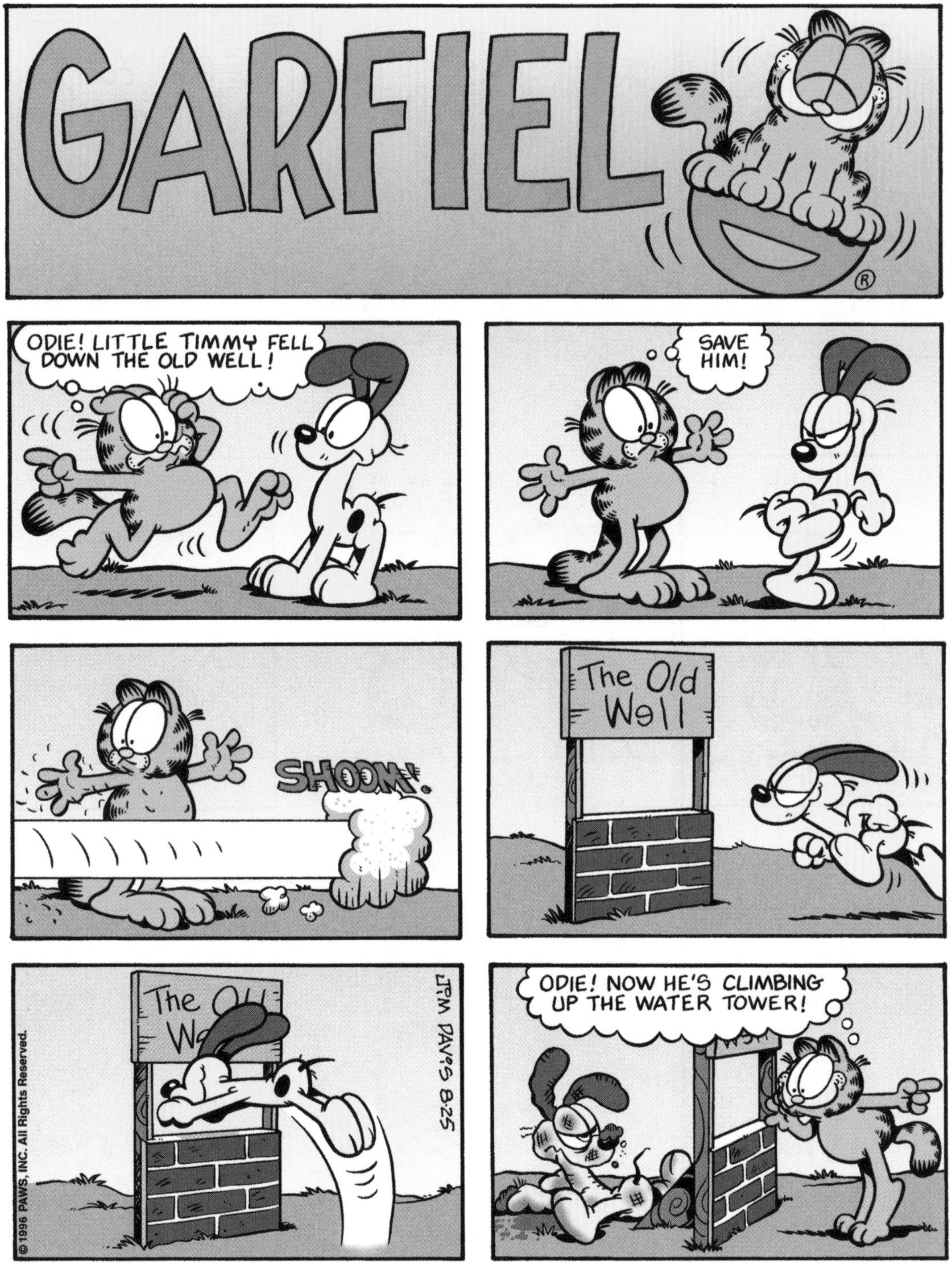
GARFIELD
ODIE! LITTLE TIMMY FELL DOWN THE OLD WELL!
SAVE HIM!
SHOOM!
The Old Well
JIM DAVIS 8-25
© 1996 PAWS, INC. All Rights Reserved.
ODIE! NOW HE'S CLIMBING UP THE WATER TOWER!

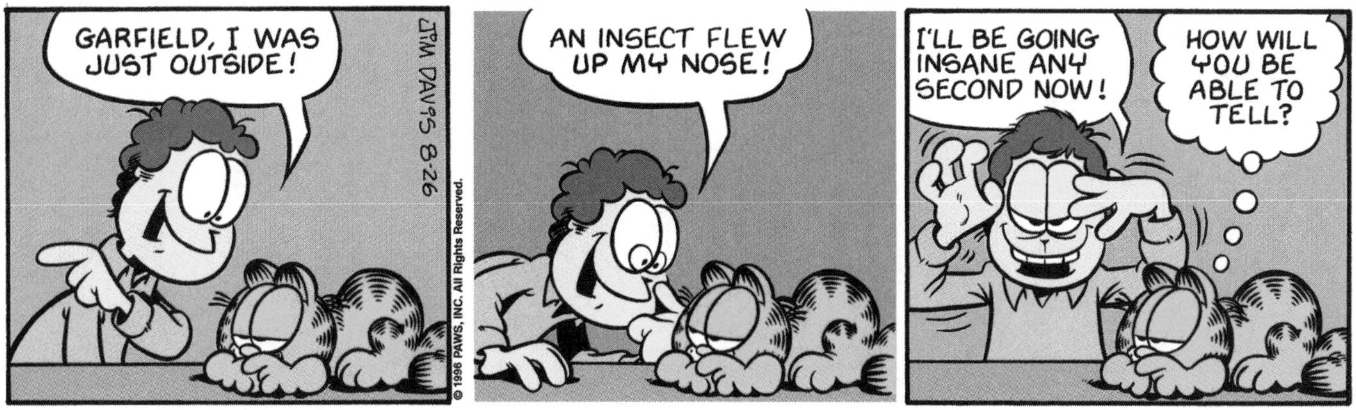
GARFIELD, I WAS JUST OUTSIDE!
JIM DAVIS 8-26
© 1996 PAWS, INC. All Rights Reserved.
AN INSECT FLEW UP MY NOSE!
I'LL BE GOING INSANE ANY SECOND NOW!
HOW WILL YOU BE ABLE TO TELL?

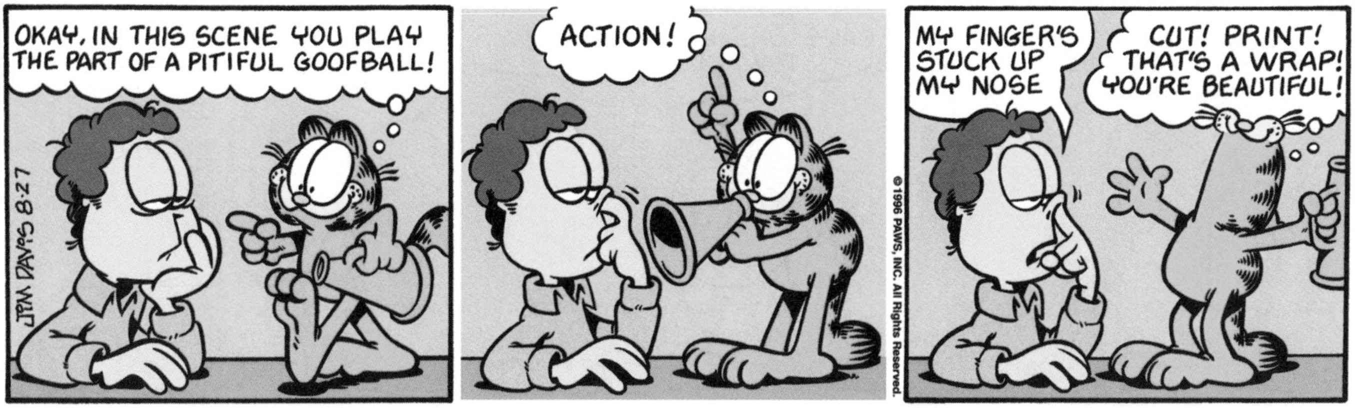
OKAY, IN THIS SCENE YOU PLAY THE PART OF A PITIFUL GOOFBALL!
JIM DAVIS 8-27
ACTION!
© 1996 PAWS, INC. All Rights Reserved.
MY FINGER'S STUCK UP MY NOSE
CUT! PRINT! THAT'S A WRAP! YOU'RE BEAUTIFUL!

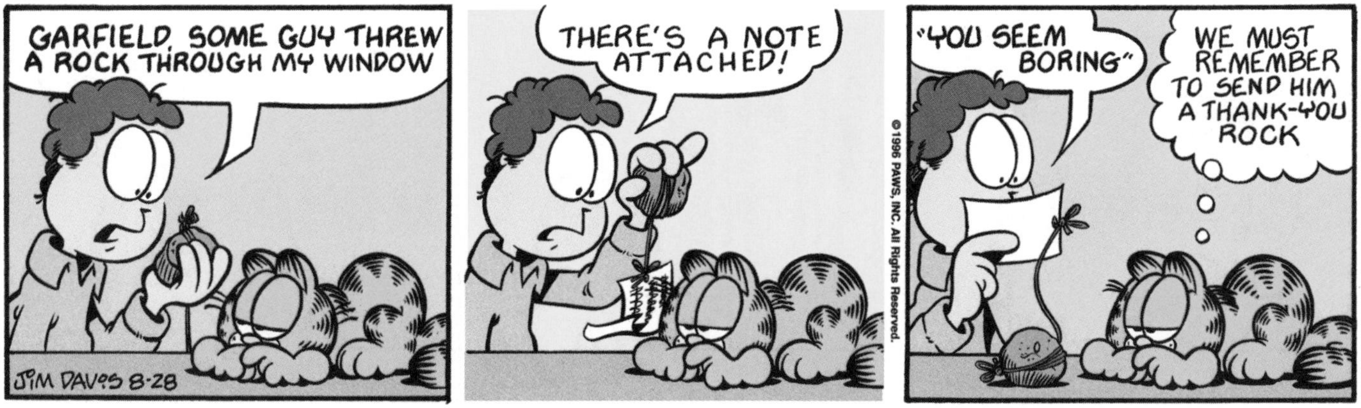
GARFIELD, SOME GUY THREW A ROCK THROUGH MY WINDOW
JIM DAVIS 8-28
THERE'S A NOTE ATTACHED!
© 1996 PAWS, INC. All Rights Reserved.
"YOU SEEM BORING"
WE MUST REMEMBER TO SEND HIM A THANK-YOU ROCK

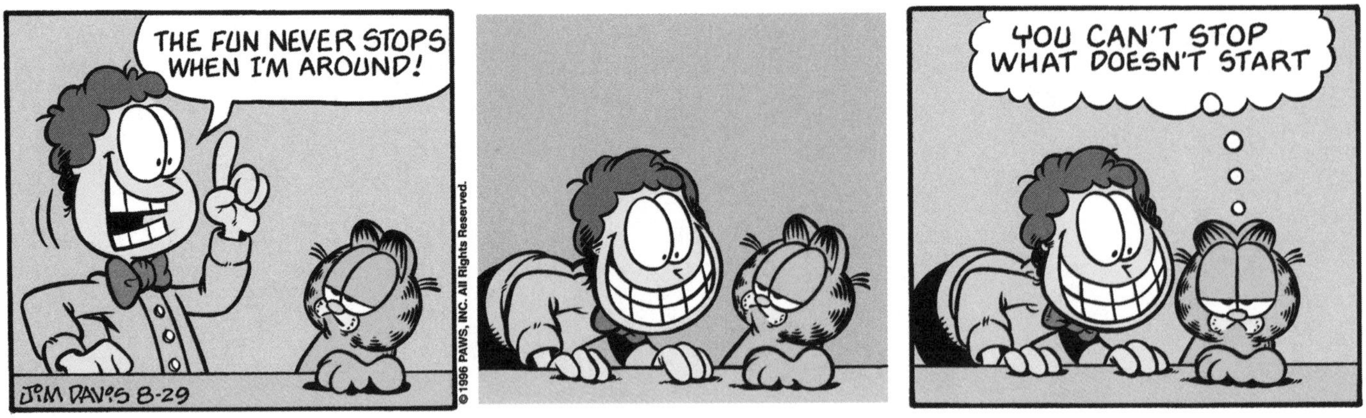
THE FUN NEVER STOPS WHEN I'M AROUND!
JIM DAVIS 8-29
© 1996 PAWS, INC. All Rights Reserved.
YOU CAN'T STOP WHAT DOESN'T START

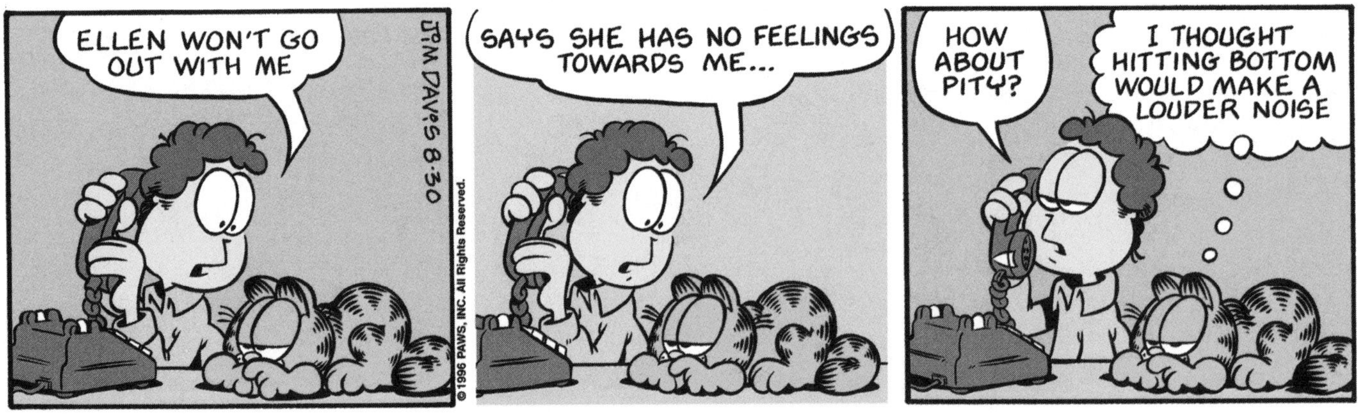
ELLEN WON'T GO OUT WITH ME
JIM DAVIS 8-30
© 1996 PAWS, INC. All Rights Reserved.
SAYS SHE HAS NO FEELINGS TOWARDS ME...
HOW ABOUT PITY?
I THOUGHT HITTING BOTTOM WOULD MAKE A LOUDER NOISE

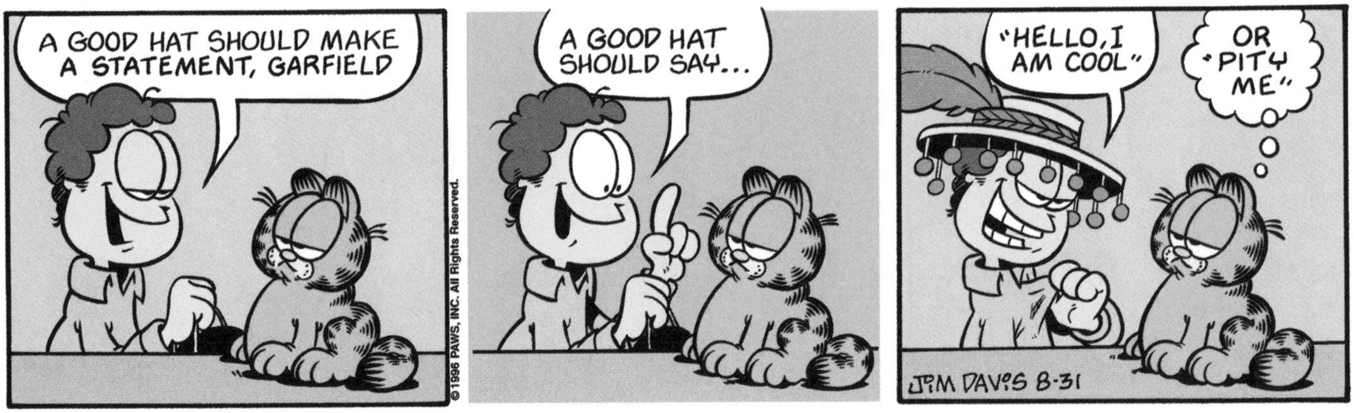
A GOOD HAT SHOULD MAKE A STATEMENT, GARFIELD
© 1996 PAWS, INC. All Rights Reserved.
A GOOD HAT SHOULD SAY...
"HELLO, I AM COOL"
OR "PITY ME"
JIM DAVIS 8-31

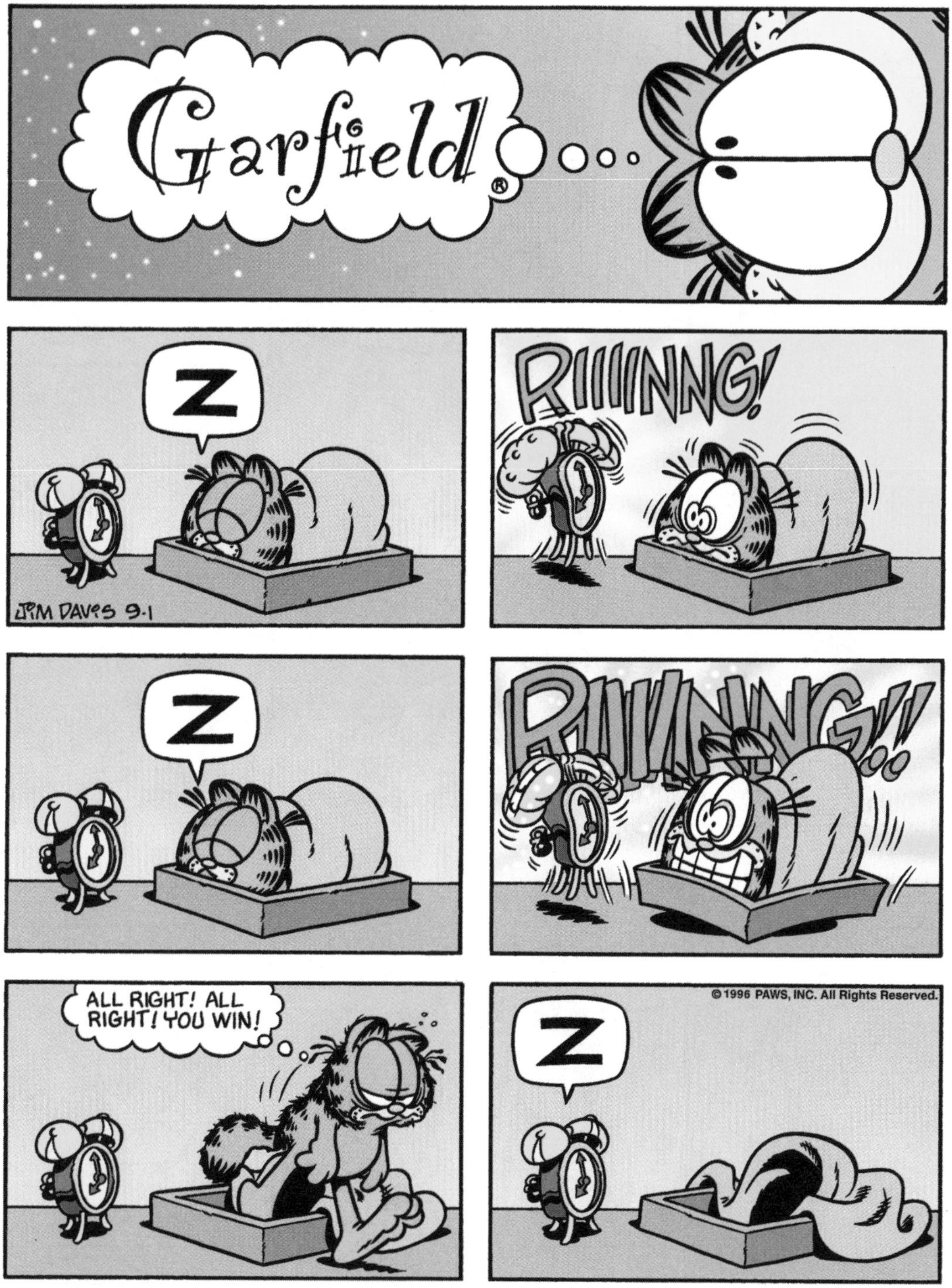
Garfield®
Z
RIIIINNG!
JIM DAVIS 9-1
Z
RIIIINNG!!
ALL RIGHT! ALL RIGHT! YOU WIN!
Z
© 1996 PAWS, INC. All Rights Reserved.

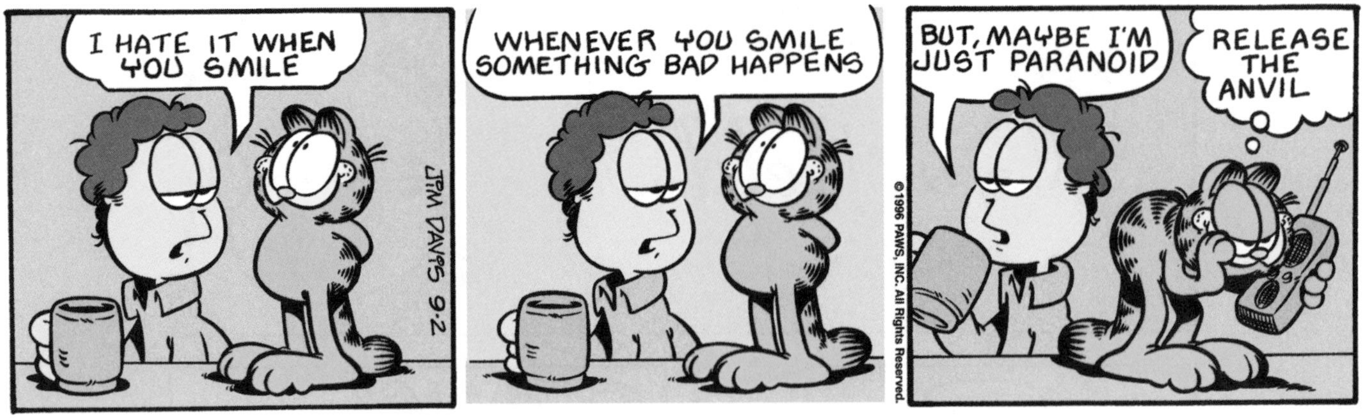
I HATE IT WHEN YOU SMILE
JIM DAVIS 9-2
WHENEVER YOU SMILE SOMETHING BAD HAPPENS
© 1996 PAWS, INC. All Rights Reserved.
BUT, MAYBE I'M JUST PARANOID
RELEASE THE ANVIL

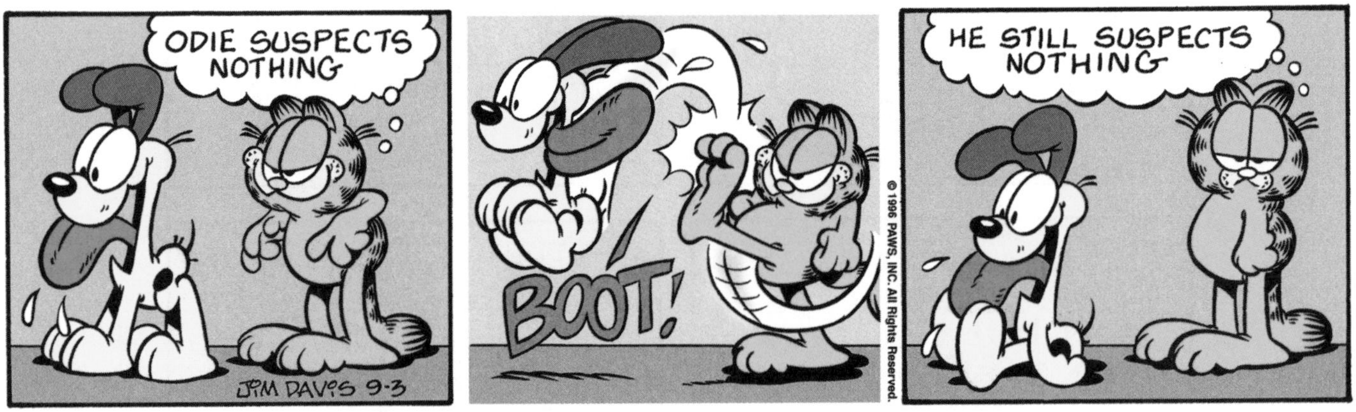
ODIE SUSPECTS NOTHING
JIM DAVIS 9-3
BOOT!
© 1996 PAWS, INC. All Rights Reserved.
HE STILL SUSPECTS NOTHING

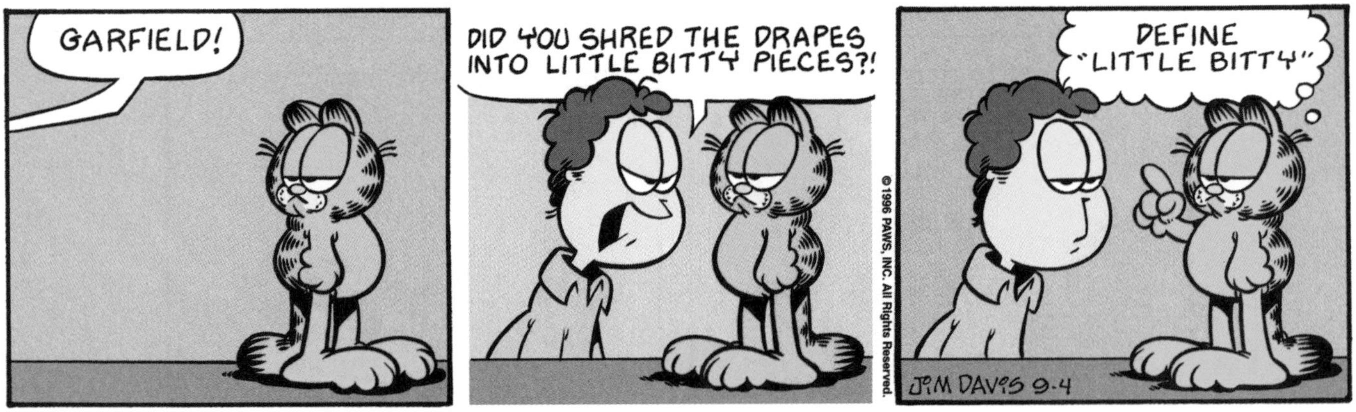
GARFIELD!
DID YOU SHRED THE DRAPES INTO LITTLE BITTY PIECES?!
© 1996 PAWS, INC. All Rights Reserved.
DEFINE "LITTLE BITTY"
JIM DAVIS 9-4

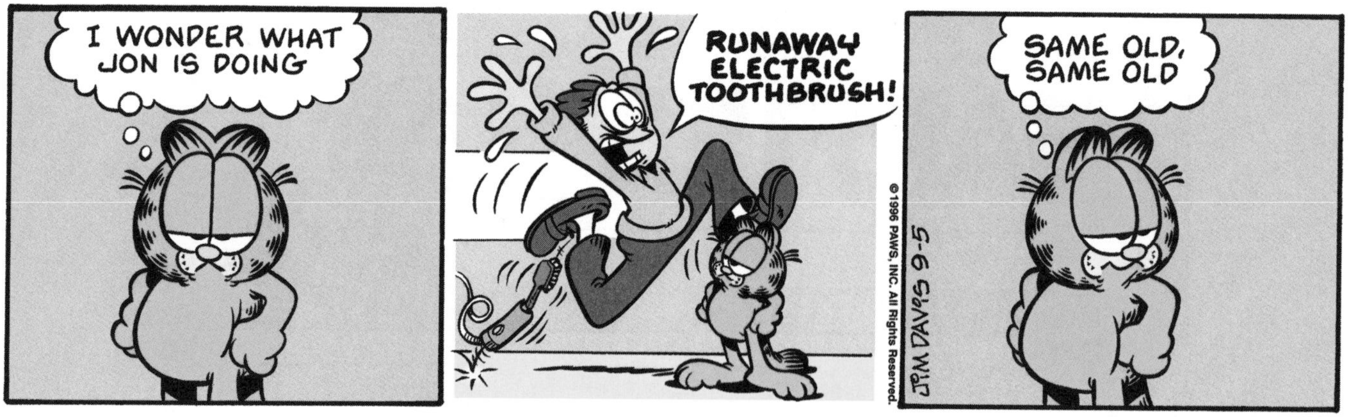
I WONDER WHAT JON IS DOING
RUNAWAY ELECTRIC TOOTHBRUSH!
SAME OLD, SAME OLD
JIM DAVIS 9-5
© 1996 PAWS, INC. All Rights Reserved.

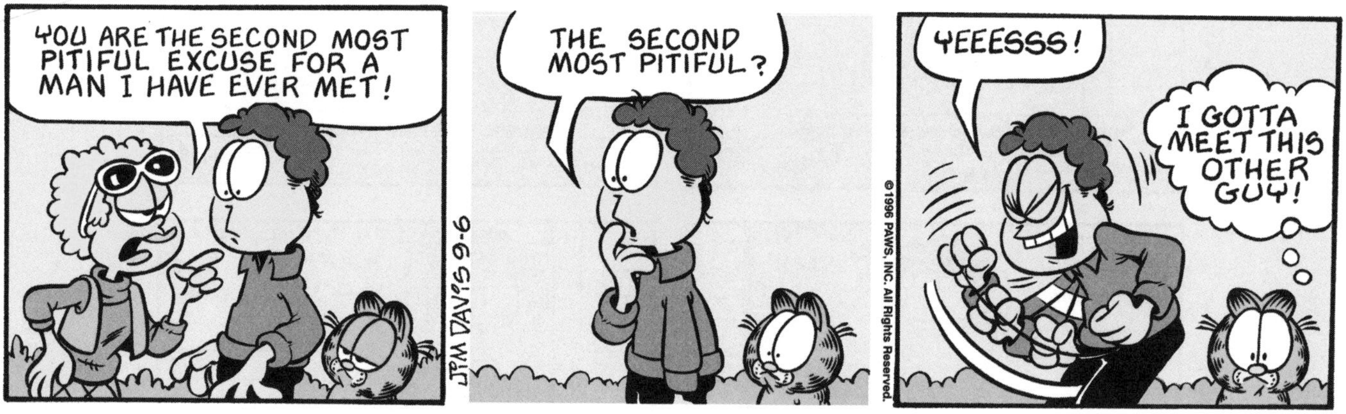
YOU ARE THE SECOND MOST PITIFUL EXCUSE FOR A MAN I HAVE EVER MET!
JIM DAVIS 9-6
THE SECOND MOST PITIFUL?
© 1996 PAWS, INC. All Rights Reserved.
YEEESSS!
I GOTTA MEET THIS OTHER GUY!

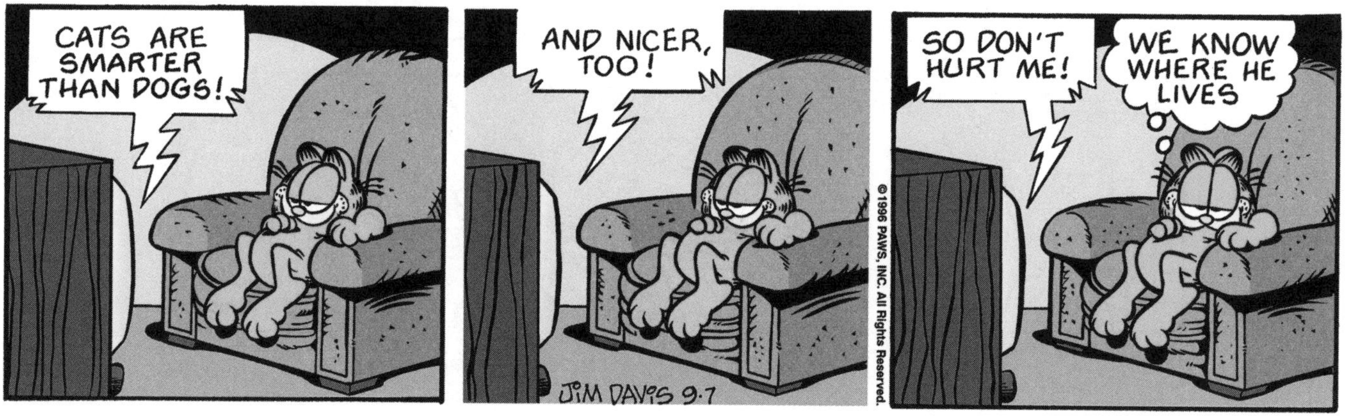
CATS ARE SMARTER THAN DOGS!
AND NICER, TOO!
JIM DAVIS 9-7
© 1996 PAWS, INC. All Rights Reserved.
SO DON'T HURT ME!
WE KNOW WHERE HE LIVES

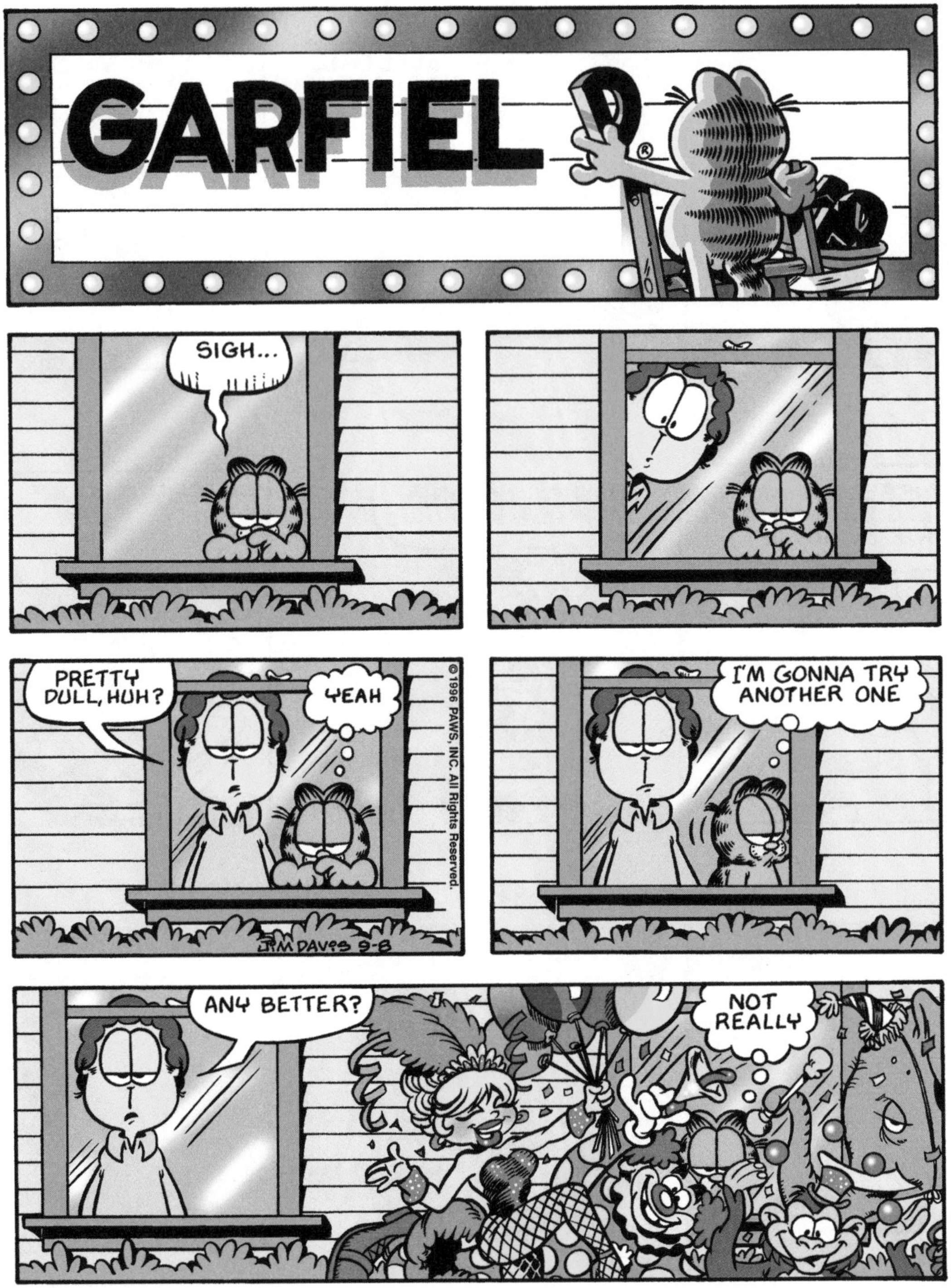
GARFIELD®
SIGH...
PRETTY DULL, HUH?
YEAH
© 1996 PAWS, INC. All Rights Reserved.
JIM DAVIS 9-8
I'M GONNA TRY ANOTHER ONE
ANY BETTER?
NOT REALLY

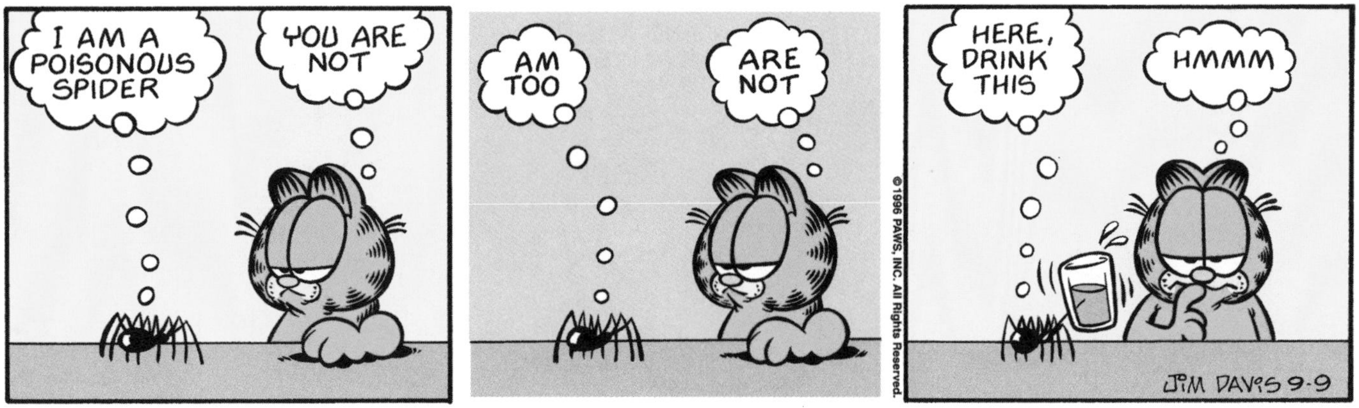
I AM A POISONOUS SPIDER
YOU ARE NOT
AM TOO
ARE NOT
HERE, DRINK THIS
HMMM
JIM DAVIS 9-9
© 1996 PAWS, INC. All Rights Reserved.

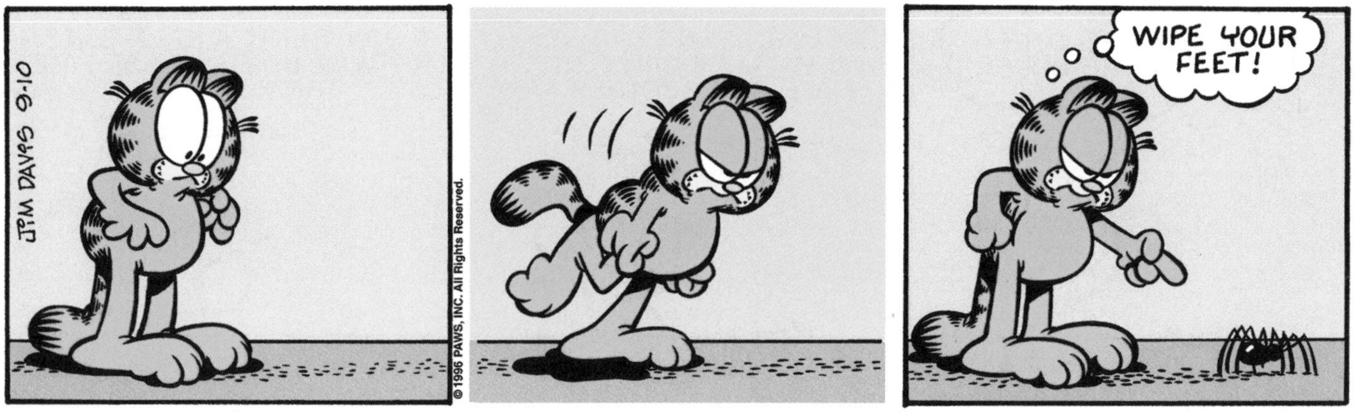
JIM DAVIS 9-10
© 1996 PAWS, INC. All Rights Reserved.
WIPE YOUR FEET!

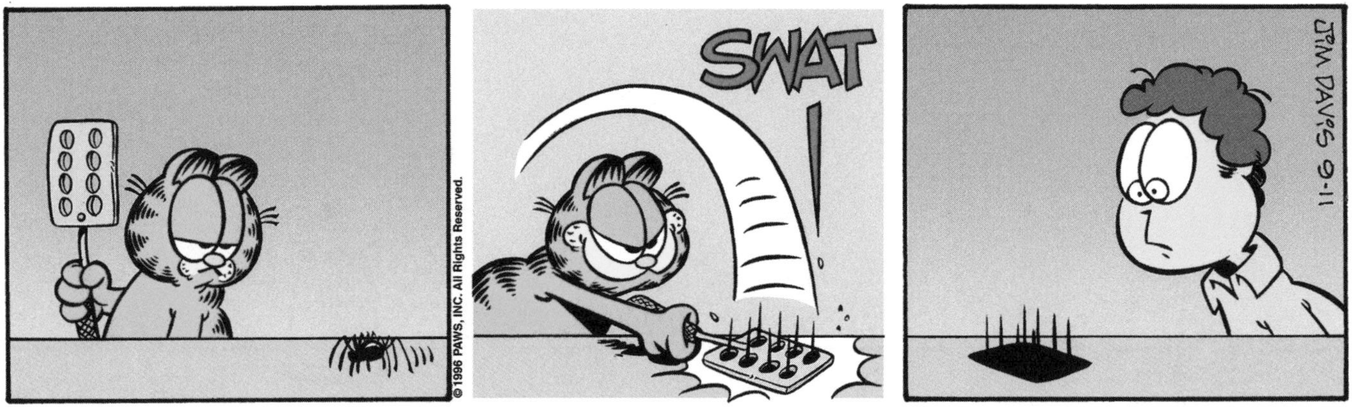
© 1996 PAWS, INC. All Rights Reserved.
SWAT
JIM DAVIS 9-11

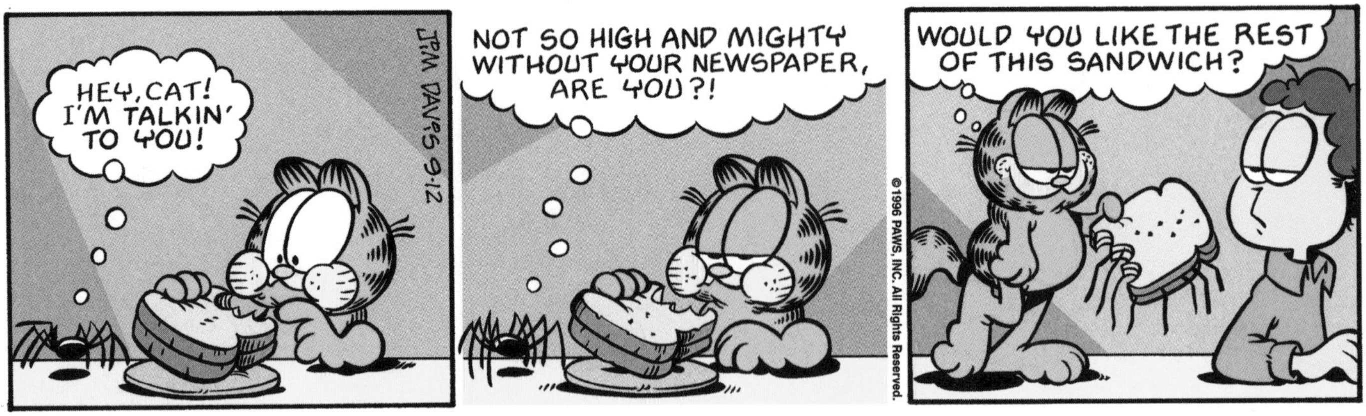
JIM DAVIS 9-12
HEY, CAT! I'M TALKIN' TO YOU!
NOT SO HIGH AND MIGHTY WITHOUT YOUR NEWSPAPER, ARE YOU?!
© 1996 PAWS, INC. All Rights Reserved.
WOULD YOU LIKE THE REST OF THIS SANDWICH?

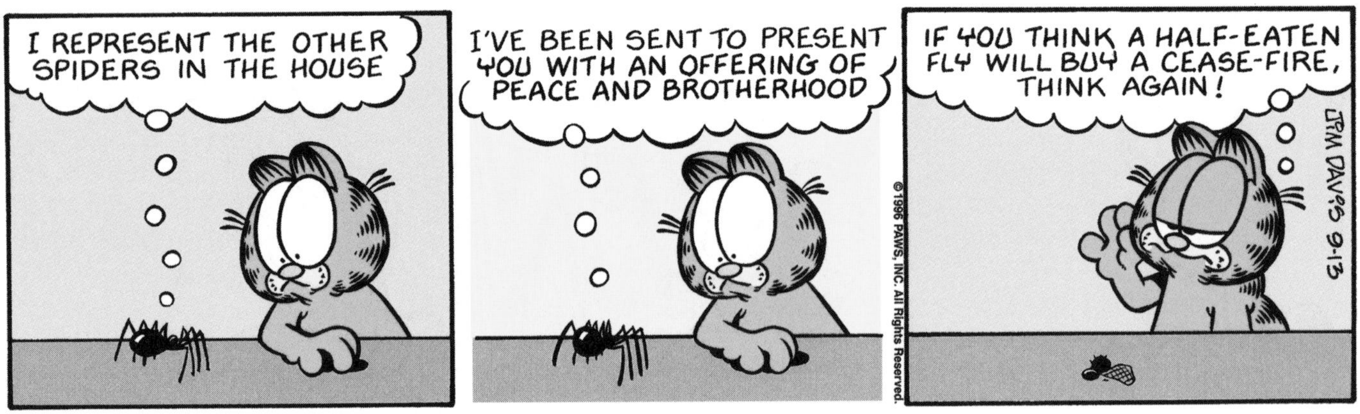
I REPRESENT THE OTHER SPIDERS IN THE HOUSE
I'VE BEEN SENT TO PRESENT YOU WITH AN OFFERING OF PEACE AND BROTHERHOOD
© 1996 PAWS, INC. All Rights Reserved.
IF YOU THINK A HALF-EATEN FLY WILL BUY A CEASE-FIRE, THINK AGAIN!
JIM DAVIS 9-13

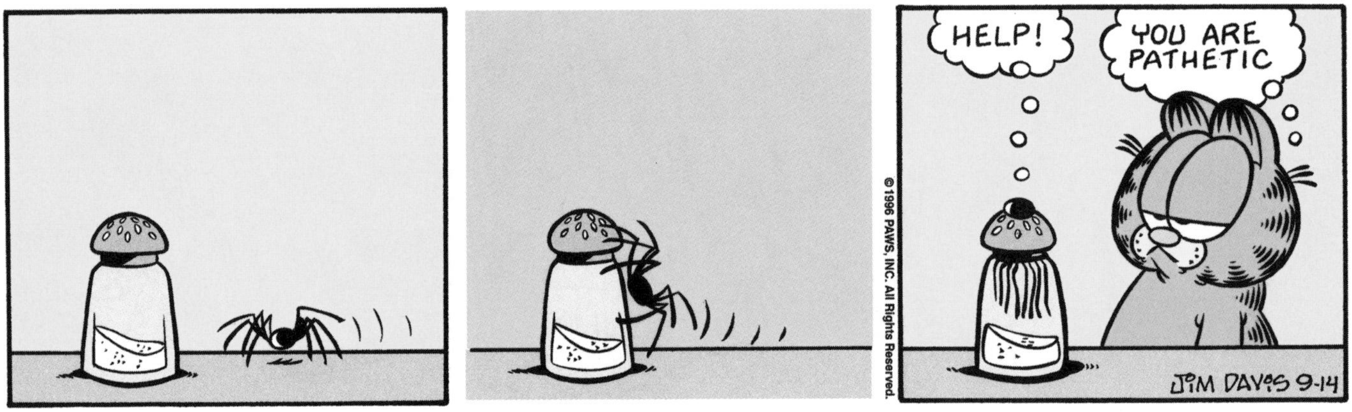
© 1996 PAWS, INC. All Rights Reserved.
HELP!
YOU ARE PATHETIC
JIM DAVIS 9-14

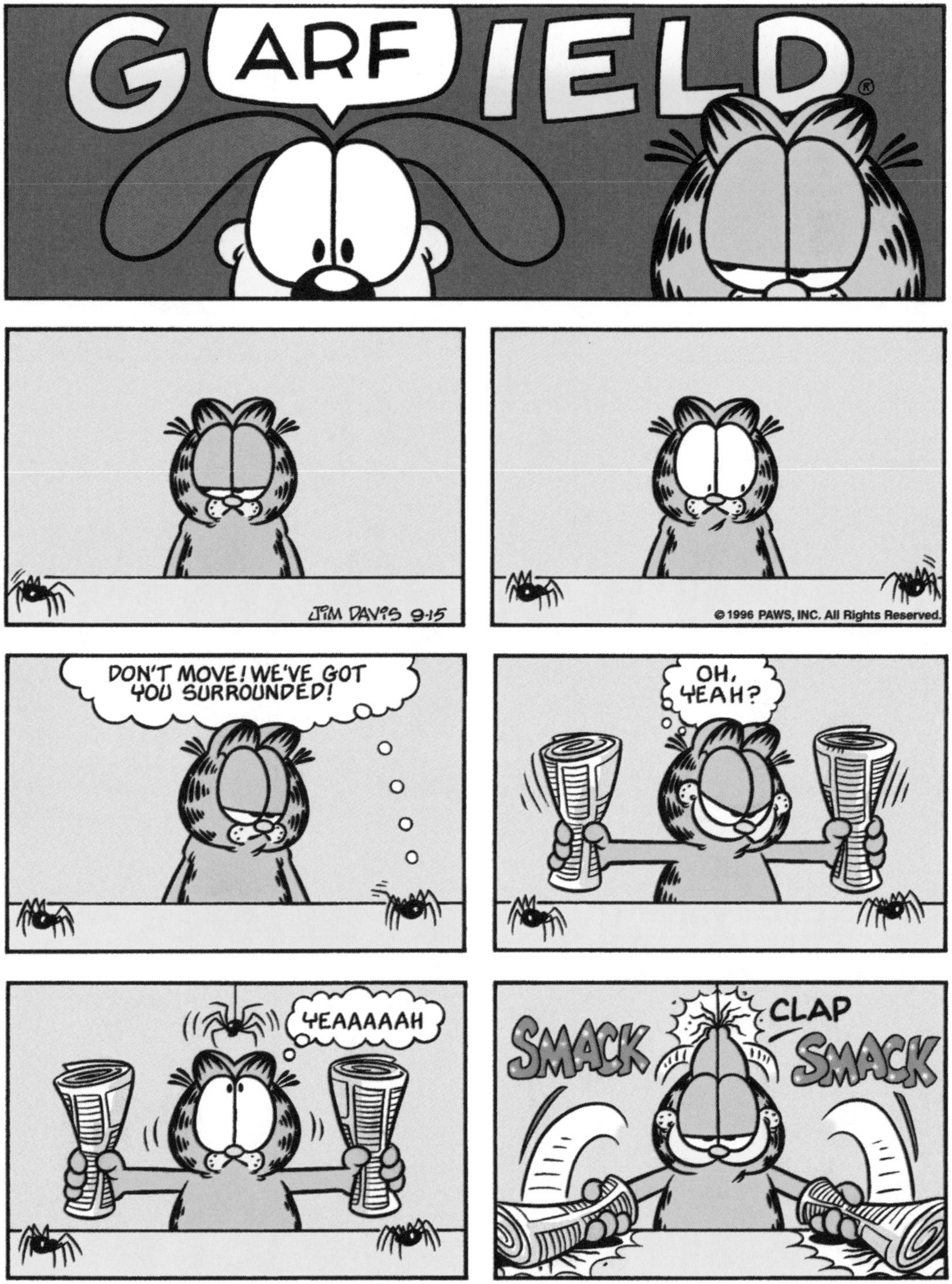
GARFIELD
ARF
JIM DAVIS 9-15
© 1996 PAWS, INC. All Rights Reserved.
DON'T MOVE! WE'VE GOT YOU SURROUNDED!
OH, YEAH?
YEAAAAAH
SMACK
CLAP
SMACK

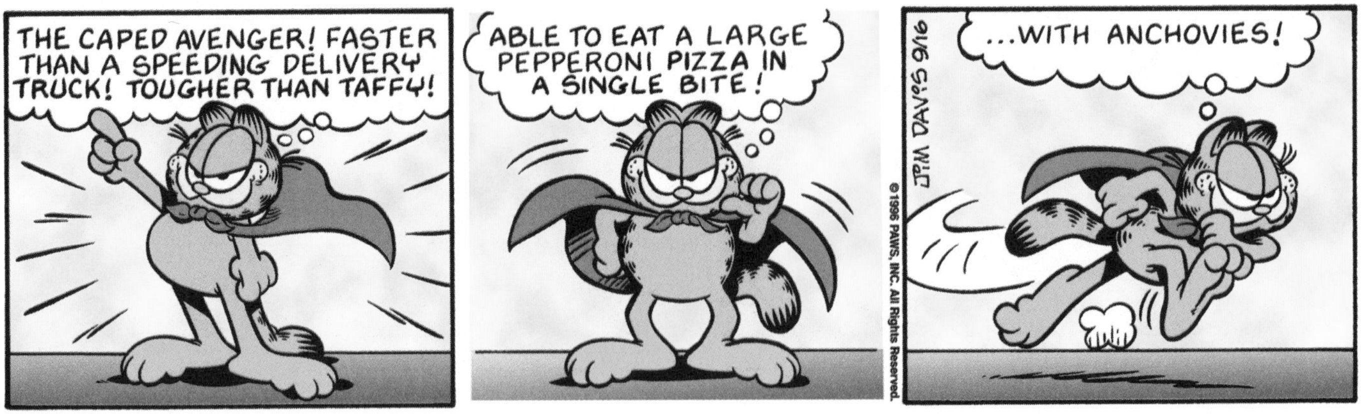
THE CAPED AVENGER! FASTER THAN A SPEEDING DELIVERY TRUCK! TOUGHER THAN TAFFY!
ABLE TO EAT A LARGE PEPPERONI PIZZA IN A SINGLE BITE!
...WITH ANCHOVIES!
JPM DAVPS 9/16
© 1996 PAWS, INC. All Rights Reserved.

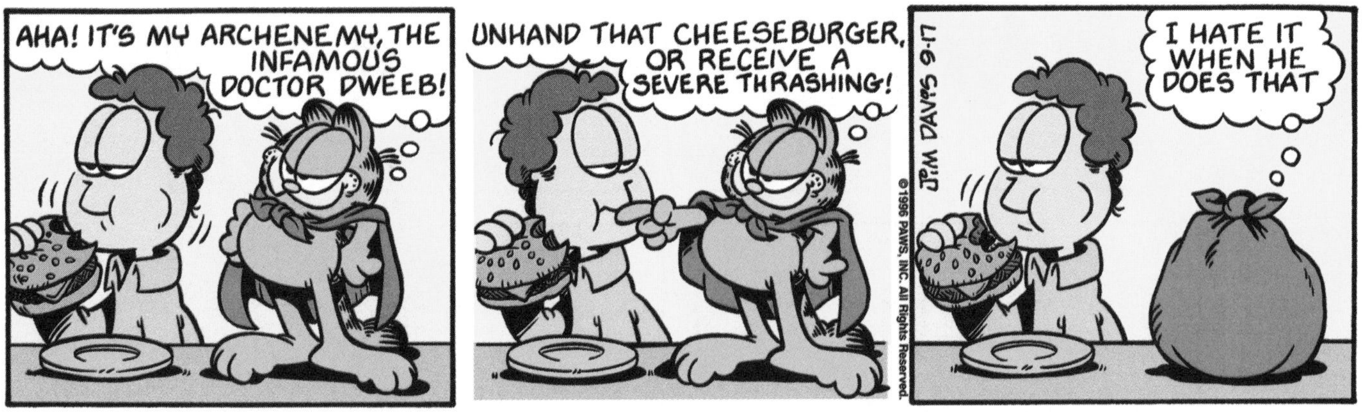
AHA! IT'S MY ARCHENEMY, THE INFAMOUS DOCTOR DWEEB!
UNHAND THAT CHEESEBURGER, OR RECEIVE A SEVERE THRASHING!
I HATE IT WHEN HE DOES THAT
JPM DAVPS 9-17
© 1996 PAWS, INC. All Rights Reserved.

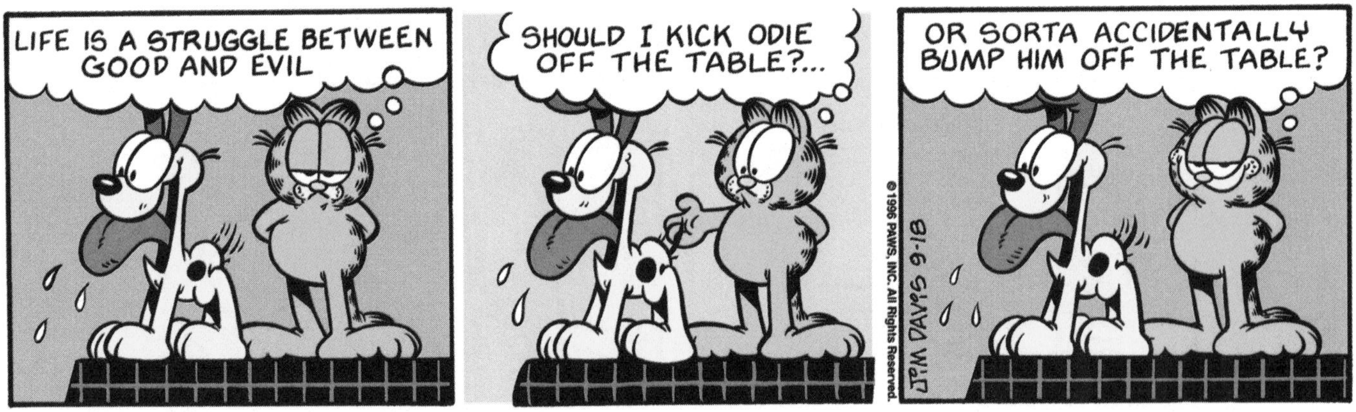
LIFE IS A STRUGGLE BETWEEN GOOD AND EVIL
SHOULD I KICK ODIE OFF THE TABLE?...
OR SORTA ACCIDENTALLY BUMP HIM OFF THE TABLE?
JPM DAVPS 9-18
© 1996 PAWS, INC. All Rights Reserved.

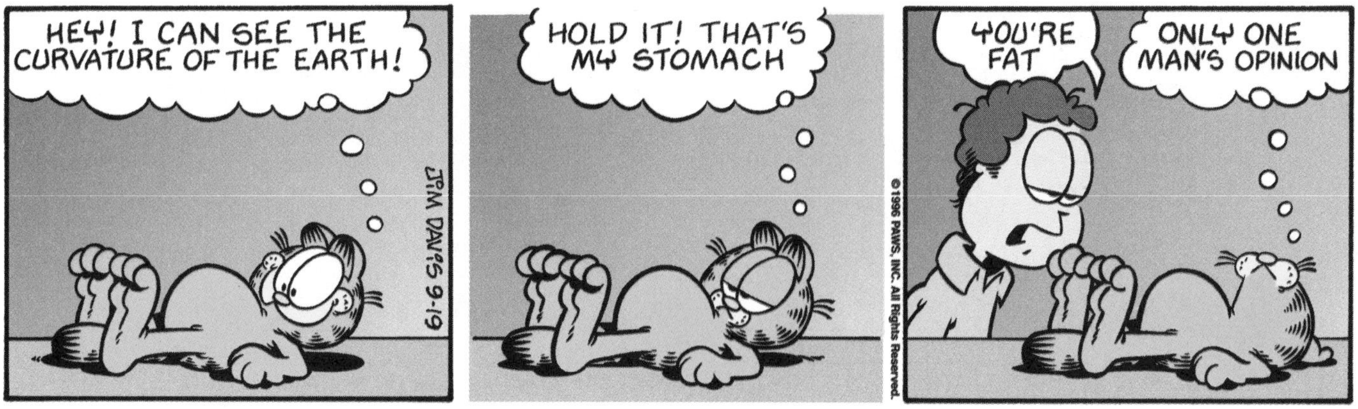
HEY! I CAN SEE THE CURVATURE OF THE EARTH!
JIM DAVIS 9-19
HOLD IT! THAT'S MY STOMACH
© 1996 PAWS, INC. All Rights Reserved.
YOU'RE FAT
ONLY ONE MAN'S OPINION

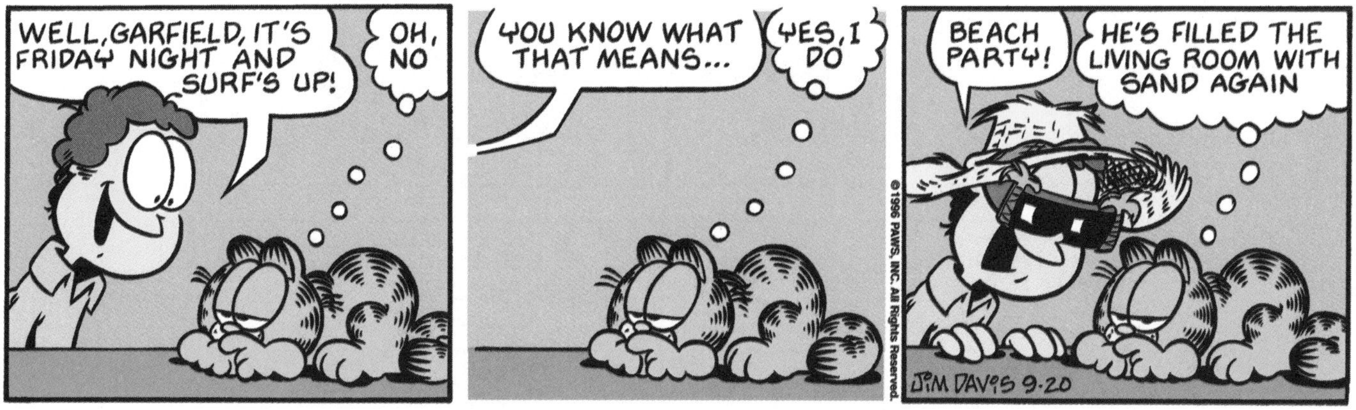
WELL, GARFIELD, IT'S FRIDAY NIGHT AND SURF'S UP!
OH, NO
YOU KNOW WHAT THAT MEANS...
YES, I DO
© 1996 PAWS, INC. All Rights Reserved.
BEACH PARTY!
HE'S FILLED THE LIVING ROOM WITH SAND AGAIN
JIM DAVIS 9-20

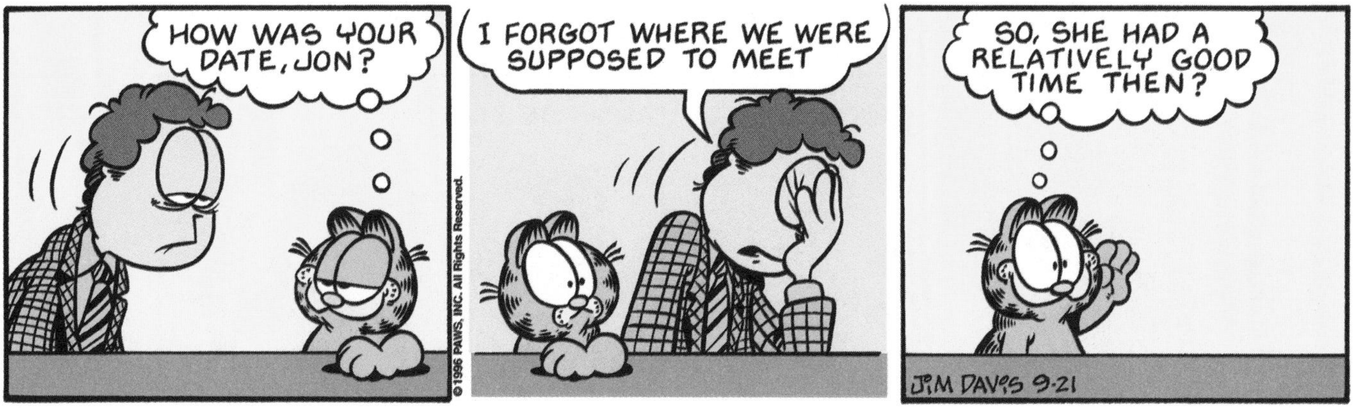
HOW WAS YOUR DATE, JON?
© 1996 PAWS, INC. All Rights Reserved.
I FORGOT WHERE WE WERE SUPPOSED TO MEET
SO, SHE HAD A RELATIVELY GOOD TIME THEN?
JIM DAVIS 9-21

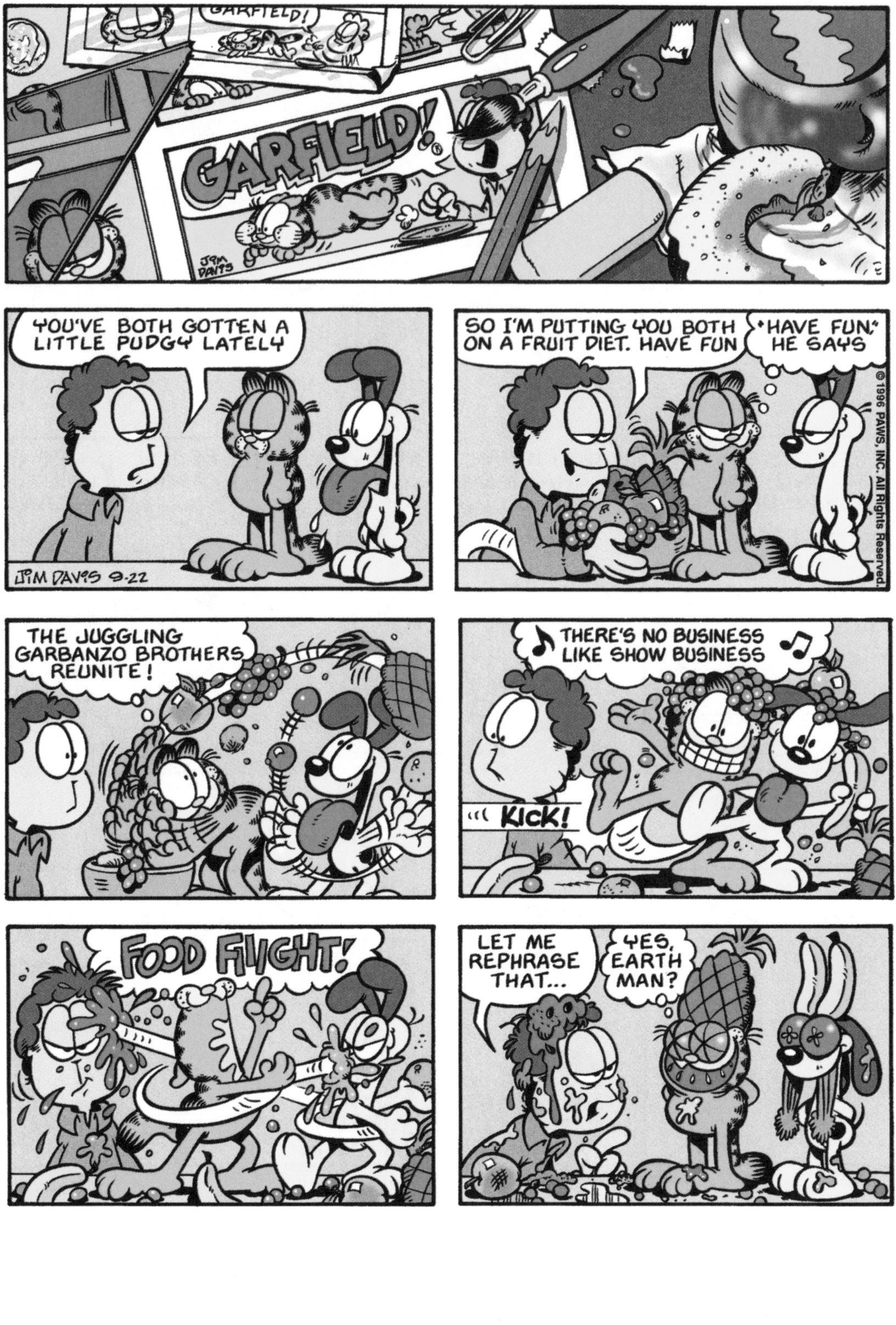
GARFIELD!
GARFIELD!
JIM DAVIS
YOU'VE BOTH GOTTEN A LITTLE PUDGY LATELY
JIM DAVIS 9-22
SO I'M PUTTING YOU BOTH ON A FRUIT DIET. HAVE FUN
"HAVE FUN," HE SAYS
© 1996 PAWS, INC. All Rights Reserved.
THE JUGGLING GARBANZO BROTHERS REUNITE!
THERE'S NO BUSINESS LIKE SHOW BUSINESS
KICK!
FOOD FIGHT!
LET ME REPHRASE THAT...
YES, EARTH MAN?

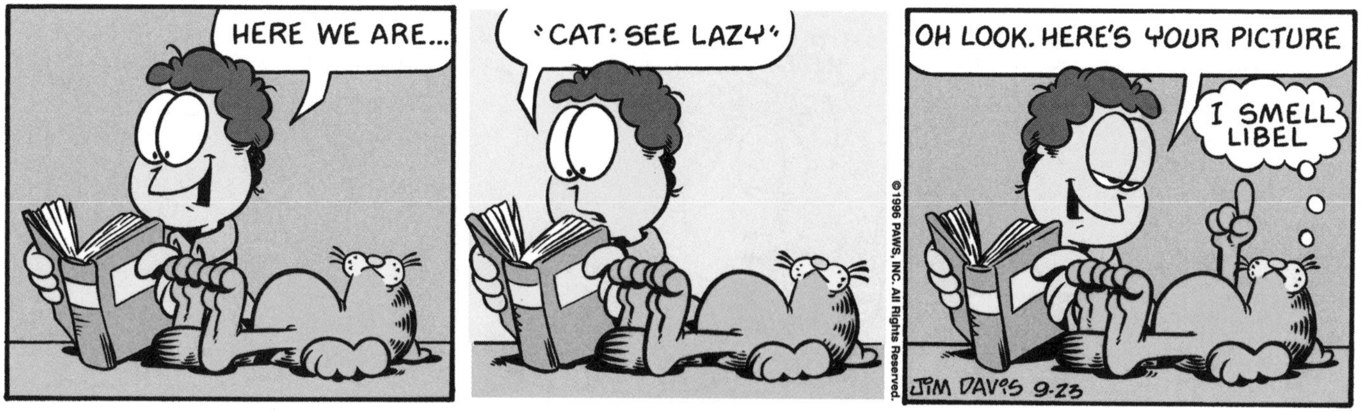
HERE WE ARE...
"CAT: SEE LAZY"
OH LOOK. HERE'S YOUR PICTURE
I SMELL LIBEL
JIM DAVIS 9-23

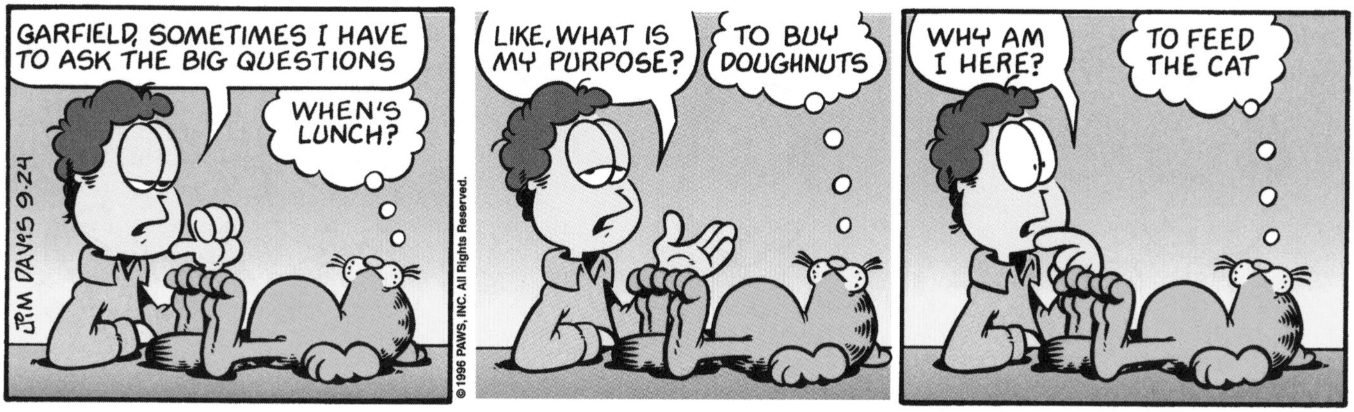
GARFIELD, SOMETIMES I HAVE TO ASK THE BIG QUESTIONS
WHEN'S LUNCH?
JIM DAVIS 9-24
LIKE, WHAT IS MY PURPOSE?
TO BUY DOUGHNUTS
WHY AM I HERE?
TO FEED THE CAT

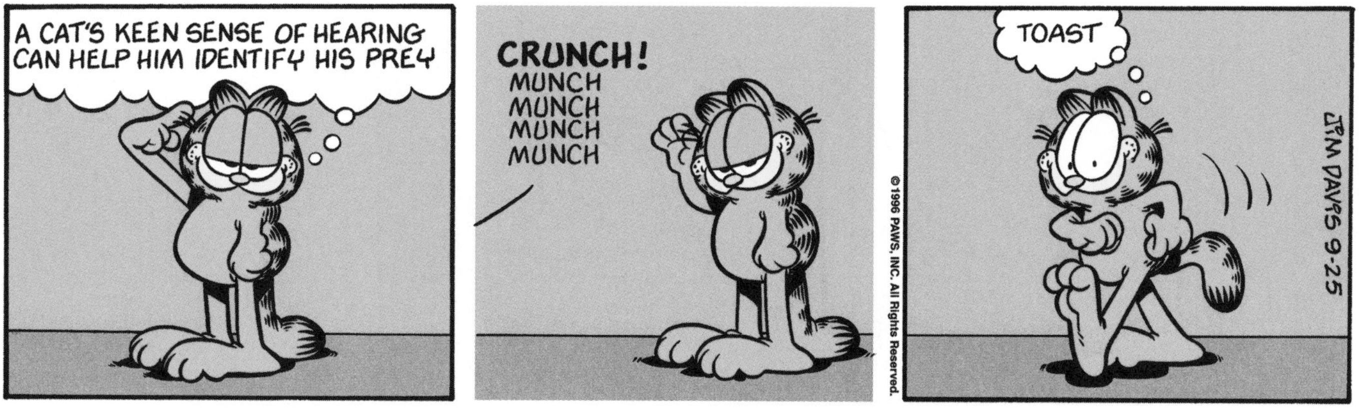
A CAT'S KEEN SENSE OF HEARING CAN HELP HIM IDENTIFY HIS PREY
CRUNCH!
MUNCH
MUNCH
MUNCH
MUNCH
TOAST
JIM DAVIS 9-25

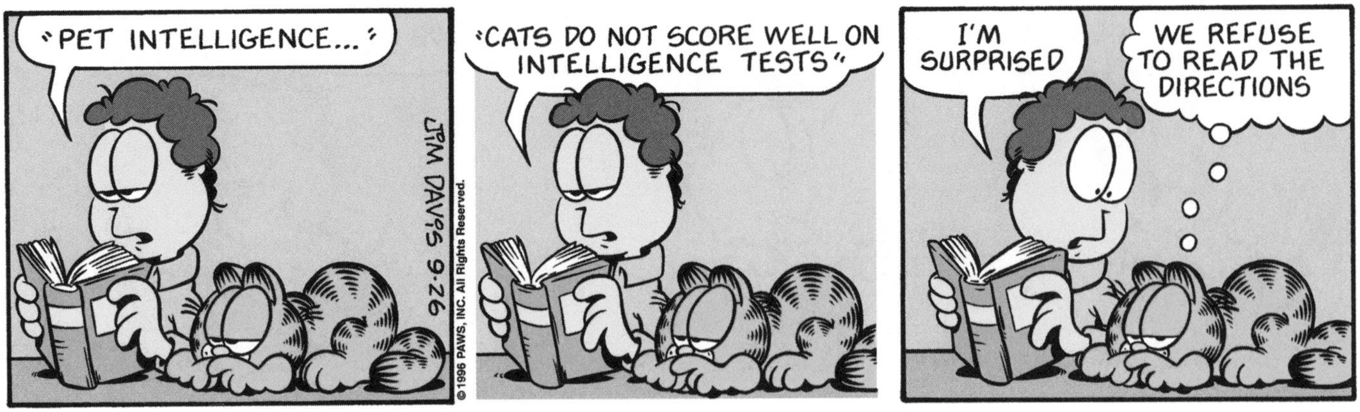
"PET INTELLIGENCE..."
JIM DAVIS 9-26
© 1996 PAWS, INC. All Rights Reserved.
"CATS DO NOT SCORE WELL ON INTELLIGENCE TESTS"
I'M SURPRISED
WE REFUSE TO READ THE DIRECTIONS

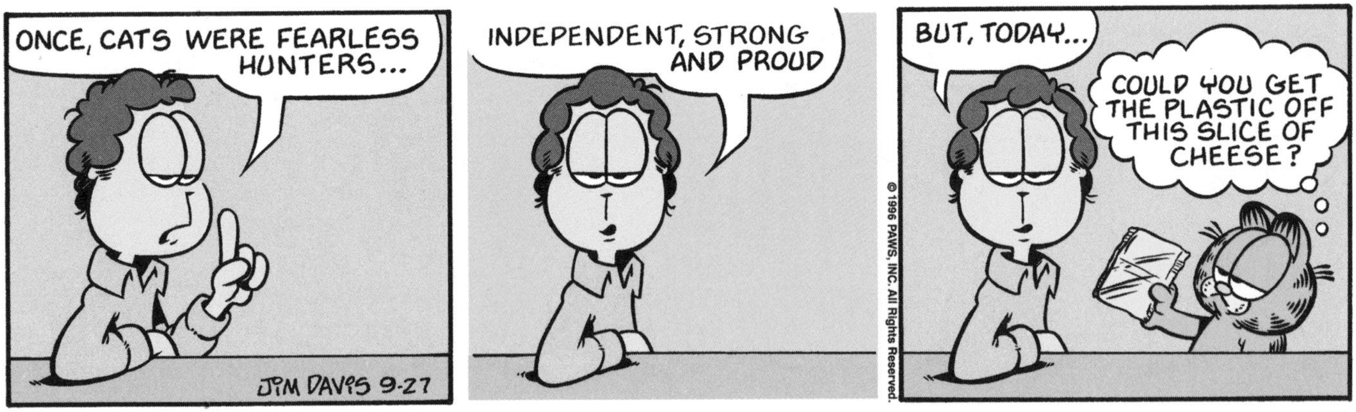
ONCE, CATS WERE FEARLESS HUNTERS...
JIM DAVIS 9-27
INDEPENDENT, STRONG AND PROUD
© 1996 PAWS, INC. All Rights Reserved.
BUT, TODAY...
COULD YOU GET THE PLASTIC OFF THIS SLICE OF CHEESE?

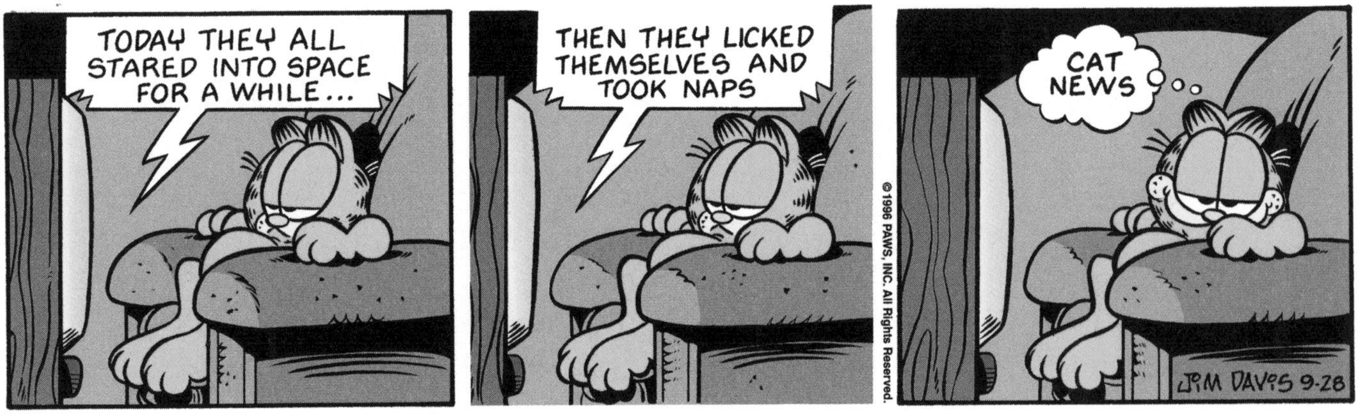
TODAY THEY ALL STARED INTO SPACE FOR A WHILE...
THEN THEY LICKED THEMSELVES AND TOOK NAPS
© 1996 PAWS, INC. All Rights Reserved.
CAT NEWS
JIM DAVIS 9-28

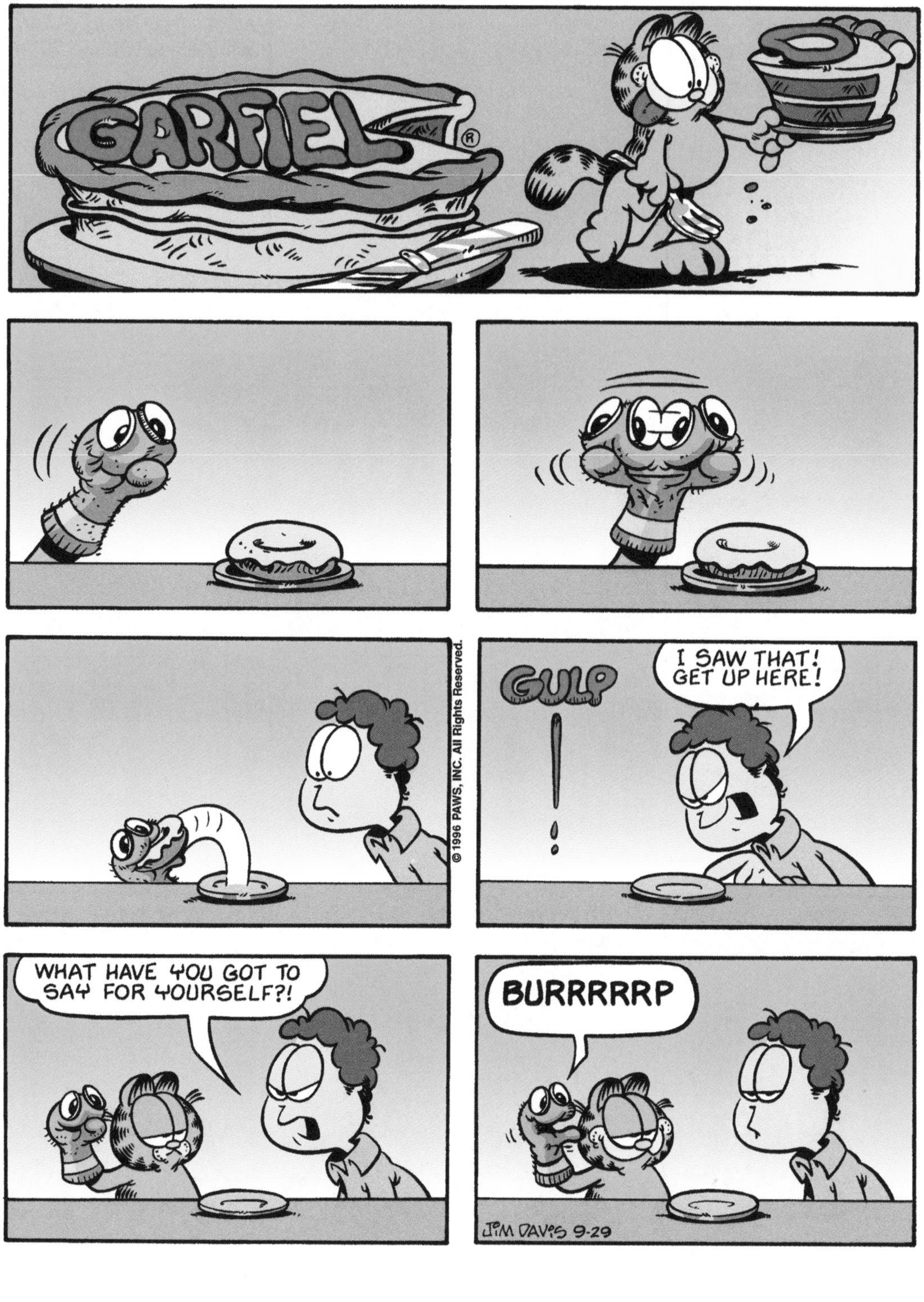
GARFIEL®
© 1996 PAWS, INC. All Rights Reserved.
GULP
!
I SAW THAT! GET UP HERE!
WHAT HAVE YOU GOT TO SAY FOR YOURSELF?!
BURRRRRP
JIM DAVIS 9-29

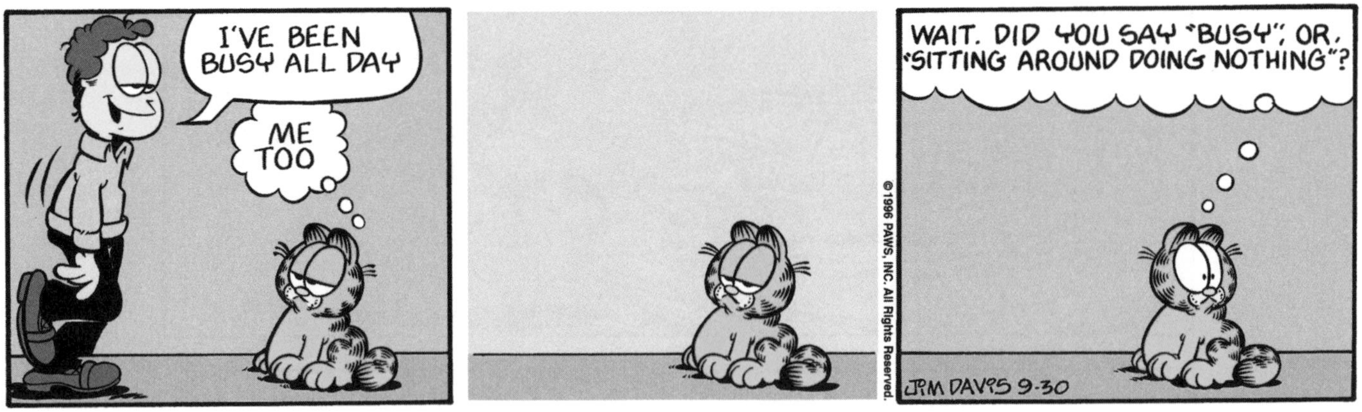
I'VE BEEN BUSY ALL DAY
ME TOO
WAIT. DID YOU SAY "BUSY", OR, "SITTING AROUND DOING NOTHING"?
©1996 PAWS, INC. All Rights Reserved.
JIM DAVIS 9-30

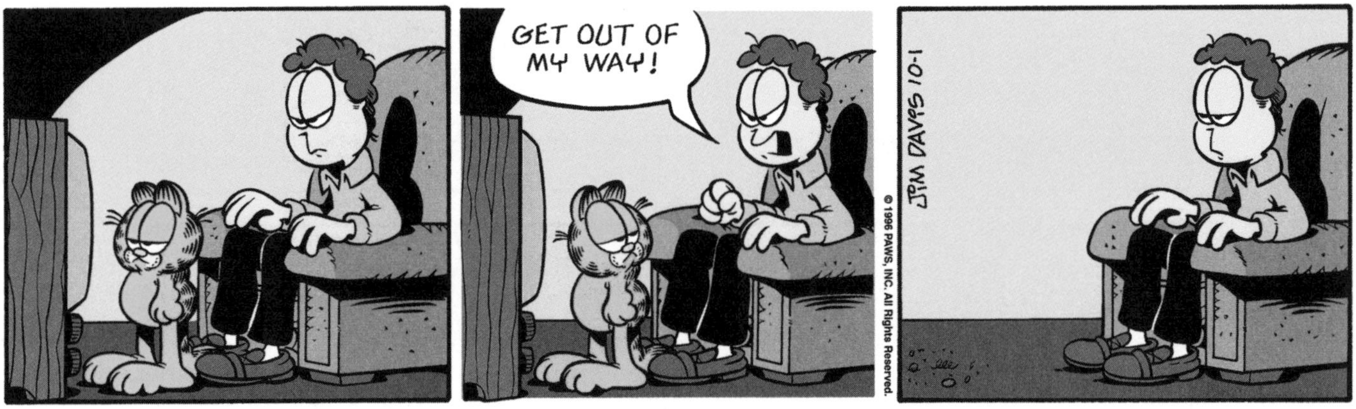
GET OUT OF MY WAY!
©1996 PAWS, INC. All Rights Reserved.
JIM DAVIS 10-1

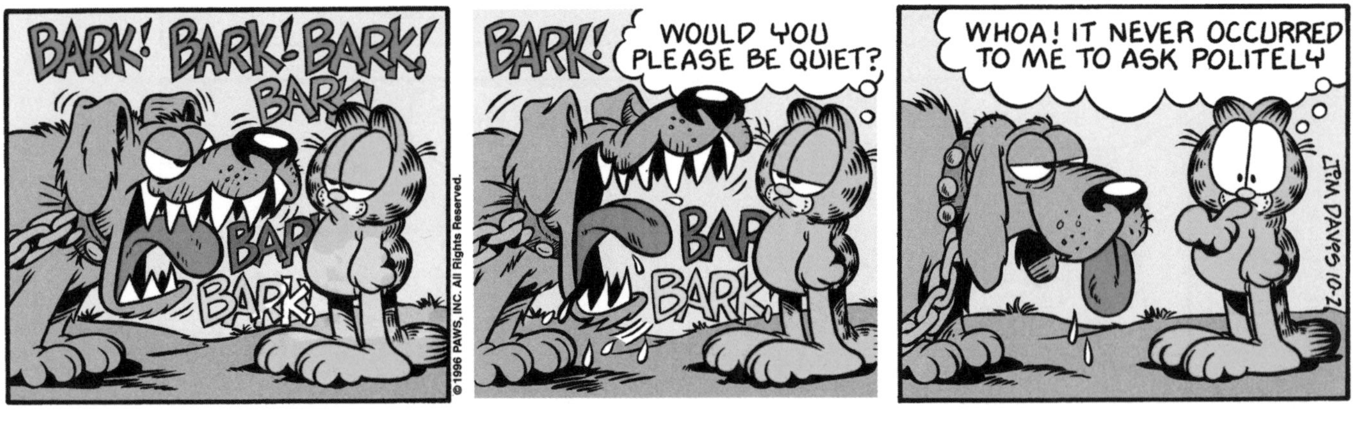
BARK! BARK! BARK!
BARK
BARK
BARK
©1996 PAWS, INC. All Rights Reserved.
BARK!
WOULD YOU PLEASE BE QUIET?
BAR
BARK
WHOA! IT NEVER OCCURRED TO ME TO ASK POLITELY
JIM DAVIS 10-2

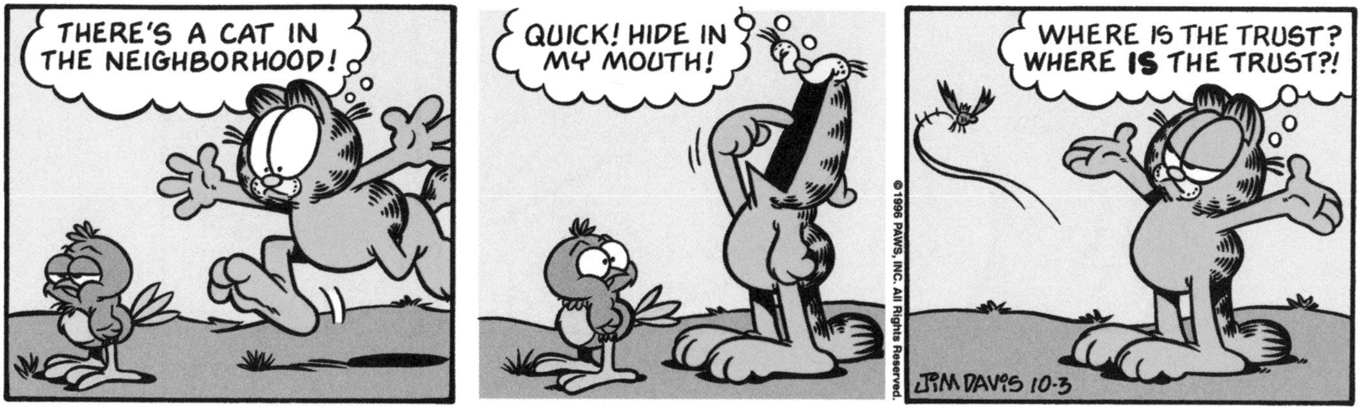
THERE'S A CAT IN THE NEIGHBORHOOD!
QUICK! HIDE IN MY MOUTH!
WHERE IS THE TRUST? WHERE **IS** THE TRUST?!
© 1996 PAWS, INC. All Rights Reserved.
JIM DAVIS 10-3

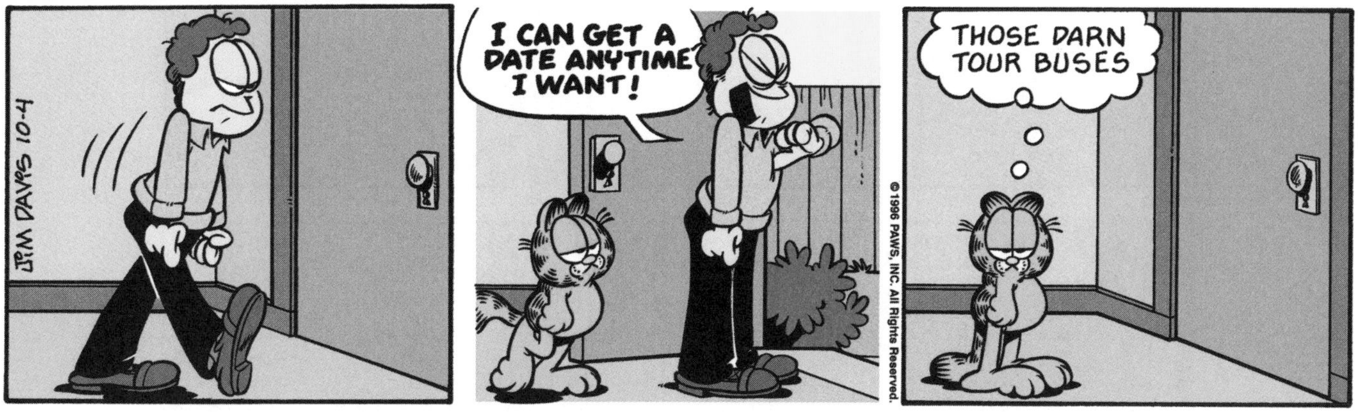
JIM DAVIS 10-4
I CAN GET A DATE ANYTIME I WANT!
© 1996 PAWS, INC. All Rights Reserved.
THOSE DARN TOUR BUSES

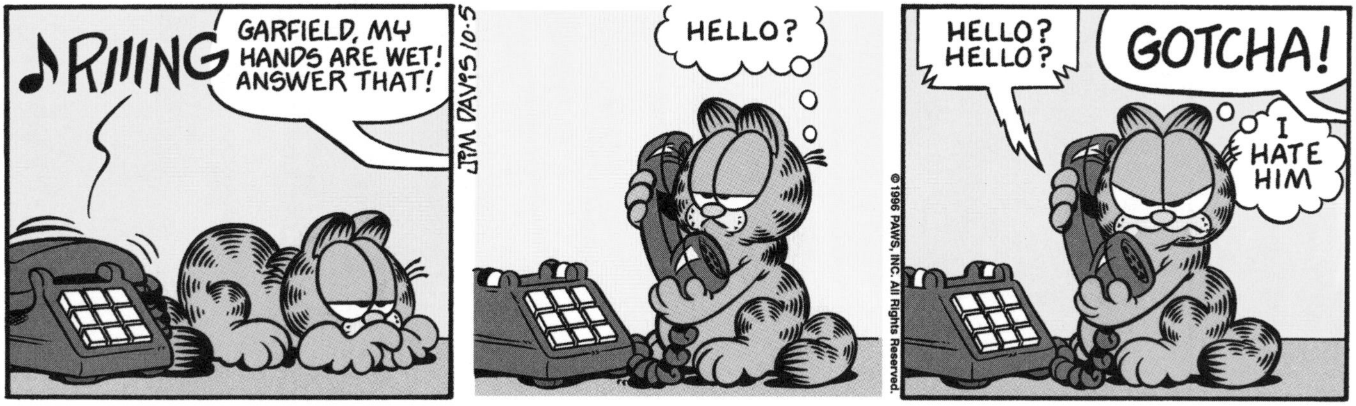
♪RIIING
GARFIELD, MY HANDS ARE WET! ANSWER THAT!
JIM DAVIS 10-5
HELLO?
© 1996 PAWS, INC. All Rights Reserved.
HELLO? HELLO?
GOTCHA!
I HATE HIM

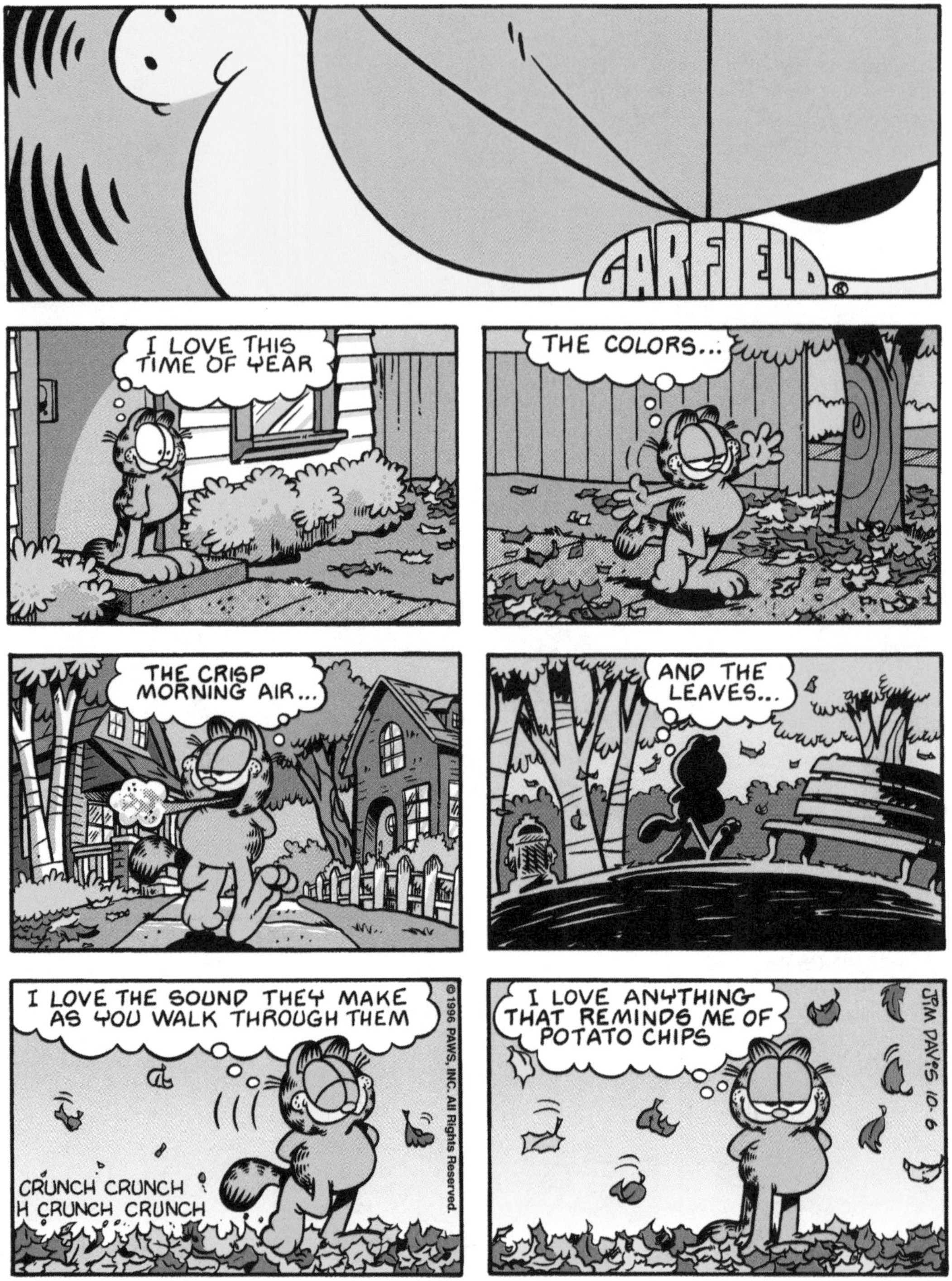
GARFIELD®
I LOVE THIS TIME OF YEAR
THE COLORS...
THE CRISP MORNING AIR...
AND THE LEAVES...
I LOVE THE SOUND THEY MAKE AS YOU WALK THROUGH THEM
CRUNCH CRUNCH
H CRUNCH CRUNCH
© 1996 PAWS, INC. All Rights Reserved.
I LOVE ANYTHING THAT REMINDS ME OF POTATO CHIPS
JIM DAVIS 10-6

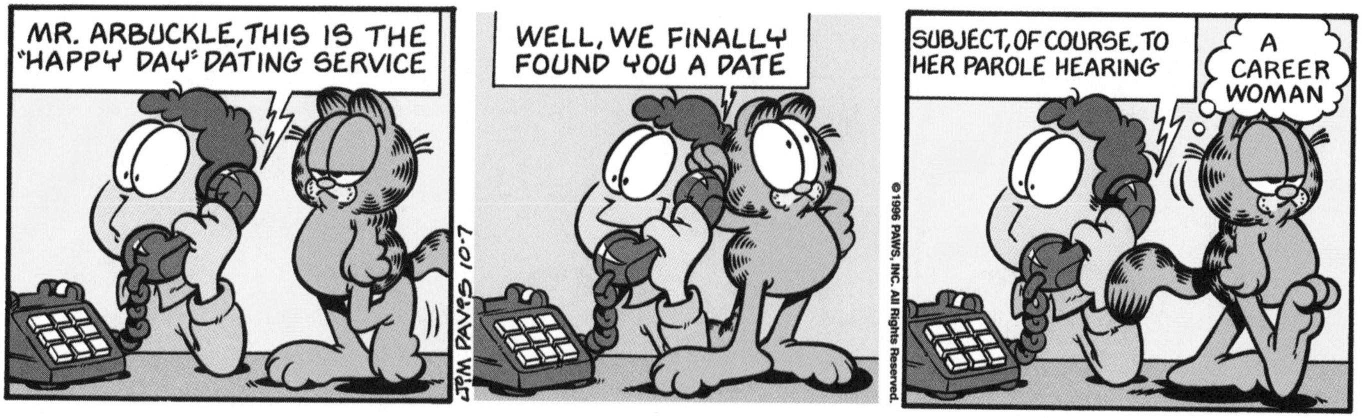
MR. ARBUCKLE, THIS IS THE "HAPPY DAY" DATING SERVICE
JIM DAVIS 10-7
WELL, WE FINALLY FOUND YOU A DATE
© 1996 PAWS, INC. All Rights Reserved.
SUBJECT, OF COURSE, TO HER PAROLE HEARING
A CAREER WOMAN

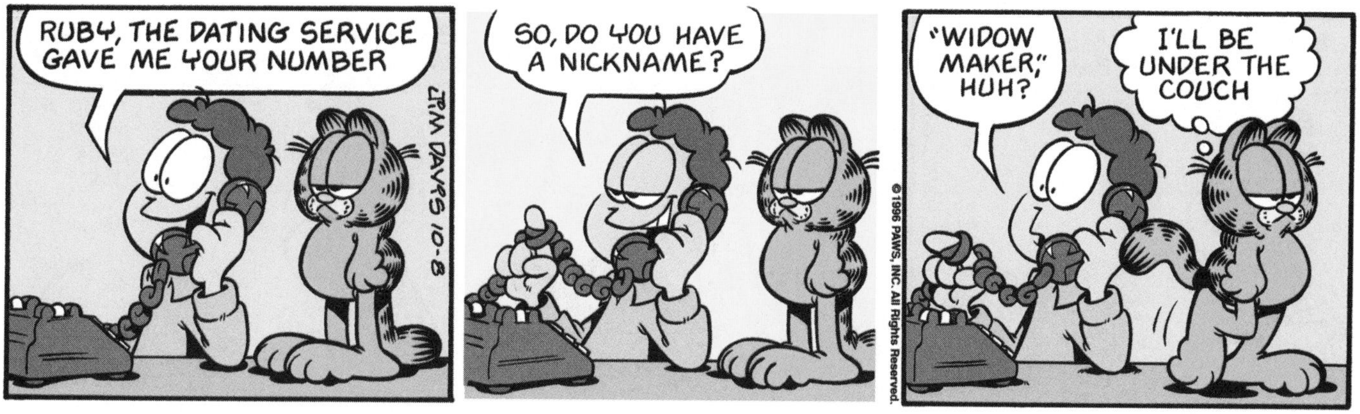
RUBY, THE DATING SERVICE GAVE ME YOUR NUMBER
JIM DAVIS 10-8
SO, DO YOU HAVE A NICKNAME?
© 1996 PAWS, INC. All Rights Reserved.
"WIDOW MAKER," HUH?
I'LL BE UNDER THE COUCH

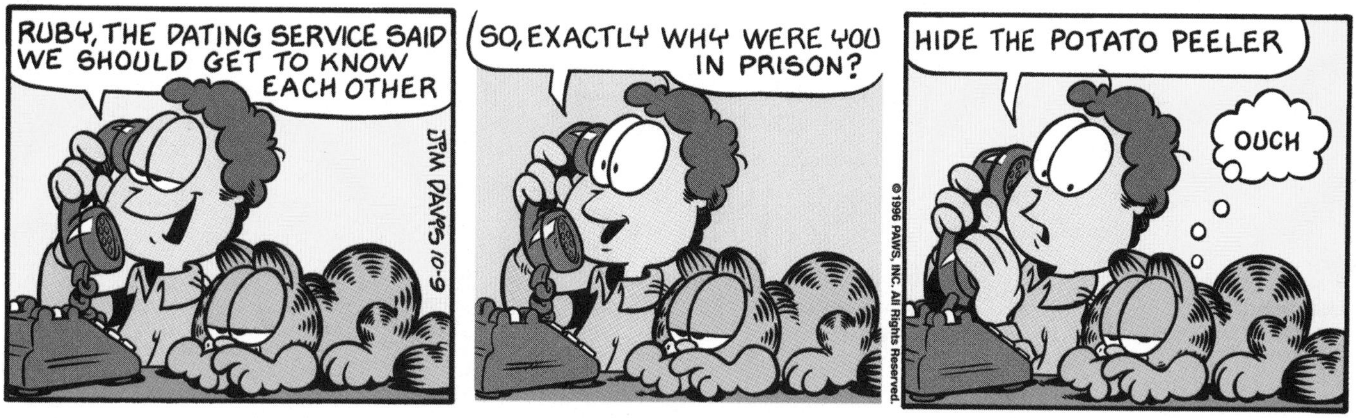
RUBY, THE DATING SERVICE SAID WE SHOULD GET TO KNOW EACH OTHER
JIM DAVIS 10-9
SO, EXACTLY WHY WERE YOU IN PRISON?
© 1996 PAWS, INC. All Rights Reserved.
HIDE THE POTATO PEELER
OUCH

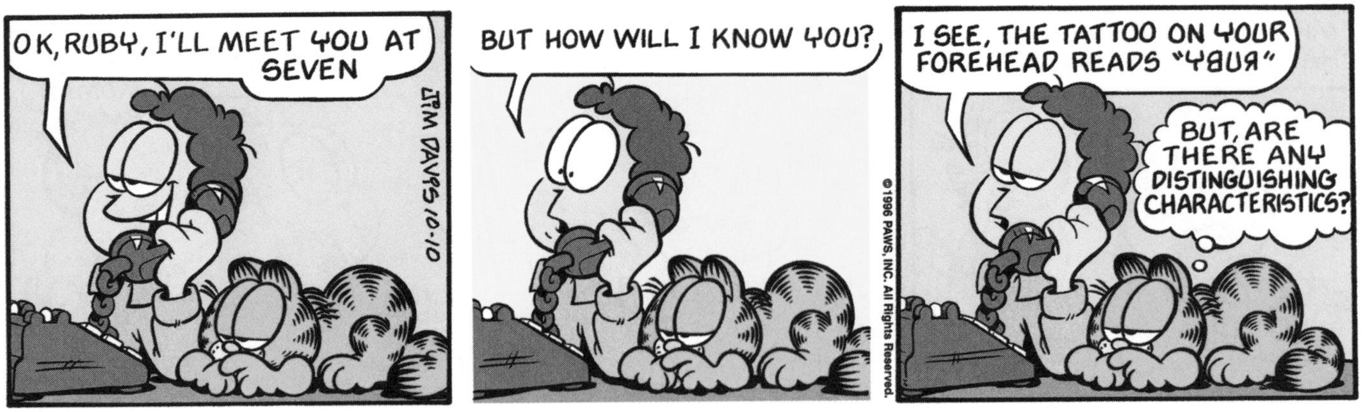
OK, RUBY, I'LL MEET YOU AT SEVEN
JIM DAVIS 10-10
BUT HOW WILL I KNOW YOU?
© 1996 PAWS, INC. All Rights Reserved.
I SEE, THE TATTOO ON YOUR FOREHEAD READS "YBUR"
BUT, ARE THERE ANY DISTINGUISHING CHARACTERISTICS?

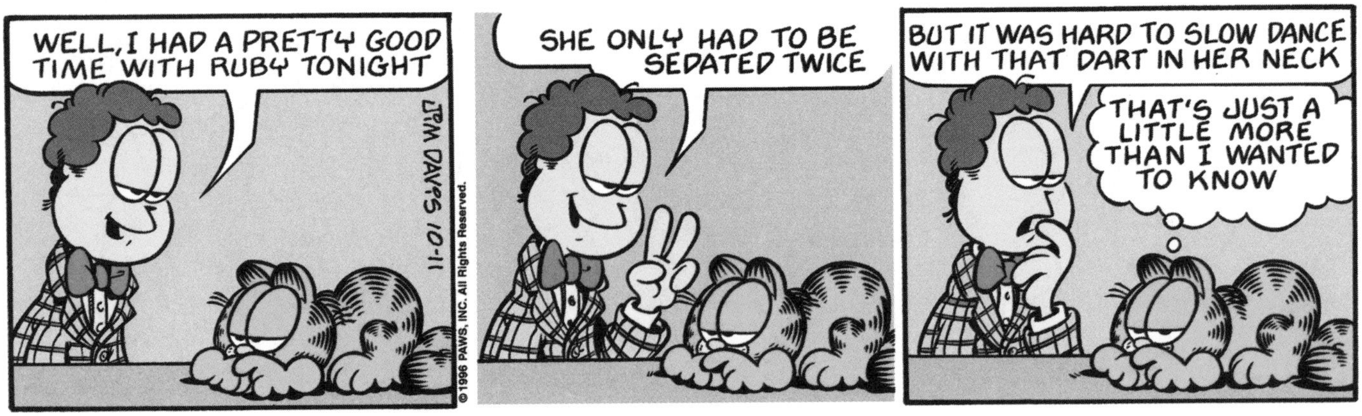
WELL, I HAD A PRETTY GOOD TIME WITH RUBY TONIGHT
JIM DAVIS 10-11
© 1996 PAWS, INC. All Rights Reserved.
SHE ONLY HAD TO BE SEDATED TWICE
BUT IT WAS HARD TO SLOW DANCE WITH THAT DART IN HER NECK
THAT'S JUST A LITTLE MORE THAN I WANTED TO KNOW

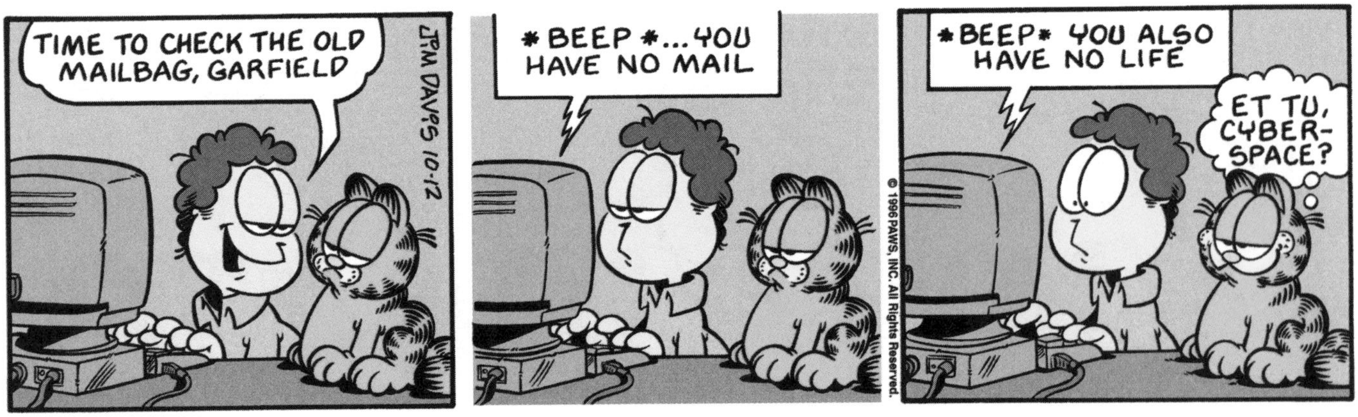
TIME TO CHECK THE OLD MAILBAG, GARFIELD
JIM DAVIS 10-12
BEEP... YOU HAVE NO MAIL
© 1996 PAWS, INC. All Rights Reserved.
BEEP YOU ALSO HAVE NO LIFE
ET TU, CYBER-SPACE?

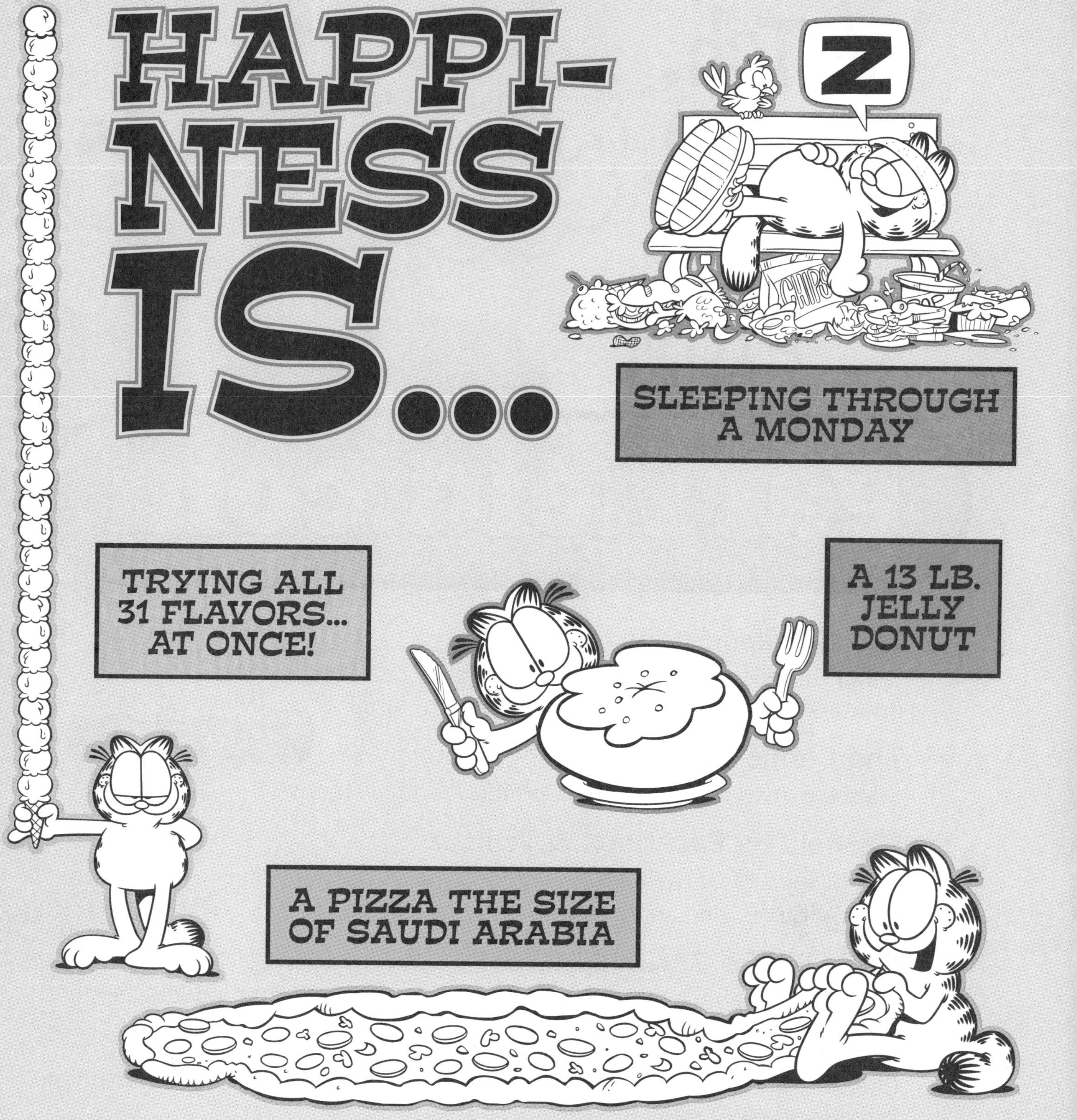
HAPPI-
NESS
IS...
Z
CHIPS
SLEEPING THROUGH A MONDAY
TRYING ALL 31 FLAVORS... AT ONCE!
A 13 LB. JELLY DONUT
A PIZZA THE SIZE OF SAUDI ARABIA